The Novel in Antiquity

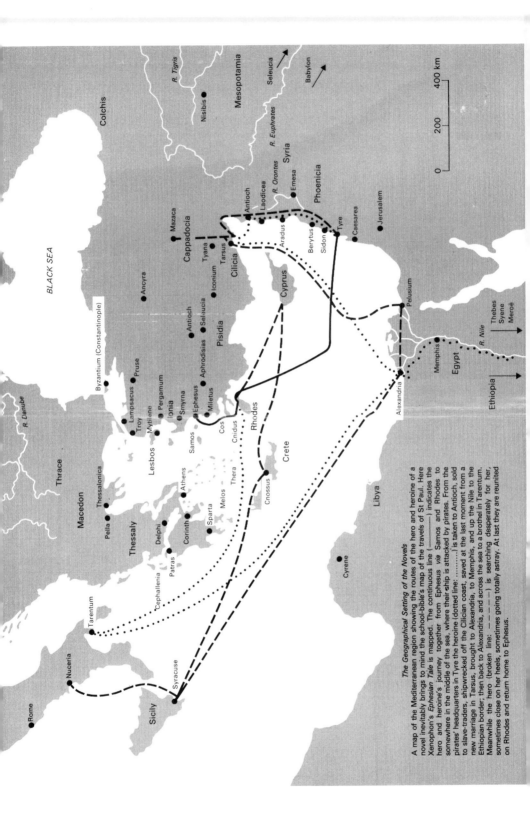

BLACK SEA

Colchis

Mesopotamia

Seleucia
Babylon

Nisibis

R. Tigris

R. Euphrates

Syria

Cappadocia

Mazaca

Antioch
Laodicea
Emesa
R. Orontes

Phoenicia

Tyana
Tarsus
Cilicia
Aradus
Berytus
Sidon
Tyre
Caesarea

Jerusalem

Ancyra

Pisidia
Antioch
Seleucia
Aphrodisias
Iconium

Byzantium (Constantinople)

Cyprus

Pelusium

0   200   400 km

Thrace

Macedon

Thessaly

Pella
Thessalonica

Lampsacus
Troy
Pergamum
Mytilene
Ionia
Smyrna
Ephesus
Miletus
Cos
Cnidus

Pruse

Lesbos

Samos

Athens

Delphi
Corinth
Sparta
Melos
Thera

Rhodes

Crete
Cnossos

Egypt

Memphis

Alexandria

R. Nile

Thebes
Syene
Meroë

Ethiopia

Patras
Cephallenia

Sicily
Syracuse

Tarentum

Nuceria

Rome

Libya

Cyrene

R. Danube

R. Nile

The Geographical Setting of the Novels

A map of the Mediterranean region showing the routes of the hero and heroine of a
novel inevitably brings to mind the school-bible's map of the travels of St Paul. Here
Xenophon's *Ephesian Tale* is mapped. The continuous line (——————) indicates the
hero and heroine's journey together from Ephesus *via* Samos and Rhodes to
somewhere in the middle of the sea, where their ship is attacked by pirates. From the
pirates' headquarters in Tyre the heroine (dotted line: ....) is taken to Antioch, sold
to slave-traders, shipwrecked off the Cilician coast, saved at the last moment from a
new marriage in Tarsus, brought to Alexandria, to Memphis, and up the Nile to the
Ethiopian border; then back to Alexandria, and across the sea to a brothel in Tarentum.
Meanwhile the hero (broken line: – – – – –) is searching desperately for her,
sometimes close on her heels, sometimes going totally astray. At last they are reunited
on Rhodes and return home to Ephesus.

The Novel
in Antiquity

TOMAS HÄGG

University of California Press
Berkeley and Los Angeles

For Bibi

University of California Press
Berkeley and Los Angeles

English edition © Tomas Hägg 1983

Swedish edition © Tomas Hägg 1980

Published in Swedish as *Den Antika Romanen*
by Bokförlaget Carmina, Uppsala

Revised by the author for the English edition
First Paperback Printing 1991

Library of Congress Cataloging Data

Hägg, Tomas.
 The novel in antiquity.
 Bibliography: p.
 Includes index.
 1. Classical fiction — History and criticism.
 I. Title.
 PA3040.H29   1983   883'.01'09   82-45906

 ISBN 0-520-07638-9

Printed in the United States of America
1 2 3 4 5 6 7 8 9

The paper used in this publication meets the minimum
requirements of American National Standard for
Information Sciences—Permanence of Paper for Printed
Library Materials, ANSI Z39.48–1984.   ∞

Contents

Preface

A book which sets out to introduce the ancient novel to readers outside the narrow circle of specialists in Greek and Latin literature
does not need many words of justification. In spite of increased
interest in the genre and considerable progress made in research in
recent years, there has been no modern, full-scale introduction to
the subject available in English. The scheme of the present attempt
to provide such an introduction may, however, require some com-
ment.

My approach is deliberately broad. In addition to the two central
forms, the ideal Greek novel and the Roman comic novel, the introduction covers also the pseudo-historical *Alexander Romance* and
the ideal novel's continuation in the apocryphal Acts of the
Apostles. The novel's social and literary contexts are described at
some length, and its reception in the middle ages and modern times
is traced. This has obviously meant sacrificing something in depth. I
have refrained from a fuller treatment of the fragments of novels
which papyrology continues to give us — a treatment which would
in any case have had to be rather technical — and I have also decided to dispense with a more profound theoretical discussion of the
genre's nature; particularly as its main characteristics will emerge,
in due course, through comparison with related literature, and are
also mirrored in the *Nachleben*.

It is my hope that the book will make its contribution, however
modest, towards redressing the balance in three respects. First, it is
my impression that even people who take a serious interest in the
modern novel, *and* its history, tend to ignore the genre's first stage,
which occurred, it is true, long before the terms 'novel' or 'romance'
were invented. The fact that there existed a 'kind of' novel in antiquity is known, but not much more. My description of the extant
examples is therefore as concrete as possible, with large extracts in

vii

translation — in the hope, of course, that once his interest is awakened the reader will pass on to the novels themselves in complete translations. Only in such a way can the ancient novel regain its legitimate place in the history of the genre. Second, I lay the emphasis throughout on the *Greek* novel, which has often had to stand in the shadow of the two Latin writers, Petronius and Apuleius. Their works are brilliant but isolated examples of their kind, whereas the ideal Greek novel of love, travel, and adventure was a flourishing popular genre for centuries. Third, there has also been a certain imbalance within the study of the Greek novel: the picture of the genre has been unduly coloured by the three late, 'sophistic' products of Longus, Achilles Tatius, and Heliodorus — the three who, in the Renaissance and baroque epochs, made their impact on European literature. To understand the rise of the genre as a whole, however, and its popular appeal in late Hellenistic and early Roman times, one has to focus on the earlier novels, those of Chariton and Xenophon of Ephesus, and the historical conditions that formed them.

The book is also addressed to readers who are not very familiar with ancient history and culture. There was a time, not long ago, when classicists began priding themselves on taking account of 'Greekless' and 'Latinless' readers. Now, in many countries, we face a situation in which well-educated people are even, to a large extent, 'Greece-and-Rome-less'. If we think our subject deserves a wider audience, we have to adjust accordingly. The author's problem, of course, is to try to supply the general background for these readers without making the account too dull or repetitive for those already initiated. The maxim to follow, as best one can, is never to overestimate the knowledge or underestimate the intelligence of the reader.

The history of the book is long and complicated, and mostly of interest only to its author. However, a few details may help to give the reader some idea of what to expect. It all started, in 1974, with an invitation from the University of Copenhagen to give a series of lectures on the narrative technique of the Greek novel, based on my Uppsala dissertation on that subject. This also entailed providing a general introduction to the genre, which is seldom on reading lists even in Classics departments. The introduction generated an appendix to a Danish translation of Heliodorus' novel, commissioned by Museum Tusculanums Forlag, and the series of lectures was later expanded for use in my teaching at the Universities of Uppsala and Bergen, until one day, much to my surprise, it proved possible to find a publisher for a book on the subject in Swedish. In the process of transforming the academic lectures into a readable book the interest and experience of the readers of Bokförlaget Carmina played a crucial role. The result was *Den Antika Romanen* (Uppsala, 1980), of which what now appears in English may most appropriately be described as the revised second edition. I have excluded some passages of interest only to Scandinavian readers, expanded others in the light of recent research, and — being my own translator — reformulated much. Some of the illustrations have been changed, and the total number of illustrations has had to be reduced.

Professor R. H. Pierce, my colleague in the Department of Classics, University of Bergen, read and corrected a first draft of my translation, and also sacrificed much of his time discussing various peculiarities of the English idiom. Professor B. P. Reardon, University of California, Irvine, generously put his expertise in the subject at my disposal for a stylistic revision of my final manuscript, thereby also saving me in places from saying something I did not really mean. The responsibility for what the book offers, in style and contents, of course rests with me alone, but had it not been for the unselfish help of these two friends I should never have ventured to assume that responsibility.

In the Swedish edition the translations from Greek and Latin were my own. In the present edition I have been fortunate enough to be able to quote in advance from a collection of new English translations of the Greek novels, to be published by the University of California Press under the editorship of Professor Reardon. In general, the translations in the forthcoming collection aim at accuracy and ease of reading; in some cases, which will be indicated in the text, the excerpts appearing in the present study try (at my request) to capture specific qualities of the original — such as the complexity of Heliodorus' style, or the sophistication of Longus' 'artistic prose' (see Appendix, p. 234). The translators are: Graham Anderson (Xenophon of Ephesus), Christopher Gill (Longus), J. R. Morgan (Heliodorus), B. P. Reardon (Chariton, *Alexander Romance*, *Acts of Paul and Thecla*, Eustathius Macrembolites), Gerald N. Sandy (Iamblichus), J. P. Sullivan (*Lucius or The Ass*, Apuleius, *Apollonius of Tyre*), and John Winkler (Achilles Tatius). To them, and to Professor Reardon for his good offices in making the translations available, I express my thanks.

My quest for illustrations was conducted mainly in the British Library, London, the Royal Libraries of Copenhagen and

Stockholm, and the University Libraries of Bergen and Uppsala.

Mrs Rita Dehlin, Bergen, with diligence and unfailing good spirits typed the successive versions of both the Swedish and the English edition.

To all those individuals and institutions mentioned above, and to others who have encouraged or assisted me in my work, I express my deep sense of gratitude.

The book is dedicated to my wife, to whose interest and constant support it ultimately owes its existence.

Bergen   Tomas Hägg

Note on Terms, Names and Historical Periods

An introduction to the ancient novel necessarily entails the use of a number of terms, concepts, and names that may be unfamiliar to those who are not daily occupied with Greek and Roman antiquity. Most terms are explained when they first occur, but it is convenient to deal with some of the more important ones at the outset. Those who feel reasonably at home in the ancient milieu can safely pass over this note and turn directly to the first chapter.

The book deals primarily with the *Greek* novel. 'Greek' always means 'ancient Greek', or possibly 'Byzantine Greek', but never 'modern Greek'. (The 'modern Greek' novel is quite another matter, not to be examined here.) One further term is employed here in a narrower sense than usual: *classical*. Throughout, by 'classical' is meant a limited period in Greek history, the classical period of 480–330 BC. The main periods of Greek history are the following (all limits are of course artificial, all dates round figures):

750 – 480 BC	Archaic Period
480 – 330 BC	Classical Period
330 – 30 BC	Hellenistic Period
30 BC – AD 330	Roman Imperial Period
AD 330 – 1453	Byzantine Period

Many put the beginning of the Byzantine period later, in the sixth century, for example. The transitional phase between imperial and Byzantine times, from the end of the third century, is called 'late antiquity'.

Most accounts of Greek literature deal with the archaic and classical periods, and with the epic, lyric, and dramatic genres. In this book, on the other hand, the *Hellenistic* period — which begins with Alexander's conquest of the Orient — is of central importance. That is when the Greek novel is 'born' (see especially chapter III).

During the *imperial* period it developed further: most of the extant Greek novels (described in chapter II) belong to the first centuries AD.

However, we shall also take account of the preceding or contemporary genres that had an influence on the novel (see especially chapter IV). At the beginning of the archaic period we find the *epic*, Homer's *Iliad* and *Odyssey*. *Tragedy*, with the three great names Aeschylus, Sophocles, and Euripides, flourishes in the fifth century; at the same time, Herodotus and Thucydides write their histories of the Persian and Peloponnesian Wars. *Historiography* was the first great prose genre of the Greeks. Xenophon of Athens, well known for his *Anabasis*, also continued the *History of Greece* where Thucydides broke off; his simple prose style influenced the first novelists. All Greek prose is also influenced by *rhetoric*; the fourth century is the century of the Attic orators (such as Lysias, a master of courtroom oratory, and Demosthenes, the most influential political orator), as it is that of the *philosophers* (Plato and Aristotle). At the transition from classical to Hellenistic times we find not only Aristotle — philosopher, scientist, literary theorist — but also the comic poet Menander: he represents the so-called *New Comedy* (to be distinguished from the 'Old Comedy' of Aristophanes, in the fifth century), apolitical comedies of manners set in the Athenian domestic milieu.

By the Hellenistic period, the Greek literary centre has moved from Athens to Alexandria in Egypt. Here Callimachus writes his hymns, epigrams, and other short poems; Apollonius Rhodius his long, learned epic in the Homeric tradition on the voyage of the Argonauts to Colchis; Theocritus his pastoral poems. The prose genres of this period — *historiography*, now strongly bent on stirring the emotions and creating sensational effects; *biography*; fantastic *travel tales* and *utopias* — will be dealt with in chapter IV.

In Roman imperial times there is a Greek cultural revival, the so-called *Second Sophistic*. It is characterized by *classicism*, a striving to return to the ideals of classical times, and by *Atticism*, an effort to shape literary works, even in the smallest detail of language, after the pattern of the ancient Athenians, the 'Attics'. The novels written under the influence of this movement are sometimes called *sophistic*; others are *pre-* or *non-sophistic*.

The map on the inside cover records most of the geographical names mentioned in the text. The index includes some additional information about persons and places.

CHAPTER I

The Novel in Antiquity — a Contradiction in Terms?

Homer, Virgil, and Heliodorus, the three great epic poets of antiquity. . . . Who today would not be taken aback by such a statement? What is this Heliodorus doing on the masters' list?

During the Renaissance our statement would not have provoked the same astonishment. Heliodorus, author of the voluminous Greek novel *Ethiopica*, or *An Ethiopian Tale*, was in vogue. The most distinguished literary theorist of the Spanish Golden Age, Alonso López Pinciano, pleads forcefully for Heliodorus' position at the side of Homer and Virgil. In his *Poetics* of 1596 he demonstrates, point by point, how Heliodorus satisfies Aristotle's requirements for epic and tragedy: the reader is brought directly into the midst of things (*in medias res*), the dramatic action 'turns' in the middle of the book (*peripeteia*), and a genuine recognition scene occurs at the end. The novel possesses verisimilitude and a high moral value. It is no problem that Heliodorus writes in prose instead of verse: even Aristotle himself objected to a classification starting from such a formal distinction. Consequently the *Ethiopica* is an epic, one of the very best, in some respects even superior to those of Homer and Virgil. And El Pinciano was not alone in ranking Heliodorus so highly. In Italy, Spain, France, and England of the sixteenth and seventeenth centuries the Greek novels of Roman imperial times — Longus and Achilles Tatius as well as Heliodorus — were much read in translation and greatly admired. Authors like Tasso, Sidney, Cervantes, Lope de Vega, Calderón, and Racine were influenced in various ways by these models, and adapted, imitated, or dramatized them.

Since then their reputation has faded. Today Heliodorus is hardly more than a name, if that, to most people with literary interests — the novel's plot and milieu are more generally known only in so far as they are mirrored in Verdi's *Aida*. *Daphnis and Chloe*, Longus'

1

pastoral novel, which is the least typical of the Greek novels, is the only one to be found more regularly on reading lists and in handbooks, perhaps to some extent because Goethe admired and recommended it. Ravel made it into a ballet; Chagall illustrated it. It still appears in new editions in various languages, often lavishly illustrated.

We shall presently allow the five extant Greek novels to speak for themselves, in chronological order, which means starting with those least known in modern times. First, however, some words about the genre in general, and the terms used for it. What El Pinciano and his contemporaries had been content to call 'epic', or sometimes 'prose epic', was as early as the following century classed as *roman*, as having more in common with d'Urfé's *L'Astrée* than with the *Iliad*. Pierre Daniel Huet's pioneering *Traité de l'origine des romans* of 1670 is much concerned with the novel in antiquity. But strictly speaking it is of course an anachronism to use the label *roman* (*Roman, romanzo*, etc.), or one of its English equivalents, 'romance' or 'novel', with reference to ancient literature. As regards most of the principal forms or genres of literature, we have taken over the terms, and largely also the definitions, from the ancient Greeks: the epic, lyric, and dramatic forms, tragedy and comedy, and so on. But for longer fictional narratives in prose we use terms of medieval origin. 'Romance' came to be used for medieval narratives in verse, later also in prose, which were composed not in Latin but in the vernacular, that is, in one of the 'Romance' daughter languages of Latin. '*Novella*' was applied to short stories of the 'new' kind Boccaccio presented in his *Decameron*, while its English derivative 'novel' in its modern sense appears to be no older than the seventeenth century.

The thought readily lets itself be guided by the word. If we judge by the term 'romance', the genre apparently begins around, say, the mid-twelfth century. Some historians of literature are even more radical, placing the real creation of the new genre at the beginning of the seventeenth century, with Cervantes' *Don Quixote*: this is the first true *roman* or 'novel'. And the influential book by Ian Watt, *The Rise of the Novel*, starts in eighteenth-century England. But if we disregard various scholars' stricter definitions of each of these terms and apply any one of them in its widest sense, collecting under one heading *Tristan and Isolde* and *Tristram Shandy*, *The Sorrows of Werther* and *Moby Dick*, James Joyce and Alain Robbe-Grillet, then there is no reason whatsoever to exclude the Greek and Roman precedents. When this is still done, the fault no doubt lies with the terminology and the inhibitions it has caused; and the root of the terminological evil is the ancient vacuum.

Antiquity never created a special term for its 'novels'. In Aristotle's day the genre did not yet exist. Only in middle or late Hellenistic times, in the last centuries BC, can we watch — or, rather, infer from the scanty evidence — how a new type of prose literature begins to be produced and distributed in the Greek-speaking countries around the Eastern Mediterranean. Mostly, we are concerned with simple adventure stories which have love, travel and violence as their main constituents. Sometimes violence is replaced by a stronger admixture of emotions, by a marked taste for sentimentality. In both cases, the result is light reading for a comparatively broad audience. The setting may be historical, but in the centre of these fictitious narratives are placed the experiences of private individuals, tossed about by fate in a world unmistakably Hellenistic.

The new genre seems to have gained a wide popularity rather quickly; numerous papyrus fragments have been found from novels other than the five which have reached us complete by way of the medieval manuscript tradition. Moreover, of these five only two belong to the earlier, more popular type of novel, namely Chariton's *Chaereas and Callirhoe* and Xenophon's *Ephesiaca*. The remaining three, identical with those disseminated and appreciated during the Renaissance and the baroque period, are the more artistic products of the Greek cultural revival of Roman imperial times. But not even then did the genre acquire a name; when works of this kind are sometimes alluded to, either very general terms are used, such as 'fictitious' or 'dramatic' tales (*plasmatika, dramatika*), or they are characterized in more detail for a particular purpose. For instance, when Emperor Julian the Apostate in a letter wishes to warn against the reading of novels, he resorts to the loose description 'fictions (*plasmata*). . . in the form of history, love subjects, and — in short — everything of that kind'.

It is true that the novel is not alone in lacking a specific name. Antiquity's 'tyranny of genres' has often been overstated; if we look more closely, there is quite a number of literary works that are outsiders, as far as the established genres are concerned, and yet they were not disregarded by the intellectuals of the time. But the novel is a whole class of literature, and a prolific one at that, lacking a learned designation of its own. The main reason for this, besides their postclassical start, seems to be that early novels, like early Christian writings, were not regarded as true literature by literary theorists and critics. There is no positive evidence for the acceptance in such quarters even of the sophisticated novels of imperial times, in spite of the obvious stylistic ambitions of their authors. Novels were most probably also read in highbrow circles, but they were not acknowledged or seriously discussed.

In accounts of the Greek novel written in English, the terms 'romance' and 'novel' are applied alternately, with some preference for the first. This alternation is indicative not only of the notorious vagueness of these terms, but also of the nature of the Greek novel. In contrast to the Roman novel, which most people nowadays agree to call 'novel', the Greek variety is chiefly 'ideal', and should thus satisfy one of the criteria often used for the 'romance'. But if we examine the first Greek novel preserved in full, that of Chariton, we also find much in common with the characteristics of the 'novel', such as the emphasis given to psychology and human relations. If the 'romance' is about incidents 'remote from everyday life', whereas the 'novel' portrays 'characters and actions credibly representative of real life in continuous plot', as one set of definitions has it, Chariton is indeed a novelist on many of his pages.

However, if I prefer to use 'novel' throughout, except in conventional titles like the *Alexander Romance*, it is not in order to inflict upon the reader the impression that we are throughout concerned with novels in the *specific* sense of the term. Both 'romance' and 'novel' can also be used globally, and it seems to me that today 'novel' is the more nearly unmarked term of the two, the one less liable to implant prejudices as to the nature of the genre. And an unmarked term is indeed needed to cover the remarkable diversity which the novel already exhibited in antiquity.

CHAPTER II

The Ideal Greek Novel

Chariton: Chaereas and Callirhoe

When writing about the Greek novels, one is never confronted with the problem of how to divide one's attention between the literary text itself and the personality and biography of the author. In all cases, we know the author exclusively through his written work and what he there discloses about himself, consciously or not. The writer of the oldest novel that survives in full introduces himself in the very first sentence, where he alludes to the way in which the classical historians begin their works:

My name is Chariton, of Aphrodisias, and I am clerk to the rhetor Athenagoras. I am going to tell you the story of a love-affair [*pathos erotikon*] which took place in Syracuse. (1.1.1)

This is all that is known, and for a long time many doubted the truth even of this scanty information. 'Chariton' was regarded as a pseudonym alluding to the Charites, or Graces, and 'Aphrodisias' seemed to be only too fitting a home town for an author writing about the intrigues of Aphrodite. But since the names Chariton and Athenagoras turned up as the names of historical persons in inscriptions precisely in Aphrodisias in Caria (SW Asia Minor), doubt has died away.

Since the authors are known from no other source and the ancient literary critics are silent about this genre, the dating of the Greek novels was a controversial issue, and still is. The controversy is not about decennia, as in the case of other ancient works of literature, but about centuries. Chariton was placed in the fifth or even sixth century AD, last in the line of novelists, in Erwin Rohde's pioneering work *Der griechische Roman* (1876). More recently discovered papyrus fragments from this novel have made it clear that it must be

5

placed at least before AD 150, and there are now good reasons for
dating it as far back as late Hellenistic times, in the first century BC.
Chariton's general attitude is highly classicistic, but as far as
language and style are concerned, his novel must be placed before,
or possibly beside, the pure 'Atticism' (see below, p. 106) which
colours the other extant novels to a greater or lesser degree.

We shall dwell in some detail upon the plot of this first novel,
since important features of its general action as well as many of its
specific motifs recur in the other novels. The alternative would be to
give one more of those standard descriptions of 'The Greek Novel'
which appear all too often in literary manuals and tend to create a
false impression. It is true that the novels all build on a common
theme, but the variations are many and the individual authors
should be clearly distinguished.

According to the only complete manuscript of Chariton's novel,
its title was *Erotic Tales about Chaereas and Callirhoe*. Callirhoe is
the daughter of Hermocrates, the leading figure in the defence of
Syracuse against the Athenian naval expedition to Sicily in
415–413 BC, which ended in total disaster for Athens. He also
occurs in Thucydides and is thus a historical person. There is, on the
other hand, no reliable evidence for the existence of Callirhoe
herself. She has a 'speaking' name: 'the beautiful-flowing (spring)';
the same applies for both hero and heroine in several of the novels,
whereas the secondary characters are often given less poetic, more
everyday names.

Callirhoe's beauty is superhuman; it can be compared only to that
of Aphrodite (figure 1) — such comparisons are legion in the
novels. Suitors gather in crowds around her, not only from all Sicily
but also from Italy and even further away. But Eros has his own
plan: he wants to couple Callirhoe with Chaereas, the equally handsome son of Hermocrates' chief political rival — here we can see the
Romeo-and-Juliet motif emerge. It is also worth noting how the action is conducted simultaneously on two levels: 'divine and human
motivation' as in Homer.

At a public festival of Aphrodite the two young people happen to
run into each other in the crowd. The result is love at first sight.
Their anguish is intense, and both, separately, are all but consumed
by passion and destroyed by it. Extremely intense emotions, streams
of tears, swooning are all characteristic of the Greek novel from its
very beginnings. The political rivalry of the fathers seems to exclude
a marital union, but the people of Syracuse stand up for the young
couple, assemble in the theatre, and force Hermocrates to give his

Fig. 1 *'Her beauty was not human but divine — not that of a sea-nymph or a mountain-nymph but that of Aphrodite the Maiden herself. . . .' This is Chariton's description of his heroine. Similarly, the hero is said to surpass everyone in beauty; he looks 'just as sculptors and painters represent Achilles and Nireus and Hippolytus and Alcibiades'. Similes of this kind are common in the novels. Instead of a lengthy verbal description, the author evokes a mental image in his reader by referring to works of art which everybody has seen in the sanctuaries and public places. So the technique also serves as a substitute for book illustration. The goddess of love depicted here, the famous Venus de Milo (now in the Louvre), belongs to the latter part of the second century BC; stylistically it looks back with nostalgia to the classical period, as does Chariton's novel.*

assent. 'There and then her knees and heart dissolved. . .' is how, borrowing a verse from Homer, Chariton describes the heroine's reaction on hearing that her father has consented to her marriage. Such borrowings from Homer, inserted in the narrative itself, form a characteristic feature of Chariton's style.

The wedding is attended by a *baskanos daimon*, a malevolent creature, who soon assumes the human guise of Callirhoe's rejected suitors. They meet and agree to take their revenge for the injury inflicted on them when Hermocrates and Callirhoe preferred Chaereas to themselves. Through a cunningly planned and executed intrigue they succeed in making Chaereas suspect his wife of infidelity. The thrilling course of events is reported as rapidly and effectively as in an Attic courtroom speech. Full of jealousy Chaereas rushes into his home and kicks Callirhoe in her stomach. She collapses, lifeless.

Through torture of the female slaves — described as a purely routine matter — Chaereas realizes that Callirhoe was innocent after all, and is seized with violent remorse. He endeavours to be sentenced to death for uxoricide, but is acquitted; he wants to commit suicide, but is prevented from doing so by his friend and constant companion Polycharmus. Callirhoe is given a magnificent burial. Honoured with rich funeral gifts she is laid to rest in a tomb by the sea.

The villain of the piece now enters the scene. This is how he is introduced:

There was a man called Theron, a scoundrel whose criminal trade it was to sail the seas and have thugs handily stationed with boats in harbours under cover of being ferrymen; from them he made up pirate crews. Theron had been about at the funeral; his gaze had fastened on the gold, and when he went to bed that night he could not sleep for thinking 'Why should I risk my life battling with the sea and killing living people and not getting much out of it, when I can get rich from one dead body? Let the die be cast; I won't miss a chance like that of making money. Now, whom shall I recruit for the job? Think, Theron; who would be suitable, of the men you know? Zenophanes of Thurii? Intelligent, but a coward. Menon of Messene? Brave, but untrustworthy.' — and he assessed each one in turn, like a man testing coins; many he rejected, but he did think some suitable. So at dawn he hurried to the harbour area and began looking them out one by one; some of them he found in brothels, others in taverns — an army fit for such a commander. (1.7.1–3)

The effective characterization and lively style, with a rich admixture of direct speech, are very typical of Chariton. His strength is not his explicit, often rather stereotyped comments on the characters and their behaviour, but rather the gradually emerging, subtle overall picture built up of the actions, reactions, and utterances of the characters, all the more effective for his observant eye for detail and grasp of psychology.

While Theron is gathering his gang of robbers and preparing to plunder the rich tomb, the author lets us have a look into the grave chamber. Here Callirhoe is just coming to life again. She has been only apparently dead and is naturally seized with horror when she catches sight of the funeral gifts and realizes what has happened. Her fear and despair are expressed in a monologue of lament, which has innumerable counterparts both in this novel and in all the others, just as the motif of apparent death recurs with persistent regularity.

But now deliverance is at hand for Callirhoe, though in the form of the pirate and grave-robber Theron. Chariton scores some comic points here: the hardboiled robbers mistake poor frightened Callirhoe for a spirit guarding the tomb and prepare for headlong flight. Theron himself, however, is not one to be seized with panic; he clears the matter up with typical common sense. The grave-robbers sit down to debate what to do with their unexpected booty. At last they decide to take Callirhoe with them on the ship, together with their plunder, and sail off.

Having been carried eastwards to Attica they go ashore for provisions and rest, and then continue to the west coast of Asia Minor, to the area around Miletus in Ionia. Theron tries to find a prospective buyer for Callirhoe, whom he offers for sale as a slave. After protracted negotiations he succeeds in selling her to the steward of a country estate and sails off with his companions, happy and relieved. The purchase itself is described with detailed accuracy, in which one can no doubt recognize the advocate's secretary from Aphrodisias, well versed in legal matters.

The owner of the country estate is Dionysius, a cultivated and sympathetic man, recently widowed. On his way from Miletus to his estate he sees his new slave for the first time:

She was standing there praying when Dionysius, jumping down off his horse, led the way into the temple. Callirhoe heard footsteps and turned to face him. So Dionysius had a full view of her — and his reaction was to exclaim: 'Be gracious, Aphrodite! May the vision of you be to my good!', and to fall to his knees. But Leonas [the steward] caught him up and said 'Sir, this is the woman we have just bought — don't be alarmed. — You, woman, come here to your master!' Now, when she heard the word 'master' Callirhoe hung her head and burst into tears — she was learning, at last, what it was not to be free. Dionysius struck Leonas: 'Impious fellow!' he said, 'do you address gods as if they were mortals? Are you telling me this woman is a bought slave? No wonder you couldn't find the seller! Haven't you ever heard where Homer himself tells us that

"The gods, in the guise of strangers from far countries
Look on the arrogance and on the harmony of mankind?"'

So then Callirhoe said 'Stop making fun of me and calling me a goddess — I'm not even a happy mortal!' Her voice, as she spoke, sounded quite divine to Dionysius; it had a musical sound, a tone like a lyre. So he was thrown into confusion. He was too awed to stay in her presence any longer, and went off to his villa, already on fire with love. (2.3.5−8)

Later the state of the Ionian nobleman is described in the following manner:

Dionysius was wounded but tried to hide the fact, like a well-brought-up man, who took particular pride in his own manly behaviour. Not wanting his servants to think him contemptible, or his friends to think him adolescent, he held out all evening: he thought that nobody noticed, but in fact his silence made his state all the more obvious. At dinner he took some food from the table and said 'Take this to the foreign woman. Don't say it's from the "master" but "from Dionysius".'

He prolonged the drinking after dinner as long as he could; knowing that he would not sleep, he wanted to stay awake among his friends. But when the night was far advanced he dismissed the company. He could not get to sleep. His whole being was in Aphrodite's shrine; he could recall every detail — her face, her hair, the way she turned, the way she looked at him, her voice, her bearing, her words; and her tears burned into him. Now there was a visible struggle between reason and emotion; desire flooded over him, but his noble character tried to resist. He kept rising from these waves and saying to himself 'Dionysius, you should be ashamed of yourself. You, the first man in Ionia in virtue and reputation, the admiration of satraps and kings and cities — behaving like a teenager! Love at first sight — and you in mourning! You haven't finished paying your respects to your poor wife's departed spirit! Is that why you came out to your estate — to celebrate a wedding still wearing black? A wedding with a slave at that — perhaps even another man's wife, because you haven't even got the bill of sale for her!' His thoughts were noble, but Eros loves trouble; Eros thought his restraint [*sophrosyne*] was insufferable [*hybris*], and so fanned to a blaze the fire in a heart in love but trying to play the philosopher. (2.4.1−5)

Callirhoe remains steadfast as long as possible; she would rather die than be unfaithful to Chaereas. Not until she realizes that she has been pregnant for two months with Chaereas' child does she yield to the will of her master and consent to marry him. Plangon, Dionysius' servant, who is a realistic and positive woman (in contrast to the heroine with her paralysing idealism), is the one who succeeds in persuading Callirhoe to take this step in order to legitimize her child; Dionysius is to believe that the child is his, only born a couple of months early. With the description of the wedding of Dionysius and Callirhoe the author leaves the Ionian scene for the time being in order to tell what has happened to Chaereas during the same period of time, since the day we left him lamenting in the funeral procession. The narrative has up to this point strictly followed the chronology of the story; now it makes a long jump backwards in time.

On his first visit to the grave after the funeral Chaereas discovers that the stone at the entrance has been moved and the chamber is empty. The city of Syracuse sends off its warships in various directions to search for the grave-robbers and the stolen goods. Tyche, the goddess of fortune or chance and a habitual figure in the Greek novels (figure 2), sees to it that Chaereas' own ship comes upon Theron's pirate vessel, where it is drifting, its crew dead of thirst. Only Theron has managed to stay alive, by stealing his fellow robbers' water. But now not even his cunning can help him any longer. Callirhoe's funeral gifts are recognized. Through torture Theron is forced to tell the truth, and is finally crucified in front of Callirhoe's tomb.

Chaereas and his friend Polycharmus — they are compared to Achilles and Patroclus of the *Iliad* — follow Callirhoe's trail to Ionia. Chaereas learns to his despair that Callirhoe is now the wife of Dionysius. Before he has time to take any further steps he is put out of action by Dionysius' steward. (It was he who had earlier arranged the purchase of Callirhoe and made his master believe that she was an ordinary slave.) In order not to put Dionysius' new-found happiness at risk, he now sees to it that Chaereas' ship is attacked and burnt, the crew killed or taken prisoner, and Chaereas and Polycharmus sold as slaves to Caria (Chariton's own native country!). It is typical of Chariton's constantly benevolent and conciliatory spirit that the instigator of this outrage is not negatively characterized; on the contrary, the steward is *philodespotos*, he is driven to the deed by love for his master. The author even to some extent exonerates the leading villain of the piece, Theron; his main characteristics are craftiness and energy, rather than deliberate wickedness.

In a dream Callirhoe sees Chaereas in chains and cries out in her sleep 'Come here, Chaereas!', and so her secret is revealed to

Fig. 2 *The goddess of fate or chance — the Greek Tyche, the Roman Fortuna — is often invoked in the novels. Works of art and coins confirm that she was in vogue in the Hellenistic Period. A signet ring with her picture could be a good-luck charm: here a carved sardonyx stone of the first century* BC*. Tyche's attributes were the horn of plenty (**cornucopia**), which symbolized her power to bestow material prosperity (cities often had her as their patron), and the rudder, which indicated that she governed individual destinies. In addition, she was sometimes depicted standing on a ball to represent her fickleness. It is this particular quality that the poor heroes and heroines of the novels get to know best.*

Dionysius. Dreams of a more or less directly symbolic kind are a common feature of the novels. With Chariton they often, in addition, serve a purely practical purpose, as here. Now begins a complex intrigue, with many twists and turns in the plot. Dionysius fights to keep Callirhoe, Chaereas strives to regain her, and a personage no less than Artaxerxes, the Great King of Persia, is smitten with love for the same wonderfully beautiful woman when the dispute between the two husbands is brought before his court in Babylon. Here Chariton has an opportunity to show off his talent for rhetoric in the speeches of the opposing parties. The court proceedings are a central item in the composition of the novel, and also its turning point, *peripeteia*. In the courtroom Chaereas can see his beloved Callirhoe again, if only for a moment; it is the first time since his fatal act of jealousy at the beginning of the novel.

While the case is still pending — it takes time since the great king is now himself emotionally involved in the subject of dispute — a rebellion breaks out in Egypt. Within four days the whole of the Persian armed forces are on the march. Callirhoe has to leave Babylon with the army baggage, together with the queen and the other women and children. Many similar items of information about Persian manners and customs are given in this part of the novel. Even Dionysius is forced to take part in the war; as an Ionian he is the great king's subject. Chaereas, for his part, manages to desert to the Egyptian camp. He soon carries out a marvellous feat of arms: at the head of three hundred picked Greek soldiers he storms and captures the city of Tyre in Phoenicia, which had up till then defied all attacks.

Dionysius, having accomplished a similar feat on the Persian side, is convinced that Callirhoe will now be his as a reward. But his expectations are frustrated: Aphrodite at last feels pity for Chaereas, who has now been punished enough for his unreasonable jealousy. He has had to wander from West to East, suffer countless torments, and Fortune shall no longer be allowed to play her cruel game with him. Aphrodite therefore stages an *anagnorismos*, a recognition scene, on the island of Aradus off the coast of Phoenicia. Callirhoe has already been brought there by the great king, and now Chaereas also arrives with his victorious Egyptian fleet.

The author himself prepares the reader for what is to come:

I think my readers will find this last book very agreeable, because it will clear away the grim contents of the earlier ones. No more piracy or slavery or trials or battles or suicide or war or capture; instead, sanctioned love, and legitimate marriage. I am going to tell you, then, how Aphrodite brought the truth to light and revealed the pair, each unrecognized, to each other. (8.1.4)

Chariton often steps forward in this way with comments addressed directly to the reader. Sometimes, imitating the historian Xenophon in his *Anabasis* (the openings of Books II–V), he gives summaries of what has happened earlier in the novel; sometimes he provides glimpses of what is to be expected, as here, or general statements about human behaviour based on some incident just related. He is the omniscient narrator who unconstrainedly communicates with his audience over the heads of his invented characters.

The happy reunion is described with drama and sentiment. Chaereas is brought to the room of an unknown female prisoner:

So he crossed the threshold, and when he saw her lying there on the ground with her head covered up, the way she breathed and held herself caused his heart to flutter; he became excited, and would certainly have recognized her had he not been quite convinced that Dionysius had recovered Callirhoe. He approached her gently. 'Don't be afraid, lady,' he said, 'whoever you are — we are not going to violate you. You shall have the husband you want.' Before he had finished speaking Callirhoe recognized his voice and uncovered her head. They both cried out at once — 'Chaereas!' 'Callirhoe!' — and embracing each other they fell to the ground in a faint. (8.1.7–8)

Chaereas' loyal companion Polycharmus endeavours to recall them to consciousness. Chariton continues:

Although he said this loudly, they were like people plunged in a deep well, who can barely hear a voice from above. Slowly they recovered their senses; then they saw each other and embraced each other passionately — and fainted again, a second time and a third time. They could say only one thing: 'You are in my arms — if you really are Callirhoe, if you really are Chaereas!' (8.1.10)

It remains to wind up Chaereas' military obligations and get him and Callirhoe home to Syracuse (figure 3). The reader is also made to witness Dionysius' grief when he receives Callirhoe's farewell letter and realizes that he has now lost her for good. The novel ends with Chaereas' and his father-in-law's detailed account, in front of the Syracusan people's assembly, of all that has happened since the day when the people themselves induced Hermocrates to give his beautiful daughter to Chaereas as his wedded wife — a broad final

Fig. 3 *The happy ending, at last! After an infinite series of adventures — 'piracy, slavery, trials, battles, suicide, war, capture' — Chaereas and Callirhoe are reunited on the little island of Aradus off the coast of Phoenicia. On board Chaereas' ship they enjoy their homeward journey together via Cyprus to Syracuse, where the whole population welcomes them with enthusiasm. Illustration by C. L. Desrais in a French translation of 1775.*

recapitulation with epic antecedents (see below, p. 110). There are
similar cases, though less detailed, in some of the later novels.

What is most characteristic of Chariton's novel might be summarized in three words: psychology, rhetoric, history. First, his
interest in the human mind. The 'inner process', the sorrow and
happiness of the characters, their hopes and fears, not least their ir-
resolution in difficult situations involving choice — the author
devotes much more attention to all this than he does to the external
course of events, which is often dismissed in a few short sentences.
The description is throughout marked by a strong sympathy for the
human being, be he Greek or barbarian, slave or king. Not without
justification, the general tone of Chariton's novel has been
characterized as 'sentimental, bourgeois, and rather similar to the
tone of stories in ladies' magazines today' (B. P. Reardon); but
Chariton is not just writing to a commercial formula, he has a
thoroughly serious view of the conflicts he depicts. He is naïve, but
sincere.

The author's second passion is rhetoric. The novel is full of
deliberations of various kinds, where the participants eloquently
present their arguments. Some are private discussions, as among the
rejected suitors or the robbers who have found the supposed corpse
alive in the grave; others are court proceedings or speeches before a
military or civil assembly, where the traditional Greek oratory
flourishes. No character in the novel is so unlearned or barbarian as
not to be able to set forth his viewpoint in a well-turned speech.
Nearly half of the novel's text consists of direct speech — a fact
worth noting, since the 'scenic' form is sometimes considered
characteristic of the modern novel alone. Besides speeches and
monologues there are also passages of lively and rapid dialogue;
among the ancient novels, *Chaereas and Callirhoe* stands closest to
the comedies of Menander.

The third characteristic is the addiction to history, or rather to
the classical historians. Chariton's classicism also manifests itself in
the quotation of Homeric verses and in the use of metaphors and
similes from classical mythology, but his main object of admiration
and imitation, both in style and content, is certainly the historians.
It seems as if he wished to legitimize the novel as literature through
its historical framework and historiographic form. Or, to put it
another way, he seeks to provide a kind of deeper justification for
our interest in the (strictly speaking) totally personal experiences of
private individuals, by letting the whole people participate in their
fortunes. The story we are reading is not just any story — the author

wants to impress upon us — but one which, once upon a time, in the great days of Greece, the Syracusan people's assembly followed in a state of breathless suspense, and the happy conclusion of which was greeted with general relief and rejoicing.

Incidentally, the historical frame turns out not to be quite correct, when examined in more detail. Hermocrates in fact died in 407 BC, before the end of the Peloponnesian War, and cannot have experienced the period of Greek internal peace which the events of the novel presuppose. Artaxerxes II Mnemon, who must be the Persian king intended in the novel, reigned from 404 to 359 BC and was consequently not contemporary with Hermocrates; nor presumably did he experience the Egyptian rebellion which inspired Chariton, since the details given about the rebellion and the storming of Tyre seem to be taken from the history of Alexander. But such anachronisms are not likely to have bothered Chariton, or his audience; at any rate they do not change our assessment of the real aim of the historical framework.

The Ninus, Sesonchosis and Parthenope Romances

Among the surviving novelists Chariton is the one who paints a historical background for his plot in the most methodical and concrete fashion. But the oldest fragment we possess, from the *Ninus Romance*, shows that Chariton had a tradition behind him in this respect. In this novel, conventionally dated to *c.* 100 BC, the hero is the Assyrian king Ninus, a youth of only seventeen years, and the heroine his cousin Semiramis (otherwise best known for her hanging gardens). In other words, this time two historical figures are themselves made the subject of a romanticized tale, creating, at least on the surface, a firmer attachment to history, or myth, than in Chariton's case. However, this does not mean that the plot itself or the characterization follow the tradition about Queen Semiramis, as we know it from other sources; on the contrary, apart from the names the points of contact seem to be extremely few. The ingredients of shipwreck, war, and eloquent love are discernible in the fragments, but they tell us very little about the general outline of the story.

Still less is preserved of a similar, though probably much later tale, which is enacted on Egyptian soil and centres on the legendary Pharaoh Sesonchosis. One of the fragments contains a conversation between father and son, where the latter seems to be opposed to the marriage planned for him by his father, a motif not unknown from comedy and novel. Whether this is really a novel of love and adventure, or perhaps rather pseudo-history like the *Alexander Romance* (see chapter V), is not revealed by the fragments.

Quite recently one further specimen of a similar kind, a novel in a historical setting, has been identified. Three papyrus fragments, written by the same hand and dated in the second century AD, give us parts of an account of a symposium at the court of the tyrant Polycrates (died 522 BC) on the island of Samos. The heroine of the novel, Parthenope, is to all appearances identical with the daughter of Polycrates whom Herodotus mentions, though not by name. The hero, Metiochus, seems to be the eldest son (born *c*. 530–520 BC) of Miltiades, the Marathon general, by an anachronism typical of the novelists. As the toast-master of the symposium we find the philosopher Anaximenes of Miletus; in Platonic tradition the topic of discussion is the nature of Eros, and the two lovers, Metiochus and Parthenope, make one contribution each. The way in which the novel relates to history reminds one strikingly of Chariton: as the latter borrows Hermocrates from Thucydides and spins the story round his daughter Callirhoe, otherwise unknown, we here meet two well-known figures from Herodotus, Polycrates and Miltiades, as the fathers of the young couple around whom the usual unhistorical intrigue — love, separation, search — has been built.

Ancient art does not provide any securely identifiable illustrations of the surviving novels. As for the fragments, we are in a somewhat better position. In a villa outside Antioch in Syria excavations have revealed several mosaic floors with motifs from novels. In one mosaic (figure 4) we see the young Ninus lying on his bed with a picture of his beloved in his right hand. In another (figure 5) Parthenope stands talking to Metiochus, who is dressed as a Roman officer: the names of both are neatly written over their heads. Other mosaics with similar pictures (figure 6) confirm that these themes were popular, even if it is just possible that some of the mosaics may illustrate not the novels but theatrical performances with the same principal characters.

Xenophon: An Ephesian Tale

Several notable similarities to Chariton's *Chaereas and Callirhoe* can be found in the novel known as *Ephesiaca*, or *An Ephesian Tale*, ascribed to a certain Xenophon with the by-name Ephesius ('of Ephesus'). Whether the author's name is a pseudonym alluding to the classical historian, who influenced both Chariton and 'the

Ephesian', or whether the by-name has perhaps been given to him simply because the novel begins and ends in Ephesus (figure 7), are matters of speculation, and there are in the text itself no firm dating

Fig. 4 *Ninus on his bed with a portrait of Semiramis in his hand. Detail from a floor mosaic from Antioch on the Orontes in Syria, c. AD 200. The identification is established by another, less well-preserved mosaic from Alexandretta, in which the same motif bears the inscription 'Ninos'. The novel has survived only in fragments, and the scene illustrated in the mosaic is not among the preserved parts. Perhaps the picture shows Ninus' fidelity to his beloved when separated from her during his military expeditions. To the right, a young girl — servant or temptress? — who offers a drink. Or is it a scene of attempted suicide, the girl bringing Ninus a cup of poison to end his distress over the supposed death of his beloved?*

criteria. Generally one is inclined to put the novel in the second century AD, the great century of this genre.

The similarities to Chariton concern in the first place some common motifs and the phraseological form they have assumed. Much
has been written in an attempt to prove who is the model and who
the imitator, and since neither of the novels is dated with absolute
certainty, this discussion is bound to continue. But the motifs in

Fig. 5 *Parthenope and Metiochus. The same summer residence at
Daphne outside Antioch that contained the Ninus mosaic (figure 4) was
also embellished with this illustration of another novel, of which only
fragments survive: the romantic tale of Polycrates' daughter Parthenope
and Miltiades' son Metiochus. The hero is dressed as a Roman officer, and
the heroine approaches him with a theatrical gesture.*

question may well have been common not only to these two but also to several Hellenistic novels lost to us, and therefore we cannot exclude the possibility of a common model, or common models, rather than direct imitation between the two accidentally preserved specimens.

In any case there is no trace in Xenophon of the humane spirit which pervades Chariton's novel. Characterization in the *Ephesiaca* is much more stereotyped, insofar as the many figures in the story are characterized at all before disappearing behind the scenes. The rhetoric has an emptier ring, and external events, partly of a violent nature, dominate. The novel is packed with narrative material; in only seventy-five pages — half the length of Chariton, a quarter that of Heliodorus — hero and heroine manage to visit an astonishingly large part of the Mediterranean world (see the map on the inside cover!), meeting in turn with shipwreck, the assaults of robbers or pirates, apparent death with ensuing burial, crucifixion, confinement to a brothel, and many other evil machinations against chastity and marital fidelity.

There is a remarkable unevenness in the narrative. Certain episodes, especially at the beginning of the novel, are embroidered with some richness of detail and with direct speech. Others are rapidly and summarily narrated. This has been explained as the result of a subsequent abridgement of an originally much longer and more 'even' novel — mistakenly, in my opinion. The style of the novel *throughout* is very simple, and the missing fullness of detail at some places may very well be accounted for by insufficient imagination or energy in the author: he simply failed to embroider all the motifs he had collected for his novel. Some contradictions and logical flaws have also been brought forward as evidence for the abridgement, but they are in fact natural features of a simple adventure story, though seldom noticed until the story in question is scrutinized under a magnifying glass, as the *Ephesiaca* has been. Add to these considerations the average risk of corruption in manuscript tradition — the *Ephesiaca* is preserved in one medieval manuscript only — and the supposed evidence for a deliberate abbreviation of the novel tends to evaporate.

The author does not totally lack a talent for telling a story, and, as already mentioned, he possesses an abundance of motifs and plots that he intends to include in his novel at any price. The plot of a whole novel has been reduced to a short secondary tale, a 'story-within-a-story': an old fisherman, Aegialeus, tells his temporary lodger Habrocomes, the hero of the novel, the story of his life:

Fig. 6 *Parthenope and Metiochus. Fragments of a floor mosaic, probably from the same house as figures 4–5. The two lovers are sitting back to back, looking intensely at each other over their shoulders. The erotic*

character of the situation is indicated by the girl's dress, which has slipped down from her left shoulder; her diadem, ear-ring, and armlets show her noble descent.

'Habrocomes my child, I am neither a settler nor a native of Sicily, but a
Spartan from Lacedaemon, from one of its leading families. I was very
prosperous, and when I was a young man enrolled in the ephebes, I fell in
love with a Spartan girl called Thelxinoe, and Thelxinoe loved me in
return. We had an encounter at an all-night festival in the city — a god
guided both our paths — and we found fulfilment for the passion that had

Fig. 7 *The shrine of Artemis at Ephesus, as it was rebuilt after the fire of
356 BC which made the arsonist, Herostratus, notorious. (Reconstruction
drawing by F. Krischen, 1938.) Through a forest of huge columns, with
Ionic capitals and decoratively sculptured bases, the view opens into the
holy of holies, where the enormous cult image of Artemis rises. Xenophon's*
Ephesian Tale *both begins and ends at this temple: Habrocomes and
Antheia first meet here at the annual festival of Artemis and fall in love,
and this is also where they finally deposit a written account of their
sufferings.*

brought us together. For some time we met in secret, and we often made pacts to be faithful unto death. But some god must have been envious. While I was still an ephebe, Thelxinoe's parents arranged to marry her to a young Spartan called Androcles; this Androcles was now in love with her as well. At first the girl found a lot of excuses for putting off the wedding; but at last she was able to meet me, and she agreed to leave Lacedaemon at night with me. So we both dressed as men, and I cut Thelxinoe's hair. We left town the very night of the wedding for Argos and Corinth, and from there we took ship for Sicily. When the Spartans found out we had gone they condemned us to death. We spent our lives in this place, poor but happy, thinking we had everything when we had each other. Thelxinoe died in this place not long ago; I didn't bury her body, but have it with me: I always have her company and adore her.' And at this he brought Habrocomes into the inner room and showed him Thelxinoe. She was now an old woman, but still seemed a young girl to Aegialeus. Her body was embalmed in the Egyptian style, for the old fisherman was an embalmer as well. 'And so, Habrocomes my child, I still talk to her as if she is alive, and lie down beside her and have my meals with her; and if I come home exhausted from fishing, she consoles me as I look at her; for she looks different to you than she does to me: I think of her as she was in Lacedaemon, my child, as she was when we eloped; I think of the festival, I think of the compact we made.' (5.1.4–11)

Xenophon prefers main clauses and uses simple words. The pace is even. Often he repeats a word or name instead of leaving it understood or replacing it by a pronoun. His style has obvious similarities with that of the folk-tale. When used for a subject that is in itself moving, and on a moderate scale, such as the story about the fisherman and his wife, this simplicity can be a real advantage. In other places it tends to make a dull and colourless impression. Therefore both the extremes that are found in judgements on Xenophon Ephesius should be avoided: most critics have seen in him a tremendously poor and untalented writer (or put the blame on the supposed abbreviator), whereas some have lavished praise on his graceful simplicity, as if this were entirely an artistic device. Compared to Chariton, Xenophon's range is no doubt very limited. Chariton also has a rather simple and seemingly artless narrative style, but in addition he can, when necessary, evade impending monotony and lend his narrative vigour and bite.

The difference between the stereotyped Xenophon and the gracefully flexible Chariton appears not only in style, in the narrower sense of the term, but also in structure, especially in their ways of handling the alternation between different lines of action. The basic theme of these novels of love, travel, and adventure, the lengthy enforced separation of the two lovers, compels the author to work with (at least) two parallel lines of action. Xenophon continually switches between the experiences of Habrocomes and those of Antheia, the heroine. An active phase in the existence of the one corresponds to a period of rest for the other, and the points of intersection exhibit a standard phraseology: 'Thus she was staying in Tarsus together with Perilaus, waiting for the wedding; Habrocomes on the other hand was on his way to Cilicia. . .', and a couple of pages later: 'They [Habrocomes and the noble robber Hippothous] were planning their return to Cilicia; for Antheia on the other hand the thirty days had passed and Perilaus was preparing for the wedding.' Resumptive elements are thus well provided for, reminding the reader of exactly where he is in the resumed line of action.

Chariton changes less often, and when he does, he usually solves the problem in a smoother way, for instance by finding organic links between the lines: letters are exchanged, (secondary) characters move between the scenes of action, and so on. If Xenophon's alternation technique may be compared to changing lanes on a dual carriageway, with Chariton the action is more akin to a relay race: one after another the characters, and not only the two principal ones, carry the action forward, but the same stretch of time is usually covered only once. (The most important exception to this rule has been mentioned above, p. 11.) The lines of action interlock so that one can speak of a single course of events, described from changing points of view. We shall in due course, when we come to Achilles Tatius, make the acqaintance of one more, specifically distinct, method of conveying parallel action.

Religion is a living agent in Xenophon's novel. While Chariton's gods may smack of literary personification — of Love, of Chance — in the *Ephesian Tale* we meet the living gods and goddesses of the time: the Ephesian Artemis, the Rhodian Helius, the Egyptian Isis, who threaten, are worshipped and conciliated, and come to the rescue (figures 8–10). An obscure oracle, interpreted by priestly expertise summoned for the purpose, sends Habrocomes and Antheia on their dangerous voyage, whereas in Chariton the corresponding obligatory change of scene is carefully worked out on the profane level: intrigues, jealousy and assault, grave-robbing. Also the ending is quite secular in Chariton's novel: Chaereas gives his report to the people's assembly. In the *Ephesian Tale* a written account of the tribulations suffered by hero and heroine is deposited in the shrine of Artemis (see figure 7).

Figs. 8–10 *Artemis, Helius, and Isis are the most important gods in
Xenophon's* **Ephesian Tale**. *Religion is a vital element in the plot, and the
multitude of gods mirrors the late Hellenistic compounding of religions,
'syncretism'.*

*Figure 8: Artemis, the chaste huntress, is young Antheia's ideal: imper-
sonating Artemis she leads the virgins' procession to the goddess's shrine at
Ephesus: 'Her dress was a purple chiton, girdled to the knee, hanging
down over the arms; her wrap was a fawnskin, a quiver hung from her
shoulder, she carried bow and javelins, dogs accompanied her. . . .' Most
of the details agree with this little terracotta statuette of the so-called
Tanagra type, c. 20 cm. high (reproduced from a drawing).*

Figure 9: On Rhodes the newly wedded couple consecrate gold armour to Helius, the sun god, and carve an epigram in which their names are mentioned. This epigram will play an important role in the reunion of the couple, which also takes place on Rhodes at the end of the novel. The sun god's face, surrounded by curly hair and an aureola of sunrays, often appears on the coins of the island; here an early Hellenistic tetradrachm (diameter 2.5 cm.).

Figure 10: Isis, the Egyptian goddess who victoriously swept over the Mediterranean world in late Hellenistic times, takes over the role of protectress for the heroine when the action reaches Egyptian soil. By invoking Isis as the guarantee of her chastity Antheia succeeds in rebuffing amorous advances. The picture shows Isis on a signet ring of the first century BC. From under her studied coiffure, decorated with lotus buds and ivy branches, the goddess melancholically looks at us with her big, deep-set eyes.

Our next extract reminds us that the novel takes place in the same Near East, governed by the Romans, as the New Testament:

Habrocomes came before the prefect of Egypt; the Pelusians had reported Araxus' death, stating that Habrocomes, a household slave, was responsible for the crime. When the prefect heard the particulars he made no further effort to find out the facts, but gave orders to have Habrocomes taken away and crucified. Habrocomes himself was dumbfounded at his misfortunes, and consoled himself in dying with the thought that Antheia, so it seemed, was dead as well. The prefect's agents brought him to the banks of the Nile, where there was a sheer drop overlooking the onrushing river. They set up the cross and attached him to it, tying his hands and feet tight with ropes; that is the way the Egyptians crucify. They went away and left him hanging there, thinking that it was safe.

But Habrocomes gazed at the sun, saw the force of the Nile, and said, 'Kindest of the gods, ruler of Egypt, revealer of land and sea to all men: if I have done anything wrong, may I perish miserably, and pay an even greater penalty if there is one; but if I have been betrayed by a wicked woman, I pray that the waters of the Nile should never be polluted by the body of a man unjustly killed; nor should you look on such a sight, a man who has done no wrong dying on your territory.' The god took pity on his prayer. A sudden gust of wind arose and struck the cross, sweeping away the soil where it had been fixed. Habrocomes fell into the torrent and was swept away: the water did him no harm, the fetters did not get in the way, nor did the animals in the river do him any harm as he passed; but the river itself escorted him along.

He was carried to the Delta where it met the sea, but there the guards arrested him and took him before the prefect as a fugitive from justice. He was still angrier than before, took Habrocomes for a hardened criminal, and ordered him to be burned on a pyre. Everything was made ready: the pyre was set up at the Delta, Habrocomes was put on it, and the fire had been lit underneath. But just as the flames were about to engulf him he again uttered the few words he could in prayer to save himself from the perils that threatened. Then the Nile rose in spate, and the surge of water hit the pyre and put out the flames. To those who witnessed it the event was a miracle: they took Habrocomes to the prefect, told him what had happened, and explained how the Nile had come to his rescue. He was amazed when he heard what had happened, and ordered Habrocomes to be kept in custody and well looked after till they could find out who he was, and why the gods were looking after him like this. (4.2)

A little later it is Antheia's turn to get into a desperate situation. She is saved too, but this time the author provides the miracle with a 'natural' explanation:

While Antheia was in the cave one of her robber guards, Anchialus, fell in love with her. He was from Laodicea, and was one of the band who had come with Hippothous from Syria: the latter had a high opinion of him, since he was a dashing and powerful member of the band. Anchialus, then, fell in love with Antheia, started making approaches and expected to talk her round and ask her from Hippothous as a gift. But she turned down all his pleas, undismayed by the cave, the fetters, or the robber's threats: she was still saving herself for Habrocomes, even if it seemed he was dead, and often when she was out of earshot she would cry out: 'I pray that I may remain the wife of Habrocomes alone, even if I have to die and suffer still more than I have already.' This made Anchialus' misery still worse, and the sight of Antheia every day fanned his passion. When he could take no more he tried to use force. One night when Hippothous was away with the others on a raid he got up and tried to rape her. In desperation she drew the sword that was lying beside her and struck him. The blow proved fatal: while he was trying to embrace and kiss her he had fallen right on top of her; she held the sword underneath and struck him in the chest.

Anchialus had paid the proper price for his wicked passion, but Antheia began to be afraid about what had happened and kept wondering whether to kill herself (yet she still had some hope for Habrocomes), or to flee from the cave (but that was impossible: the road was difficult and there was no one to show her the way). So she decided to wait in the cave and take whatever Providence had in store.

That night she waited, unable to get any sleep, and with a great deal on her mind. When day came, Hippothous arrived with his band. When they saw Anchialus dead and Antheia beside the body, they guessed what had happened, interrogated her, and found out everything. They were furious about it, and decided to take revenge for their dead companion. Different suggestions were made about Antheia, one man telling them to kill her and bury her with Anchialus' body, another to crucify her. Hippothous for his part was distressed over Anchialus, and decided on a harsher penalty: he gave orders to dig a big, deep trench and throw Antheia in with two dogs beside her, to make her pay dearly for her daring.

The robbers obeyed, and she was brought to the trench. The dogs were particularly huge and fearsome Egyptian hounds. When they had thrown them in, they shut the trench with large planks and piles of earth on top, not far from the Nile, and put one of the robbers, Amphinomus, on guard. Amphinomus had already fallen in love with Antheia, so that he now felt all the more sorry for her and sympathized with her plight. He found a way of keeping her alive and stopping the huge dogs molesting her; every so often he would remove the covering of the trench, throw in bread, give her water, and so keep her spirits up. By feeding the dogs he prevented them from doing her any harm; soon they were tame and docile.

Antheia reflected about herself and her current plight: 'What perils, what a revenge — to be shut in a trench for my prison, with dogs much tamer than the robbers! I share your own fate, Habrocomes, for you were once in the same straits; and I left you in prison in Tyre. If you are still alive, then my plight is nothing, for some day, perhaps, we shall be together; but if you are already dead, there is no point in striving to stay alive, no point in this man taking pity on me, whoever he is — pitiable though I am.' She kept mourning and moping in this vein.

And while she was shut in the trench with the dogs, with Amphinomus consoling her and pacifying the dogs with his feeding, Habrocomes had ended his journey from Egypt and. . . . (4.5.1−5.1.1)

Thus the story winds its way forward, adventure is added to adventure. On one occasion Antheia succeeds in maintaining her chastity by pretending that she is consecrated to Isis; on another, having arrived in a brothel in South Italy, she simulates an epileptic fit for the same purpose. When at last she is reunited with Habrocomes at the shrine of Isis on Rhodes, she can perform a veritable catalogue aria of her rejected suitors, and Habrocomes similarly swears that no other woman has seemed beautiful to him and that he is still as pure as when they parted in the prison in Tyre.

Iamblichus: A Babylonian Tale

A number of other novels as well, known only through papyrus fragments or Byzantine summaries, should probably be placed in the second century AD. We know most about Iamblichus' *Babyloniaca*, or *A Babylonian Tale*, which was summarized by the Patriarch Photius in the mid-ninth century in his great composite work, the *Bibliotheca*. The summary is a rather rapid one: Photius compresses into a dozen pages what had in the original been developed in no less than sixteen 'books'. (According to other information, the *Babyloniaca* had even extended over thirty-nine 'books'.) The picture is supplemented by a great number of short fragments of the original version, preserved as quotations in later writings, above all in the Byzantine encyclopaedia called the *Suda* (tenth century). The story throughout keeps to the Babylonian milieu; otherwise the novel seems to have been typical of its genre, with love, violence, and exoticism in large quantities.

The main characters are called Rhodanes and Sinonis. They are already married when the story begins, but the King of Babylon, the cruel tyrant Garmus, has fallen in love with the beautiful Sinonis and wants to marry her. She refuses; in revenge Rhodanes is crucified, but is saved by Sinonis. 'They both flee, he from the cross, she from the marriage.' Close on their heels they have two of the tyrant's creatures, the eunuchs Damas and Sakas, who have had their ears and noses cut off as a punishment for letting Rhodanes and Sinonis escape. The flight and pursuit fill large parts of the novel, as one breath-taking or macabre episode follows another. Here are some of them in Photius' summary:

They [Rhodanes and Sinonis] stop at the house of a robber who robs travellers and makes a meal of them. The soldiers sent by Damas capture the robber and set fire to his house. They are surrounded by flames and scarcely manage to escape destruction by killing their asses and placing the dead creatures on the flames as a pathway.

During the night they are seen by those who set the fire and when asked who they are they answer, 'The ghosts of those killed by the robber.' Because of their pale and emaciated appearance and their weak voices they convince the soldiers and frighten them. They flee again from there, overtake the funeral cortège of a young woman and join the crowd to watch. An aged Chaldaean astrologer arrives and stops the burial, saying that the young woman is still breathing. That proves to be true. He prophesies to Rhodanes that he will be a king.

The grave of the young woman is left empty, and there are left behind several robes that were to be burned on the grave and food and drink. Rhodanes and Sinonis feast on the food and drink, take some of the clothing and lie down to sleep in the young woman's grave. As daylight takes hold, those who set fire to the robber's house realize that they have been tricked and follow the footprints of Rhodanes and Sinonis, supposing that they were henchmen of the robber. They follow the footprints right up to the grave and look in at the motionless, sleeping, wine-sodden bodies lying in the grave. They suppose that they are looking at corpses and leave, puzzled that the tracks led there. Rhodanes and Sinonis leave there and. . . . (Chapters 5–7)

More blood is shed in Iamblichus' novel than in any of the others. One favourite theme is suicide or attempted suicide. Another is any kind of poison, causing death, apparent death, or sleep: deadly honey rendered poisonous because the bees have fed on venomous snakes; a rose in which a poisonous fly is hiding; or poisoned drinks of a more ordinary type. Magic also fascinated the author; in a special excursus he describes various magic practices in Babylonia. There is a sub-plot as well: the priestess of a shrine of Aphrodite has two sons, Euphrates and Tigris, and one daughter, Mesopotamia, who was born ugly but endowed with beauty by the goddess of love. Their fates are later woven into the main plot: the brothers resemble to the point of confusion both each other and Rhodanes; the girl after her metamorphosis resembles Sinonis; and thus the ground is prepared for a play on identities, of which the author makes the most in the continuing pursuit. More or less well-founded jealousy between hero and heroine complicates things further; during the latter part of the action the two are separated from each other, but the ending is happy and Rhodanes becomes King of Babylon, exactly as predicted by the Chaldaean astrologer.

The date of the novel seems for once to be certain. According to Photius the author states that he writes in the reign of Marcus Aurelius (AD 161–80) and is Babylonian by birth, although he has acquired a Hellenic education. A marginal note in the oldest Photius manuscript (tenth century) gives different information: Iamblichus was a Syrian by birth and learned Babylonian from a native Babylonian, who as a prisoner of war had been sold to Syria and become a private tutor to the young Iamblichus; in that way the latter had obtained materials for his novel. Whichever information we choose to believe, the interesting thing is that the author of the *Babyloniaca* obviously was not a Greek — neither a native Greek nor a descendant of Greeks living in the Orient — but an Oriental by birth. This may also have been the case with Achilles Tatius (Egyptian) and Heliodorus (Syrian), even if it is not explicitly stated anywhere. Thus oriental narrative traditions could flow freely into the Greek genre of the novel. The form of the novel may have remained unaffected by this, but not the narrative content. There is a big difference between the 'barbarians' who inhabit the Babylon of Chariton, viewed as they are through the coloured spectacles of the Greek literary tradition, and the more genuine Orientals who are glimpsed through Photius' summary of Iamblichus.

The Sophistic and the Non-Sophistic Novel

Chariton and Xenophon are usually regarded as the representatives of the 'pre-sophistic' or, since the dating and sequence are somewhat uncertain, the 'non-sophistic' novel. This label implies simply that the other three novels that survive complete are clearly, though in different ways, influenced by the Greek cultural revival of the imperial age known as the 'Second Sophistic'. (This is dealt with in more detail in the next chapter.) The novel has thus been drawn into the predominant literary trend of the time, and this has left its mark on both form and content.

If we want to learn about the novel as it might have looked in its original shape and — to judge from the number of papyrus fragments — as it was read by a fairly broad audience in the centuries round the birth of Christ, then we have to stick to Chariton

and Xenophon, even if they too of course are, to some extent, subject to literary pretensions and fashionable stylistic trends. Longus,
Achilles Tatius, and Heliodorus, on the other hand, had the greater
influence on posterity, as models for the 'learned' Byzantine novel
and for European novelists of still later times. That is why these
three have to an undeservedly great extent coloured the general picture of the Greek novel. In fact their novels are three highly individual works of literature, ill suited to serve as typical representatives
of a popular genre. These authors aimed at a narrower and more
refined audience than that of their predecessors, an audience which
was apt to make considerable demands of even its leisure reading.

Longus: Daphnis and Chloe

The most marked individualist among the writers of Greek novels is
Longus, whose pastoral story *Daphnis and Chloe* presumably
belongs to the latter part of the second century AD. The theme of
travel which is basic in the others is replaced in Longus' novel by a
detailed depiction of a single milieu, the island of Lesbos and its
rustic life. Nature is at the centre of the story: it is neither just
background nor pure embellishment, but the basis of the action
itself. The two principal characters were as infants each exposed by
their parents, but saved by animals: Daphnis was suckled by a goat,
Chloe by a sheep. Also, as they grow up as fosterlings in goatherd
and shepherd families, they retain their special ties to plants and
animals; they are said to love their goats and sheep more than is
customary, and Nature is their school in everything.

The novel covers a period of less than two years. We follow the
changes of seasons, at the same time witnessing the development of
the young goatherd Daphnis and the young shepherdess Chloe from
childish innocence to greater and greater sexual awareness. Each
season corresponds to one phase of this development. This is the
description of the arrival of the first spring:

It was the beginning of spring and all the flowers were in bloom, in the
woods, the meadows and on the mountains. There was now the hum of
bees, the sound of sweet-singing birds, the skipping of new-born lambs.
The lambs skipped on the mountains, the bees hummed in the meadows,
the birds filled the copses with their song. Everything was filled with the
beauty of spring; and Daphnis and Chloe, tender young creatures that they
were, imitated what they heard and saw. They heard the birds singing and
they sang; they saw the lambs skipping and they took little jumps; they imi-

tated the bees and gathered flowers. They scattered some of the flowers in
the folds of their clothes; and they used the rest to weave little garlands, as
offerings to the Nymphs.

They did everything together, grazing their flocks near each other.
Often Daphnis rounded up those of her sheep that wandered off, and often
Chloe drove the more adventurous of his goats down from the crags.
Sometimes one of them looked after both the flocks, while the other was
absorbed in some toy. Their toys were of a pastoral and childish type. She
picked stalks of asphodel from here and there and wove a trap for
grasshoppers, and while she was working on this she paid no attention to
her sheep. He cut slender reeds, pierced them at their joints, fastened them
together with soft wax, and practised piping until night-fall. They also
shared their drink of milk or wine, and they divided whatever food they
brought from home. You would be more likely to see the sheep and the
goats separated from each other than Chloe and Daphnis. (1.9–10)

Correspondingly winter is described as a barren and inhibitory
season. The snow falls heavily on Lesbos, the water freezes, the
roads become impassable. The country people enjoy being excused
from their labour for a while, being able to sleep longer and have
their breakfast in peace and quiet; but Daphnis and Chloe suffer all
the more from being isolated from nature and from each other. But
a new spring arrives — longed for as a 'rebirth from death' — with
a profusion of flowers and with new, more advanced games of love.

Thus the gradual awakening of love in two children of nature is
the main theme, in contrast to the 'love at first sight' motif in the
earlier novels. Travel and long periods of enforced separation are
absent. But there are also a number of obvious connecting links between this prose pastoral and the traditional novel of love, travel,
and adventure. An attack by pirates occurs, although this time the
Phoenician pirates are forced to leave their ship and make a raid inland. The recognition motif is also there, though in the form it had
in New Comedy: thanks to certain tokens, clothes and pieces of
jewellery, which their foster-parents had found together with the
children Daphnis and Chloe are at last recognized by their real
parents, who are town dwellers. Rivals and villains of various shades
set their snares, as in the other novels, and try to prevent the final
union of the two lovers. Without success, of course: Daphnis and
Chloe are allowed to celebrate their rural wedding and, in spite of
their newly acquired wealth and enhanced status, they choose to
stay in their simple pastoral surroundings, feeding on milk and fruits
and revering the Nymphs, Pan, and Eros, the triad of gods to whom
the whole novel is dedicated.

Longus is also the most conscious artist among the Greek novelists. He knows what he wishes to achieve and has full control of his means of expression. The novel is carefully polished, down to the smallest detail. The possibilities inherent in the parallel action are exploited as in no other novel: each stage in Daphnis' development has its counterpart in Chloe's line of action. Parallelisms and antitheses form the basic pattern in the stylistic design as well. The rhythm — the interchange of short and long syllables — is studied, as is the use of rhyme, alliteration, and other types of sound effects. In some particularly poetic passages the whole is built up of a series of short, parallel units, each consisting of the same number of syllables (or with a regular variation of the number). This prose-poem character can be illustrated to some extent if we break up the translated text into these smaller units (without, however, any attempt to reproduce rhyme or syllable numbers). The passage chosen (2.7) is one of the show-pieces, the old cowherd Philetas describing the power of Eros:

> Love is a god, my children;
>> He is young,
>> Beautiful,
>> And winged;
> And so he enjoys youth,
>> Pursues beauty,
>> And makes souls take wing.

> Zeus has not so much power as he:
>> He rules the elements,
>> He rules the stars,
>> He rules his fellow gods —
> More completely than you rule your goats and sheep.

>> All the flowers are the work of Love,
>> All the plants are his creation;
>> Thanks to him, the rivers flow,
>>> The winds blow.

>> I have seen a bull in love,
>> Bellowing as though stung by a gadfly,
>> And a he-goat in love with a she-goat,
>> Following her everywhere.

> I was young myself once and fell in love with Amaryllis.
>> I forgot to eat,

> I didn't drink,
> I wouldn't sleep.
> My soul was in pain,
> My heart pounded,
> My body was frozen.
>
> I cried out as though being struck,
> I was silent as though dying,
> I plunged in rivers as though on fire.
> I called on Pan to help me,
> Since he himself had been in love with Pitys.
> I praised Echo
> For calling after me the name of Amaryllis.
> I smashed my pipes,
> Because they charmed the cows,
> But they failed to draw Amaryllis to me.
>
> There is no remedy for Love,
> No potion,
> No drug,
> No spell to mutter,
>
> Except a kiss,
> And an embrace,
> And lying down together in nakedness.

The pastoral milieu in which Longus has set his love story is of course a literary milieu, a translation into prose of Hellenistic bucolic poetry. The main source was Theocritus, but the whole tradition, perhaps even including Virgil, seems to have made its contribution. Daphnis is the very prototype of the lovesick shepherd in this tradition. Philetas, the old and experienced herdsman in Longus' novel, has borrowed his name from Theocritus' forerunner, the poet Philetas of Cos. Longus' relationship to Theocritus himself — investigated in depth by Georg Rohde — is a complex one. At the same time as Longus quite openly alludes to his master, and on the whole makes the latter's picture of rural life and nature his own, in some ways he also distances himself from the idyll. Some supernatural elements are given a more realistic touch through subtle changes. For instance, the cattle do not actually dance to the music but graze in the neighbourhood and 'as it were' participate in the festivity. Other things are ascribed to the shepherds' own way of thinking or reported as hearsay, for which the author assumes no responsibility. It is all the easier to slip reservations of various kinds into the narrative since Longus — in contrast to both Theocritus and the other novelists — makes great use of indirect speech. Where Theocritus is mimetic and graphic, Longus, as Rohde observes, is often content to relate. On the other hand, prose as the medium for the description of nature inevitably leads to a greater wealth of detail: poetry selects graphic and striking traits, prose strives more towards completeness. Thus Longus embroiders the motifs which were depicted in a more impressionistic manner by Theocritus.

The reader of *Daphnis and Chloe* is expected to know his Theocritus, or else he will miss some of the finer nuances. For instance, the homage to Eros quoted above ends with an ironic dissociation from Theocritus' more idealistic approach to the subject, which reads as follows:

No other remedy is there for love, Nicias, neither unguent, methinks, nor salve, save only the Muses; and this remedy is painless for mortals and pleasant, but hard to find. . . . (11.1–4, trans. A. S. F. Gow [Cambridge, 1952])

For Theocritus poetry, referred to as 'the Muses', is the only efficient medicine; Longus, as we have seen, twists poetry into incantations, a 'spell to mutter', only to reject this remedy as well and write out his personal prescription, Nature's own medicine against the pains of love.

Even if much of Longus' depiction of country life and nature is traditional bucolic matter, the novel is hardly an armchair essay throughout. Lesbos is not one of the traditional pastoral milieux, but may very well have been chosen by the author because he was familiar with it, through either belonging to a Roman family living in the town of Mytilene or just having the island as his holiday resort. Realistic traits in the description of nature and life on the island seem to indicate some personal experience. Attention has been drawn especially to the description of bird-hunting in winter by means of glue-sticks, and also to that of the plague of flies when the goat's-milk cheese is being prepared. But Theocritus too mixes realistic traits with purely idealizing ones. All in all it would seem that Longus fits pretty well into the traditional theory of pastoral poetry having sprung from the town dweller's nostalgic yearning for the country and the simple life (even if Longus himself actually speaks in a slightly contemptuous manner of a rich youth from the city who goes to the country only to enjoy its exoticism). There is a precedent in Greek prose, the charming description of the hunters' life on Euboea in a speech of Dio Chrysostom (late first century AD) — 'a picture of life in a remote corner of Greece, a Greece that had by this time itself become a poor and remote corner of the world' (A. Wifstrand). But in Dio it is the country dwellers themselves, with their unspoiled and positively naïve disposition, who lie at the centre; Longus has given the principal parts to Nature and its prime mover, Eros.

Longus' novel has some interesting points of contact with contemporary pictorial art. The author himself declares in the introduction that he took his inspiration from a series of paintings in the Grove of the Nymphs on Lesbos. The main theme of the paintings was love, and among the separate scenes he mentions are exposed children, suckled by domestic animals and taken in by shepherds, as well as attacks of robbers and enemies. He was seized with a desire to add words to the pictures, found a man who could explain them, and so wrote his novel. This literary fiction — for a fiction it surely is — has induced several scholars to look for a closer connection between Longus' narrative style and the pictorial art of the imperial age. In particular, some wall paintings from Roman villas and graves of the period AD 130−60 — the culmination of the philhellenic movement under the Emperors Hadrian and Antoninus Pius — are parallel to Longus in both style and subject-matter: the idyllic rural milieu is depicted with a delicate play of colours and an elaborate composition (figure 11).

Whether we should follow Michael Mittelstadt and accept that Longus has deliberately 'translated' an existing type of narrative pictorial cycle into the literary medium, is perhaps more open to question. He demonstrates how the *Odyssey* wall paintings from the Esquiline, made in the middle of the first century BC in an 'illusionistic' style, place the illustrated scenes against a continuous background of pastoral landscape in the same way that Longus does in his novel. The common landscape ensures the continuity of the 'narrative'. There is no doubt some truth in this comparison, but to my mind the differences are more important. Longus' scenery is not static; on the contrary, the emphasis is on *change*, the constant cycle of the seasons. To describe the awakening and gradual development of love in two young people, in harmony with the changing phases of nature, is to choose a theme which can be treated only in literary form, even if pictorial art may be able to contribute something in the way of colour and atmosphere.

Fig. 11 *A rural idyll. A Roman landscape painting, representative of the so-called philhellenic style (mid-second century AD). In its idyllic peacefulness, delicate play of colours, and elaborate composition it has much in common with Longus' pastoral novel from the latter part of the same century. To the left a man with a heavy load on his back is on his way towards a bridge; a cowherd is just driving his animals over the bridge. On the tree to the right pious herdsmen have suspended ribbons to some deity, and between the tree and the grazing cattle there is a simple altar, against which a long torch is leaning. The cult of rural deities, such as Pan and the Nymphs, also plays an important part in* **Daphnis and Chloe.**

Achilles Tatius: Leucippe and Clitophon

Achilles Tatius and Heliodorus retain the traditional travel theme. One difference in the organization of the plot, however, should be noted. In Chariton, Xenophon Ephesius, and Iamblichus the hero and heroine are united in marriage at the outset; they are separated and constantly strive to return to home and marriage. In Achilles Tatius and Heliodorus, on the other hand, as in Longus, marriage is the conclusion of the novel, its happy ending, and the story is about the struggle of the two young people first to win each other and then to clear away all the obstacles which the surrounding world, deliberately or accidentally, places in the way of their union. In these two novels the heroine protects her chastity, her *sophrosyne*, not only against robbers and other temporary admirers, but also in her relations with the man she loves. Incidentally, the Greek novels, as we know them, are not at all pornographic; they usually communicate a romantic and idealistic view of love. In the five surviving specimens there is nothing corresponding to the naturalistic sexual descriptions in the Roman novels of Petronius and Apuleius (and in the Greek model of the latter), although it is true that at least Longus and Achilles Tatius like to dwell on the physical aspects of love as well. The Lollianus fragment (see the caption to figure 26) may be taken to indicate, however, that the novels chosen by the Byzantines for preservation are perhaps not quite representative in this respect.

The novel *Leucippe and Clitophon*, probably written some time before AD 200, breaks up the established novel pattern in a number of ways. The whole story is narrated in the first person. The hero himself, Clitophon, with the author as his audience, recounts the story of his and Leucippe's fortunes from their first meeting in Tyre in Phoenicia, through thrilling adventures among robbers in the Nile Delta, up to the conclusion in Ephesus, which is described at great length. To begin with this narrative fiction is quite strictly maintained: only what happens to Clitophon himself, or in his presence, is reported to the reader; other people's reactions are described only through their visible or audible emotional expressions; incidents taking place elsewhere are mentioned only if and when the hero is informed about them.

In this way also the problem of parallel action is solved: Leucippe's experiences during the periods when she is physically separated from Clitophon are communicated to us partly through Clitophon's simultaneous observations, as he passively witnesses them from a distance, and partly through other people's subsequent reports. The first fragmentary and deliberately enigmatic account means that the reader shares Clitophon's perspective and limited knowledge; later reports supplement, correct, and explain. The full facts were of course available to Clitophon the *narrator* from the start, but for the sake of suspense and illusion the author lets him keep his knowledge to himself and no more than hint at the denouement. The restricted narrative perspective which dominates the subtle description of Clitophon's awakening feelings for Leucippe and his attempts to approach her is, however, later replaced by a fairly unrestricted omniscience, and consequently also by an alternation technique reminiscent of that of Chariton; the distinction between first-person and third-person narrative is partly eliminated.

But whenever suspense demands it, we are back in the restricted narrative perspective. The best example is a scene played in the inaccessible swamps of the Nile Delta, a favourite haunt of robbers. Leucippe is in the hands of brigands; Clitophon has been saved by a detachment of soldiers. From the military camp he is made the passive and suffering witness of what happens to his beloved Leucippe:

We could in fact see brigands aplenty and fully armed, standing on the opposite side of the chasm. They had improvised an altar of earth and near it was a coffin. Two of them were leading a girl to the altar with her hands tied behind her back. I couldn't see who they were under their helmets but I did recognize Leucippe. They poured a libation over her head and led her around the altar to the accompaniment of a flute and a priest intoning what I guessed was an Egyptian hymn — at least, the movements of his mouth and the distension of his facial muscles suggested a hymn.

Then at a signal they all moved far away from the altar. One of the attendants laid her on her back and tied her to stakes fixed in the ground, as sculptors picture Marsyas bound to the tree. [1] He next raised a sword and plunged it into her heart and then sawed all the way down to her abdomen. Her viscera exploded. The attendants pulled the entrails out with their hands and placed them on the altar. When they were well roasted, they carved the whole lot into pieces and all the pirates shared the meal.

As each of these acts was performed the soldiers and the general groaned aloud and averted their eyes from the awful sight. But I, contrary to all reason, just sat there staring. It was a case of sheer shock: I was simply thunderstruck by the enormity of the calamity. Perhaps the myth of Niobe was no fiction after all: faced with the carnage of her children, she felt just as I did, and her emotional paralysis had given the appearance of petrification. [2]

When the ceremony was concluded, so far as I could tell, they placed her body in the coffin, put the lid on, razed the altar and ran away, leaving her there, without looking behind them. All this was done according to the rubrics chanted by the priest. (3.15)

---

[1] The satyr Marsyas had ventured to compete with Apollo himself in playing the flute; he was not only defeated, but also sentenced to the cruel punishment of being hung up in a tree and flayed alive. Sculptors loved this scene; Myron's statue group is the most well known example.

[2] Niobe, the mother of six sons and six daughters, ventured to speak disdainfully of Leto, who had brought but two children into the world. However, these two were Apollo and Artemis, who took their revenge by shooting all Niobe's children dead. In her boundless grief the mother is said to have been turned into a rock.

In this gruesome account we get to know only what Clitophon himself saw from his look-out (with the exception of the very last sentence). Afterwards he and the reader are informed of what *really* happened: the two unrecognizable figures were in fact Clitophon's own friends, who simulated a sacrifice to cheat the brigands. The sword which seemed to be plunged deeply into Leucippe was a weapon designed for use on the stage: most of the blade disappeared into the hilt, the point cut open a goatskin bag filled with animal entrails and blood, which they had attached to Leucippe's own stomach!

Another remarkable feature is the great number of long digressions that interrupt the action proper, mainly in the first half of the novel. A couple of times we find extremely detailed descriptions of paintings. One has as its motif 'Europa and the Bull', the myth of Zeus turning himself into a bull and kidnapping the Phoenician princess Europa. It is situated in the first chapter, where it sets the tone and subject, as it were, of the whole novel. Another depicts Andromeda and Prometheus each fettered to a rock; Perseus is descending from the sky in order to save Andromeda from the sea monster, while Prometheus is already in the claws of his tormentor, the eagle which gorges itself on his liver. Rhetorical descriptions, so-called *ecphrases*, of works of art were a popular genre in the imperial age. But most of the digressions in Achilles Tatius are of a different kind; they describe and discuss various phenomena of nature: exotic animals and plants, the Nile and its inundations, or physiological and psychological processes in man — kissing, weeping, loving. Many such expositions are also put into the mouths of the characters, for instance a long discussion of the relative advantages of homo- and heterosexual love.

Homosexuality also occurs elsewhere in the Greek novels (and is one of the predominant themes in the Roman Petronius). Chariton is the most discreet. He has his hero constantly accompanied by his loyal friend Polycharmus, but hints at the nature of Polycharmus' friendship only by comparing him to Patroclus, Achilles' brother-in-arms in the *Iliad* — a hint that should have been quite sufficient for any reader who was looking for it. At the end of the novel Polycharmus receives Chaereas' sister as his wife, expressly as a recompense for his loyalty, and a rich dowry; no romantic strains are evident. Xenophon is much more straightforward. The most important character of the novel, next to the hero and heroine, is the robber Hippothous, now with Habrocomes, now with

Antheia — but there can be no doubt about whose company he prefers. As far as Antheia is concerned, he is at one point prepared to sacrifice her to Ares, the war god; on another occasion he throws her into the pit together with hungry dogs; and when at last he helps to bring about the reunion of the loving couple, he does so out of friendship for Habrocomes. By that time he has himself found a beautiful boy whom he adopts; earlier he has told Habrocomes about the great love of his youth, the beautiful Hyperanthes, whom he lost in a shipwreck off Lesbos — it was in despair at this loss that he entered the robber's trade. Achilles Tatius, however, true to his insatiable hunger for knowledge, also investigates the matter theoretically. During the trip from Berytus (Beirut) to Alexandria, while Leucippe is asleep below decks, the men debate whether women or boys are the more worthy object of a man's desire; the pederasts have the last word, but no shadow is allowed to fall upon the disposition of the hero himself; he is totally devoted to his Leucippe.

Back to the digressions. It would be wrong to regard them as unnecessary padding in the novel, something that did not 'organically' belong there. First, at least the introductory *ecphrasis* has, as already mentioned, a thematic connection with the novel's plot, and many of the other descriptions are directly attached to the action. Second, it is evident that the author himself took special care with these components of the novel. To them is devoted the most scrupulous stylistic chiselling: short, asyndetic units for the description of people, and a more fluent style when the surroundings are depicted; graphic quality and richness of detail; rhythm, assonance; in short, all the rhetorical devices which the time, the Second Sophistic, gives access to. Here is an example from the description of 'Europa and the Bull' (figures 12–14), although a translation into a modern language can never do full justice to such a piece of ancient 'artistic prose':

The sea itself was dichromatic — it had a red tinge near land, but was dark blue towards the deep. Then a composition of foam and rocks and waves: rocks rising above the land, foam splashing the rocks white, waves swelling to peaks which shattered into foam around the rocks.

A bull was painted in mid-sea riding on the waves, which rose like a steep hill under the bent curve of the bull's foreleg. The maiden sat on his back, not astride but side-saddle, with her feet together towards the right, and on the left her hand holding the horn as a charioteer would hold the reins. And the bull in fact had turned his head somewhat in the direction

Figs. *12–13* '*Europa and the Bull' is a favourite motif with ancient artists and writers. The Phoenician princess Europa is picking flowers on the
beach with her girl friends, when Zeus discovers her. The god falls in love,
turns himself into a bull, and approaches the young girls. Only Europa
dares to stay, and even caresses the bull and mounts his back
— whereupon the bull rushes into the water and swims away in the
direction of Crete with his beautiful victim.*
    *Figure 12: The mosaic belongs to the first century AD; it was found in
Palestrina and later kept in the Palazzo Barberini in Rome. The upper
field shows Europa's friends fleeing in dismay (and possibly her father
Agenor to the right); in the lower field Europa (with bare back) on the
bull. The two figures in the lower right corner have not been identified.
The painting which Achilles Tatius describes similarly depicted both the
meadow with the terrified girls and Europa on the bull.*

Figure 13: Another variation on the same theme in an unusually well-preserved Roman mosaic now in Copenhagen (first century AD).

of the pressure of her guiding hand. There was a chiton[3] over the maiden's chest down to her modesty, from there on a robe covered the lower part of her body: the chiton was white, the robe red, and the body showed subtly through the clothing — navel well-recessed, stomach flat, waist narrow, but with a narrowness that widened downwards towards the hips. Breasts gently nudging forward: a circumambient sash pressed chiton to breasts so that it took on her body's form like a mirror.

Both her arms were outstretched, one to the horn and one towards the tail; connecting them from either side was her veil, which fluttered behind her in a long arc above her head. The bosomy folds of this garment billowed out in all directions, puffed full by a wind of the artist's own making. She rode on the bull as if on board a cruising ship, using this veil as a sail.

---

[3] Garment worn nearest to the body, fastened together at the shoulders, leaving the arms bare. Women's *chitons* reached to the feet, men's ended at the knees.

Around the bull dolphins danced and Loves cavorted: you would have said their very movements were visibly drawn.

And Eros was leading the bull: Eros, a tiny child, with wings spread, quiver dangling, torch in hand. He had turned to look at Zeus with a sly smile, as if in mockery that he had, for Love's sake, become a bull. (1.1.8–13)

This introductory *ecphrasis* may thus be looked upon as a symbol of the plot: love is the main theme of the novel, as it is of the painting, and Europa is like Leucippe carried away over the sea. Various interpreters have regarded further elements of the *ecphrasis* as alluding to specific events of the novel, but it is difficult to decide exactly how far symbolic thinking has really guided the author in his description. The same is true for the interpretation of the *ecphrases* inserted further on: there is some general agreement with the action, but when one tries to go into detail the result tends to be rather strained and arbitrary. As in the Homeric similes, the starting point

Fig. 14 'Europa and the Bull' is a motif which also occurs in Byzantine art, following ancient models, in the same way that the sophistic novels were still read and imitated by the Byzantines. This small ivory relief (5 x 13 cm.), in the Victoria and Albert Museum, London, is strikingly similar in detail to Achilles Tatius' description: Europa sits turned towards the spectator, side-saddle and with her feet together, the lower body turned slightly to the rear of the bull but the torso and head facing forwards; with her left hand she grasps a horn, with her right she holds her veil, which flutters in a curve over her head; and Eros, torch in hand, turns and looks (triumphantly?) at the bull, who is Zeus transformed. The veil over Europa's head is to be found in many ancient representations of the scene as well, for instance on coins from Phoenician Sidon, the very town in which Achilles Tatius situates his painting.

and possibly also the terminal one may be directly connected with the context, but in between pure delight in narration or description prevails.

Of course, it is in itself quite legitimate to look for symbols and forebodings, particularly in Achilles Tatius: a net of foreshadowings, mostly of a straightforward and easily interpreted kind, is spread over his whole narrative. However, the fact that they are usually straightforward is one of the reasons why we should be extra careful in seeking *hidden* symbols: Achilles Tatius is not a man to understate things. Some of the foreshadowings belong to the narrative frame itself, either as vaguely worded hints of coming misfortunes or as direct revelations, from author to reader, of what is going to happen. Others are integrated into the action and understood as forebodings by the characters themselves, exactly as they would have been in real life: premonitions, oracles, omens, dreams. Clitophon, for instance, dreams that his body is joined, up to the navel, with that of a girl. Then comes a horrifying figure, with bloodshot eyes and snakes for hair, who with her sickle cuts the united bodies in two. Perhaps this symbolizes, in a general way, the novel's separation-motif. Most immediately and concretely, however, the dream prefigures what takes place in the second book of the novel: immediately before the wedding Clitophon's betrothed (who is not Leucippe) is kidnapped. The terrifying woman of the dream was Tyche, Fortune. But before this happens the author has for safety's sake prepared the reader both through a further dream — Clitophon's father dreams that the wedding day has come, that he lights the wedding torch, but that it goes out — and through an omen: at the sacrifice on the day before the wedding an eagle snatches away the victim from the altar before the eyes of those making the sacrifice.

On another occasion the opposite is true: a single dream has a double function. Leucippe's mother sees in her dream how a robber with his sword cuts her daughter's belly open. Terrified, she rushes to her daughter's room and arrives just in time to prevent Clitophon, who has slipped into the room and into Leucippe's bed, from carrying out his intentions (figures 15–16). The dream alludes immediately to Clitophon 'stealing' Leucippe's innocence, but at the same time it prefigures the later scene (quoted above) when Leucippe is literally in the hands of robbers and the dream-vision seems to have become tragically real. The former interpretation is obvious to the reader even as the dream is being described, of the latter he can be aware only with hindsight.

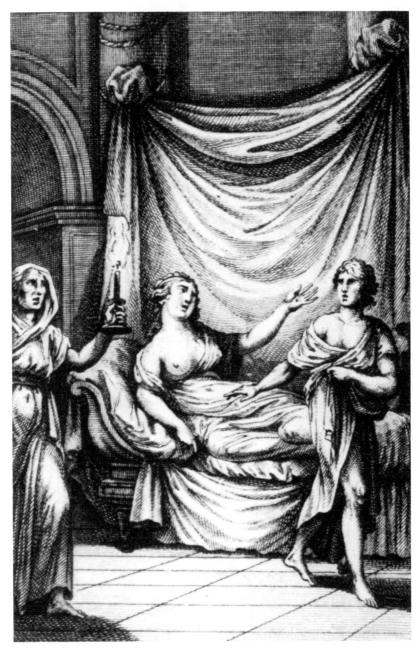

Fig. 15 *Clitophon escapes from Leucippe's bed as her mother enters from the left. Illustration in a French translation of 1796.*

There is one further quality of Achilles Tatius as an author that is worth remarking on: his art of characterization. In his novel it is not simply a matter of course that after the first meeting the heroine should immediately reciprocate the hero's violently growing passion; rather, the author lets us follow the development step by step. First he describes Clitophon's happiness simply at being placed in such a position at the table that he can watch Leucippe. Then comes the first meeting in private, and the first kiss; at last, Leucippe consents to fly with Clitophon from the town and from her mother's supervision. By this point we are a quarter of the way through the

Fig. 16 *Woman surprising two lovers? Wall painting from Pompeii. The parallel with the novel-scene illustrated in figure 15 is obvious, although here the loving couple are just taking some refreshments, when the woman (followed by a small boy) intrudes. Whether this painter had some particular episode from a novel in mind is impossible to say; but it may be suspected that many an ancient work of art, conventionally described as a 'scene from contemporary life' or 'unidentified mythological subject', in reality illustrated some lost novel.*

novel — in Chariton hero and heroine are married after three pages!

Here is the first kiss:

At the end of this conversation I suddenly realized that Leucippe was nearby. I blanched at the sight of her so sudden, then I blushed. She was alone, not even Clio [her maid] was with her. Yet like one not knowing what to say in my confusion, I said, 'Greetings, my lady.' She smiled a winsome smile; though her amusement said clearly that she understood why I called her 'my lady', she asked, 'I? Your lady? Don't say that!' 'Ah, but a certain god has sold me into your service as surely as Heracles was sold as slave to Queen Omphale.'[4] 'You mean Hermes? — whom Zeus ordered to sell Heracles?' and again she smiled. 'Hermes? Hermes?! Why are you quibbling? You know very well what god I mean.'

While the conversation was shuttling back and forth like this, circumstance came to my assistance: on the previous day, around noon, she had happened to be playing her lyre; Clio had been sitting there with her, and I was walking by. Suddenly a bee had come buzzing out of nowhere and stung Clio on the hand. She cried out, Leucippe started up, and putting aside her lyre, diagnosed the wound and comforted her, telling her not to worry. For she could stop the pain with a simple two-line spell, taught her once by an Egyptian woman as a remedy for bee- and wasp-stings. She chanted her formula over the sting, and after a little while Clio said she felt better. Well, as chance would have it, at this very moment a wasp or a bumblebee was circling round my head with a menacing zzzzzzzzz. In a moment of inspiration I clapped my hand to my face and pretended that I had just been painfully stung. The girl came close and took my hand, asking where I had been stung. 'On my lip,' I said; 'Why don't you recite your spell, dearest?' She moved closer and put her mouth near mine in order to mumble her charm over the wound. In whispering the formula she lightly grazed my lips with hers. I silently kissed her in return, just suppressing the noise kisses make. And as she formed the words, opening and closing her mouth, she transformed that incantation into a steady stream of kisses. Then I took her in my arms and really kissed her. She stepped back. 'What are you doing?' she cried; 'Is that some spell you know?' 'I'm in love with your formula,' I replied, 'it brought relief to my pain.' Since she understood my meaning and even smiled, I went on boldly, 'Oh dear, my dearest, I'm stung again and still more harshly. The wound has spread to my heart and still needs your magical remedy. You

---

[4] Heracles tried to steal the Delphic tripod from his half-brother Apollo. Their father Zeus intervened and sentenced Heracles to be sold as a slave for three years. Hermes arranged the sale, and a Lydian queen by the name of Omphale bought the demigod for her personal service, a tale 'not without its touch of piquancy', as Martin P. Nilsson remarks.

must have some bee inherent in your lips, for they are full of honey and their kiss leaves a wound. Say the spell again, but this time don't run through it so hastily, which merely irritates the wound.'

I put my arms around her more firmly and kissed her with greater abandon. She allowed me this freedom with only a token resistance. But when we saw the maid in the distance coming towards us we broke apart, with reluctance and regret on my side, I don't know with what feeling on hers. This episode relieved my tension and raised my hopes. I could feel her kiss still resting on my lips like a material thing, and I carefully guarded it as a secret store of pleasure. For a kiss is a premier pleasure, lovechild of the mouth, and the mouth is the loveliest member of the body, for it is the organ of speech and speech is a shadow of the soul itself. The union and commingling of two mouths radiates pleasures down into the bodies and draws up the souls toward the kissing lips. I cannot remember any previous experience when my heart was happier. I learned then for the first time that for sheer pleasure nothing can compete with an erotic kiss. (2.6−8)

In a sub-plot of this novel it is possible to speak of character development proper. In Chariton too we observed a strong interest in psychology, but with him it is always a matter of one particular type or character being put in different situations, of his or her different reactions being aptly described. But there is never a development in the sense that a character is changed by enduring changing fortunes. Chaereas may seem to be two different people in the first and second half of the novel, the emotional lover and the brave warrior, but what changes is his situation, not his character. However, the description of the minor character Callisthenes in Achilles Tatius' novel is a different matter. Young Callisthenes undergoes a wonderful change, a *metabole*, from living an irresponsible and debauched life to being a paragon of virtue: he becomes well-behaved and efficient, he rises from his chair in the presence of older people, he makes a point of being the first to utter a greeting when meeting someone, and so on. What causes the change is of course love, and the reward is the hand of his beloved.

It has been suggested that Achilles Tatius' novel was intended as a parody of the serious novel in the manner of Heliodorus. Now chronology seems to preclude such a relationship to Heliodorus, but that aside it would be a strange parody indeed which worked so discreetly that it escaped being identified as parody for more than seventeen hundred years! It is true, however, that this novel — in contrast to Heliodorus — is characterized by a light, perhaps even an ironic tone. But this is a consequence of the author's ironic distance from his narrator hero, hardly of his repudiation of the genre as such. Or, as R. M. Rattenbury aptly notes, Achilles Tatius is to the novel what Euripides is to tragedy: he sets out to 'humanize' the novel, with the result that some of its conventions tend to appear slightly ridiculous.

Heliodorus: An Ethiopian Tale

Heliodorus of Emesa left behind the heaviest novel, in terms of both volume — some 300 standard printed pages — and style. The technique of composition of his *Ethiopica* is incomparably more complicated than that of any of the earlier novels. Heliodorus took Homer as his chief model, and this means, among other things, that following the pattern of the *Odyssey* he brings his reader directly *in medias res*:

The smile of daybreak was just spreading across the sky and the sunbeams picking out the hilltops when a group of men in brigand gear peered over the mountain which overlooks the place where the Nile flows into the sea at its mouth that men call the Heracleotic. They stood there for a moment scanning the expanse of sea beneath them: first they gazed out over the ocean but, as there was nothing sailing there that held out hope of spoil and plunder, their eyes were drawn to the beach nearby.

This is what they saw: a merchant ship was riding there, moored by her stern, empty of crew but laden with cargo. This could be surmised even from a distance, for the weight of her cargo forced the water up to the third line of boards on the ship's side. But the beach! — a mass of newly slain bodies, some of them quite dead, others half alive and still twitching, testimony that the fighting had only just ended. To judge by the signs, this had been no proper battle. Amongst the carnage were the miserable remnants of festivities that had come to this unhappy end. There were tables set with food, and others upset on the ground, held in dead men's hands; in the fray they had served some as weapons, for hostilities had broken out on the spur of the moment; beneath other tables men had crawled in the vain hope of hiding there. There were wine bowls upturned and some slipping from the hands that held them; some had been drinking from them, others using them like stones. The suddenness of the catastrophe caused objects to be put to strange new uses and taught men to use drinking vessels as missiles.

There they lay: here a man felled by an axe, there another struck down by a stone picked up there and then from the shingly beach; here a man battered to death with a club, there another burned to death with a brand from the fire. Various were the forms of their deaths, but most were the victims of arrows and archery. In that small space the deity had contrived an infinitely varied spectacle, defiling wine with blood and unleashing war at the party, combining wining and dying, pouring of drink and spilling of blood, and staging this tragic show for the Egyptian bandits. (1.1.1–6)

Instead of describing omnisciently the scene on the beach Heliodorus has deliberately chosen to let the whole be presented to the reader through the medium of a third party, the band of brigands appearing on the mountain ridge. Step by step they register and interpret the spectacle as it unfolds before their eyes. At the beginning they are as ignorant as the reader: that the merchant ship is heavily loaded, that the struggle has just ended, that it started unexpectedly — these are all inferences drawn by the brigands from what they see before them. Their curiosity and wonder inevitably infect the reader; this is a deliberate means of creating suspense. It is only in combination with this device that the *in medias res* technique achieves its full effect. (Homer takes the opposite course: he reduces the effect of shock with his invocation of the Muse, in which the hero and his general situation are introduced, in spite of the fact that his material is mythical, not fictional, and he narrates with omniscience.) Heliodorus' procedure is bold, and apparently brand new. In the other third-person novels the authors in similar situations immediately explain the true state of things with self-evident authority. Only in Achilles Tatius does there occur at some places a corresponding restriction of the narrative perspective, but there this technique follows more naturally from the fact that his is a first-person novel. Heliodorus has transferred the technique into the third-person narrative, and as is well known he has had many followers in modern fiction.

Because the author concentrates on the visual aspect, the whole introductory scene, and many other parts of the novel as well, seem almost to have been written directly for film, as O. Weinreich first remarked. We now zoom into close-up: when the robbers, still unable to understand what has happened, rush down to lay their hands on the booty, we focus on a small area of the beach (figure 17):

On a rock sat a girl, a creature of such indescribable beauty that one might have taken her for a goddess. Despite her great distress at her plight, she had an air of courage and nobility. On her head she wore a crown of laurel; from her shoulder hung a quiver; her left arm leant on the bow, the hand hanging relaxed at the wrist. She rested the elbow of her other arm on her right thigh, cradling her cheek in her fingers. Her head was bowed and she gazed steadily at a young man lying at her feet. He was terribly

wounded and seemed to be barely conscious, coming round almost from
death as if from a deep sleep. Even so, he had a radiant manly beauty, and
his cheek appeared more gleaming white because of the red streak of blood
running down it. His pain made his eyes heavy, but the sight of the girl
drew them upwards to her. What forced them to see was that it was her
they saw. (1.2.1−3)

The characters introduced in this way are of course the protagonists
of the novel. Their names, Theagenes and Charicleia, are disclosed
as soon as the action makes this natural. Only much later do we
learn how they landed, in this miserable condition, at one of the
mouths of the Nile. Through a series of retrospective narratives the
whole prehistory is eventually unravelled. Charicleia is revealed as
the beautiful, white-skinned daughter of the dark King and Queen
of Ethiopia, Hydaspes and Persinna, conceived in a moment when
the queen happened to have her eyes turned on a painting of
Perseus and Andromeda (see figure 62). The child is a copy of
Andromeda, and on account of her white skin she is exposed. But
she is rescued, grows up with strangers, is adopted by a Greek and
finally, as chaste as she is beautiful, she becomes the priestess of
Artemis at Delphi. A young Thessalian nobleman, Theagenes, a
descendant of Achilles, comes to the Pythian Games and they fall
deeply in love (figure 18). But not until the last page of the novel,
after many misfortunes and seemingly hopeless situations, are they
united in marriage, being at the same time consecrated as priest and
priestess in the Ethiopian sun cult.

   In fact the whole action of the novel takes place under the sign of
the sun god, Helius. Heliodorus himself is descended from him, according to the final words of the novel. His name, 'gift of the sun',

Fig. 17 *'On a rock sat a girl, a creature of such indescribable beauty that
one might have taken her for a goddess. . . . On her head she wore a
crown of laurel; from her shoulder hung a quiver; her left arm leant on the
bow, the hand hanging relaxed at the wrist. She rested the elbow of her
other arm on her right thigh, cradling her cheek in her fingers.' Illustration for a French translation of Heliodorus' novel (1626). The attributes
bow and quiver indicate that Heliodorus wants his readers to think of the
chaste hunting goddess Artemis as they will have seen her represented in
art. It is interesting to compare this seventeenth-century Charicleia, superficially so true to the author's description, with the picture of Artemis
which an ancient reader might have called forth in his imagination (see
figure 8).*

indicates this, and Emesa, his Syrian hometown, actually was a centre of the sun cult during the imperial age. The *Ethiopica* has a markedly edifying nature; chastity and piety are constantly glorified, and even the robber chief turns out to be a noble character. The novel's success in Byzantine times is probably to some extent due to this pious tone. It is quite natural that the author was said to have converted to Christianity and become a bishop (of Tricca in Thessaly). The same story is told, more surprisingly, of Achilles Tatius. Tradition also has it that during a synod at which Heliodorus' novel was declared to be a danger to youth, its author, the bishop, was given the choice between burning his book or re-signing. Heliodorus is said to have preferred the latter alternative.

In reality we do not even know to which century Heliodorus belongs. Scholars, looking for evidence in the subject-matter of the text as well as in its diction and style, have opted for various dates between the early second and late fourth centuries AD. The historical setting in which the action is supposed to take place, with Egypt governed by the Persians, is indistinct and, as usual, grossly anachronistic. Many have regarded the religious attitude of the novel as best in harmony with the third century, the century of the sun-worshipping Roman Emperors Heliogabalus and Aurelian; others, however, and notably Martin P. Nilsson, assign it to the fourth. In recent years the most concrete material for the dating debate has been drawn from the passage of the novel where the siege of Syene (Aswan) in Egypt is described in great detail. The account has some striking similarities with Emperor Julian's description of the siege of Mesopotamian Nisibis in AD 350. Provided that Julian really is giving an authentic report of an historical event, the matter would be settled: Heliodorus is the imitator and must have written in the second part of the fourth century. However, the sources for the siege of Nisibis are conflicting, and there remains the possibility that Julian's version is influenced by literature rather than founded on history.

Fig. 18 *The abduction: the young Thessalian nobleman Theagenes has carried away the chaste Charicleia, Artemis' priestess at Delphi, and now brings her on board a Phoenician ship. This is the beginning of their long and adventurous journey south, towards Ethiopia, Charicleia's homeland, and towards marriage. The old man in the middle of the boat is the Egyptian priest Calasiris, who chaperoned the abduction. Illustration of 1626, with ship and architecture of not exactly ancient appearance.*

Maybe the possibility of correctly dating Heliodorus will increase in the near future. The conclusion of the novel takes place in *Aithiopia*, that is in the northern part of the modern Sudan, and in its capital Meroë. The archaeological investigation of Meroë and its surroundings, which is at present in full swing, may perhaps give us a picture of Meroitic history and religion concrete enough to be fruitfully compared to Heliodorus' account. It has long been clear, from both archaeological and other literary evidence, that a sun cult was practised in Meroë (figure 19), even if other cults were predominant. But it goes without saying that extreme caution is called for: even with a general agreement between novel and historical fact it is still by no means certain that the details of Heliodorus' description are authentic. This is fiction, by a novelist who strives for effect and splendid spectacle, not for documentary accuracy. For confirmation of this, we have only to look somewhat more closely at one of the show pieces, the magnificent description of a sacrificial feast at Delphi, reported in the first person by one of the characters of the novel.

Two men are sitting in a small village in the Egyptian countryside, engaged in conversation (figure 20). They converse in Greek: the younger of the two is himself a Greek, Cnemon of Athens, while the other, Calasiris — an elderly man with long white hair and a full beard — comes from Memphis in Egypt, where he was a priest. For some time, however, he has been staying in Delphi, and the narrative is his. Each time he tries to curtail or conclude his description, he is met by wild protests from his partner: the insatiable curiosity of the Athenian (a national characteristic, see Acts 17:21!) thus serves as the motivation for Heliodorus' detailed depiction of the Delphic spectacle. At the time of the Pythian Games, Calasiris relates, a delegation from Thessaly arrived in Delphi, in order to perform the annual propitiatory sacrifice to Neoptolemus, the son of Achilles — at the very altar of Apollo in Delphi where Neoptolemus had long ago been treacherously murdered by Orestes. The delegation was led by a young Thessalian nobleman, Theagenes, who could trace his genealogy back to Achilles. The culmination of the feast was the impressive offertory procession; its splendour is described by Calasiris, with all the amazement and admiration of the foreign visitor:

'At the head of the procession came the sacrificial animals, led on the halter by the men who were to perform the holy rites, country folk in country costume. Each wore a white tunic, caught up to knee length by a belt. Their right arms were bare to the shoulder and breast, and in their right hands they each brandished a double-headed axe. Each and every one of the oxen was black; they carried their heads proudly on powerful necks that thickened to a hump of perfect proportions; their horns were flawlessly straight and pointed, on some gilded, on others wreathed with garlands of flowers; their legs were stocky, their dewlaps so deep that they

Fig. 19 *The sun god ensures the Meroitic King Sherkarer victory over his enemies. Detail of a rock drawing at Jebel Qeili in the Butana (east of Khartoum in the Sudan), dated at the beginning of the first century AD. In the capital, Meroë, archaeologists have excavated a building which they identify as a sun temple. These finds confirm that there is a kernel of truth in Heliodorus' account of the Meroitic sun cult, even if it should not be taken as documentary description.*

brushed their knees. There were exactly one hundred of them — a hecatomb in the true sense of the word. Behind the oxen came a host of different sorts of beasts for the sacrifice, each kind separate and in its due place, while flute and pipe began a solemn melody as prelude to the sacred ceremony.

'After the animals and the cowherds came some Thessalian maidens, in beauteous raiment girdled deep, their hair streaming free. They were divided into two companies; half — the first company — carried baskets full of flowers and fresh fruit, while the others bore wickerwork trays of sweetmeats and aromatics that breathed a sweet fragrance over the whole place. They carried their baskets on their heads, so leaving their hands free, and moved at right angles to one another in a formal dance, so that their every forward step was a dance movement. They were given the signal to begin by the second group launching into the introduction to the ode, for this group had been granted the privilege of singing the hymn through from beginning to end. The hymn was in praise of Thetis and Peleus, and their son and finally their son's son. [5] After them, Cnemon. . . .'

'What do you mean "Cnemon"?' interrupted Cnemon. 'For a second time, father, you are trying to cheat me of the best part of the story by not giving me all the details of the hymn. It is as if you had provided me only with a view of the procession, without my being able to hear anything.'

'Very well,' replied Calasiris. 'If such is your wish, I shall tell you. Their song went something like this:

'"Of Thetis I sing, the golden-haired goddess,
Daughter of Nereus, the Lord of the Ocean,
Married to Peleus at mighty Zeus' wishing,
Our Aphrodite, the star of the sea-waves.
The child of her womb was the noble Achilles,
Who fought like the War-God and raged in the battle,
Whose spear flashed like lightning, whose fame lives forever.

[5] Thetis, the daughter of the sea god Nereus, celebrated her wedding with a mortal, Peleus. She bore him a son, Achilles, who in his turn with the princess Deidameia (called 'Pyrrha' in the hymn) had a son Neoptolemus (or Pyrrhus), to whose tomb in Delphi the sacrificial procession is now on its way.

Fig. 20 *Calasiris and Cnemon conversing. The Egyptian priest tells the young Athenian of his experiences at Delphi, above all of the magnificent offertory procession to Neoptolemus' tomb, represented in the balloon above. Through this device the artist manages to illustrate Heliodorus' narrative technique as well: the first half of the novel is filled with retrospective narratives, which like the pieces of a jigsaw puzzle eventually join to give a coherent picture of past events, from the conception of the heroine right up to the novel's introductory scene at the mouth of the Nile.*

Neoptolemus, the son Pyrrha bore him,
Dealt death to the Trojans, but to Greece gave great glory;
Neoptolemus, we pray you, be gracious;
Showered with blessings in your tomb here at Delphi
Smile and accept the offering we bring you.
From all tribulation deliver our city.
Of Thetis I sing, the golden-haired goddess."

'To the best of my recollection, then, Cnemon, the hymn was along these lines. So exquisite were the harmonies of the singers, so exactly did the rhythms of the sound of their steps keep time with the music that one's ears charmed one's eyes to be blind to what they saw. As the procession of maidens passed, the onlookers moved in step with them, as if drawn along by the cadences of the song, until behind them the troop of young horsemen and their leader rode up in splendour to prove the vision of beauty more potent than any sound.

'The young men numbered fifty, divided into two groups of twenty-five to escort the leader of the sacred mission who rode at their centre. They wore boots woven from straps of scarlet leather and bound tightly above their ankles; their cloaks were white and clasped with a golden buckle across their chests; a dark blue band ran around the hems of their mantles. Their mounts were all Thessalian steeds, and the light of the freedom of the plains of Thessaly shone in their eyes; they resented the mastery of the bit, foaming and champing and trying to dislodge it, yet they allowed their riders' thoughts to guide them. The horses were caparisoned with silver and gold frontlets and cheek-pieces so splendid that you might have thought the young men had held a competition on this point.

'But splendid though they were, Cnemon, the crowd hardly spared them a second glance. Every eye was turned towards their captain — my beloved Theagenes; it was as if a flash of lightning had cast all we had seen before into darkness, so radiant he was in our eyes. He too was on horseback, in full armour and brandishing a spear of ash-wood tipped with bronze. He wore no helmet but led the procession bare-headed, cloaked in a flowing scarlet mantle with gold embroidery depicting the battle of Lapiths and Centaurs and a clasp with, at its centre, an amber figure of Athene with her Gorgon's head talisman on her breast plate. A sweetly blowing breeze added to the charm of the scene, for its gentle breath tenderly caressed the hair that cascaded over his neck and parted the curls on his forehead, and also swept the hem of his mantle over his horse's back and shanks. The very horse seemed to understand his master's beauty and to realize what a fine thing it was to carry such a fine rider on his back, so proudly he flexed his neck and carried his head high with ears aprick; there was arrogance in the way his brows arched over his eyes, and pride in his step as he pranced along with his master on his back; he obeyed the rein's every command and with each pace he paused for an instant in perfect balance with one leg uplifted, gently clipping the ground with the tip of his hoof so as to give a smooth and gentle rhythm to his gait. The sight took everyone's breath away, and they all awarded the young man the prize for manhood and beauty. And all those women of the lower orders who were incapable of controlling and concealing their emotions, pelted him with apples and flowers in the hope of attracting his good will.[6] The verdict was unanimous: nothing in the world could surpass the beauty of Theagenes.

'But when rosy-fingered dawn, the child of morning, appeared — as Homer would say — when from the temple of Artemis came forth my wise and beautiful Charicleia, then we realized that even Theagenes could be eclipsed, but eclipsed only in such measure as perfect female beauty is more lovely than the fairest of men. She rode in a carriage drawn by a pair of white bullocks [see figure 60], and she was apparelled in a long purple gown embroidered with golden rays. Around her breast she wore a belt of bronze; the man who had crafted it had locked all his art into it — never before had he produced such a masterpiece and never would he be able to repeat the achievement. It was in the shape of two serpents whose tails he had intertwined at the back of the garment; then he had brought their necks round under her breasts and woven them into an intricate knot, finally allowing their heads to slither free of the knot and draping them down either side of her body as if they formed no part of the clasp. You would have said not that the serpents seemed to be moving but that they were actually in motion. There was no cruelty or fellness in their eyes to cause one fright, but they were steeped in a sensuous languor as if lulled by the sweet joys that dwelt in Charicleia's bosom. They were made of gold but were dark in colour, for their makers' craft had blackened the gold so the mixture of yellow and black should express the roughness and shifting hues of their scales. Such was the maiden's belt. Her hair was neither tightly plaited nor yet altogether loose: where it hung long down her neck it cascaded over her back and shoulders, but on her crown and temples where it grew in rosebud curls golden as the sun it was wreathed with soft shoots of bay that held it in place and prevented any unseemly blowing in the breeze. In her left hand she carried a bow of gold; the quiver was slung over her right shoulder and in her right hand she held a lighted torch. But the light from her eyes shone brighter than any torch.'

'It's them!' exclaimed Cnemon. 'It is Charicleia and Theagenes. . . .

'So now, Cnemon, when the procession had wound three times around the tomb of Neoptolemus, and the young men had ridden around it three times, the women cried aloud and the men raised a loud war-cry. As if at one sign, cattle, sheep and goats were sacrificed; it was as if they were slaughtered by a single hand. On an enormous altar they heaped countless twigs and on top they laid all the choicest parts of the sacrifices as custom demanded. Then they asked the priest of Pythian Apollo to commence the libation and light the altar fire. Charicles [the priest of Apollo] answered

---

[6] The apple was Aphrodite's fruit; to throw an apple meant a declaration of love.

that it was his office to pour the libation, "but the leader of the sacred mission should be the one to light the altar, with the torch that he has received from the hands of the acolyte. This is the usage laid down by ancestral custom."

'With these words he began the libation, and Theagenes made to take the fire; and in that very instant it was revealed to us, Cnemon, that the soul is something divine and partakes in the nature of heaven. For at the moment when they set eyes on one another, the young pair fell in love, as if the soul recognized its kin at the very first encounter and sped to meet that which was worthily its own. For a brief second full of emotion they stood motionless. With exaggerated slowness she handed him the torch and he took it from her hands — and all the while they gazed hard into one another's eyes, as if calling to mind a previous acquaintance or meeting (figure 21). Then they smiled a fleeting, furtive smile, visible only as a slight softening of their expressions. And then they blushed, as if they were embarrassed at what had happened, and a moment later — I suppose as their passion touched their hearts — the colour drained from their faces. In the space of an instant, an infinity of expression passed across their faces, as every imaginable kind of alteration in complexion and countenance bore witness to the waves that pounded their souls. No one but me seemed to see any of this; they were all taken up with their own concerns and thinking their own thoughts; even Charicles failed to notice, as he was pronouncing the traditional prayer and invocation; but I had nothing to do but watch the young pair. . . .

'Eventually and with a great effort of will, Theagenes wrenched himself away from the maiden, and lit the altar fire with the torch. The procession was at an end, and the Thessalians went off to celebrate; the rest of the people departed, everyone to his own home.' (3.1.3–6.1)

We recognize the detailed, graphic style from Achilles Tatius' *ecphrases*. Heliodorus does not, like Achilles, describe works of art as if they were reality, but sometimes views reality as a work of art (J. Palm).

The first half of the novel is dominated by the complex, interlaced retrospective narratives of what had happened before the arrival of the hero and heroine in Egypt. Some of the minor characters have their life stories surveyed as well, among others the young Athenian Cnemon, whom we have just met. His story is a variant of the Hippolytus–Phaedra motif. The latter part of the novel is a more straightforward account, in chronological sequence, of the arduous and adventure-packed journey south from the Nile Delta to Meroë; war, politics, and passionate barbarians constantly frustrate the hopes of the young lovers. One of the most dramatic events takes place in Memphis. Theagenes and Charicleia have been temporarily reunited and are staying in the palace of the Persian satrap. The satrap's wife Arsace has been seized with a violent desire for Theagenes. This barbarian woman is depicted as the opposite of Charicleia in all respects; she is licentious by nature and chronically unfaithful to her husband, while Charicleia is unchangeably chaste and true. Arsace is impulsive, passionate, and quite ruthless in her passion; Charicleia is rational almost to the point of coolness and can always control her feelings.

Arsace now accuses Charicleia of having murdered an old female servant with poison. Charicleia is of course innocent of the crime, but in spite of this she refuses to defend herself in front of the court and pleads guilty:

For having during the night in the prison cell related the whole of her story to Theagenes and learnt in turn of his ordeals, and having made a compact that they should of their own free will welcome any death that might be inflicted on them and so be rid forever of a life without hope, an exile without end, and a fate without pity, and having — so she thought — embraced him for the last time; while always taking care to wear secretly the necklaces that had been exposed with her, but now girding them around her loins under her clothes and wearing them like a kind of funeral ornament, she admitted every crime with which she was charged, and invented crimes with which she was not charged. (8.9.8)

In this first section the translation is deliberately made to follow Heliodorus' own sentence structure, as far as this is possible in a modern language. The whole section is one long period in the Greek; the first finite verb comes just a couple of lines from the bottom. All that goes before — the whole retrospect of what happened in the preceding night — is expressed by a series of co-ordinated participles, all ending in the same way (*anatheméne, pythoméne, syntheméne*, etc.). The sound effect of this rhymed row of participles can of course not be reproduced. The rest of the description of Charicleia's ordeal will be translated in a way more enjoyable to a modern ear, with the periods cut up into shorter sentences.

Her judges did not hesitate; indeed they very nearly sentenced her to the excessive cruelty of a Persian execution, but, perhaps in pity for her youth and matchless beauty, they condemned her to be burnt at the stake. At once she was seized by the executioners and taken to a place just outside the city wall. All this time a crier was proclaiming that she was being led to the stake as a poisoner, and a large crowd from the city followed behind them; some had actually seen her being led away, others had heard the

Figs. 21–22 *On the ceiling of the King's Room in Kronborg Castle, Elsinore (Denmark), the Dutch painter Gerard van Honthorst (1590–1656) of Utrecht depicted four scenes from Heliodorus' **Ethiopian Tale**, two of which are reproduced here.*

The first meeting (figure 21): Charicleia hands the torch over to Theagenes, and their eyes meet. . . . Between them stands Charicleia's foster-father, Charicles, who is priest of Apollo.

The recognition (figure 22): thanks to a ribbon embroidered with Ethiopian characters Charicleia is at last recognized as the daughter of the black-skinned Ethiopian royal couple; the queen had had her exposed immediately after her birth, because her skin was white. To the right Theagenes, still a prisoner, waits to be sacrificed to the sun god.

story that raced through the town and had hurried to see for themselves. Arsace was there too, watching from the wall, for she was determined to feast her eyes on the sight of Charicleia's punishment.

The executioners built a gigantic bonfire and then lit it. As the flames took hold, Charicleia begged a moment's grace from her guards, promising that she would mount the pyre without the use of force. She stretched her arms skywards towards the beaming sun and prayed in a loud voice, 'O Sun and Earth, and you spirits above and beneath the earth who watch and punish sin, bear me witness that I am innocent of the charges laid against me, but that I gladly suffer death because of the unendurable agonies that fate inflicts on me. Have mercy on me, and grant me your peace; but with all possible speed exact retribution from that she-devil, that evil adultress who has contrived all this to rob me of my beloved — Arsace!'

At these words, pandemonium broke loose. Some of the crowd were making up their minds to halt the execution for a second trial, others were already moving to do so, but Charicleia forestalled them all by climbing up on to the pyre and positioning herself at the very heart of the fire, where she stood for some time without taking any hurt. The flames flowed around her rather than licking against her; they caused her no harm but drew back wherever she moved toward them, and served merely to encircle her in splendour and present a vision of her standing in radiant beauty in a frame of light, like a bride in a chamber of flame [figure 23]. Charicleia was astounded by this turn of events, but, still eager to die, she leapt from one part of the blaze to another. But it was pointless; for the fire always drew back and seemed to retreat before her onset. The executioners did not let up but redoubled their efforts, encouraged by threatening signs from Arsace, hurling on logs and piling on reeds from the river, fuelling the flames by whatever means they could — but all to no avail. The city was in uproar; this deliverance seemed to show the hand of god. 'She is innocent,' they yelled, 'she has done nothing wrong.' (8.9.9–15)

The end of this exciting episode is that Charicleia jumps down from the pyre, to the enthusiastic cheering of the crowd. Arsace is however still the stronger, and Charicleia again lands in gaol with Theagenes (figure 24). The motif of 'miraculous escape from certain death' recurs with many variations in the Greek novels, as we have already seen. In this case it is soon disclosed that the heroine's salvation was due to a magic stone which she was carrying with her on the pyre.

The *Ethiopica* is the classic among the Greek novels, and not only in the sense that later times canonized it. It is also classic in the deeper sense that Heliodorus stands as both the climax and the termination of a long tradition; he assembles the typical elements used by his predecessors and recasts them into a new whole. His sense of form is strong and his ambitions great — greater than his ability, many would say. The restricted point of view is carried through with success, whereas the author is sometimes less fortunate in mastering the complicated pattern of retrospective narrative and the gradual unveiling of the 'prehistory' in the first half of the novel. The reader may now and then have difficulties in keeping up with events and, when checked in detail, everything does not come out quite right. But the story as a whole is forcefully told and exciting to read; it is full of magnificent scenes and colourful characters.

Moreover, Heliodorus has ambitions beyond the traditional novel form. He sets out to include in his work classical literature at large.

Fig. 23 '. . .like a bride in a chamber of flame.' Charicleia at the stake, as a French illustrator of 1633 imagined her. Her prayer to the sun god (top right!) has proved successful; the people marvel; her adversary and rival Arsace (on top of the wall) is furious.

Epic of course offers the narrative frame and much of the subject-matter, but also drama, Euripides in particular, has obviously exercised a profound influence on Heliodorus. Add to this historiography — the detailed descriptions of campaigns and sieges show the author's martial interests — as well as philosophy, with a number of Platonic reminiscences. The novel is the 'open' genre which accepts such an influx from various quarters without losing its identity, and Heliodorus succeeds in setting his own mark on the different constituents.

Heliodorus can hardly hold his own against his great classical models, like Homer and the drama, or against the modern masterpieces of prose fiction. But measured by more reasonable standards his novel exhibits artistic qualities that cannot be altogether expected in a work of entertainment. Becoming acquainted with him is all the more exciting in that he reveals beneath his classical veneer glimpses of unclassical, even un-Greek traits: the novel testifies to a time and a cultural milieu far from both classical Athens and Hellenistic Alexandria.

The Byzantine Revival

For all we know, the *Ethiopica* is the last novel of love, travel, and adventure to have been written in antiquity. But after an interval of some 800 years the genre suddenly reappears, as if nothing, or next to nothing, had happened in between. From the twelfth century — the century of the Comnenian Dynasty, one of the renaissance periods of Byzantium — we know of four novels, written in a learned literary Greek (in contrast to the popular language of the age): one in prose, *Hysmine and Hysminias* by Eustathius Macrembolites, and three in verse: *Rhodanthe and Dosicles* by Theodore Prodromus, *Aristandros and Callithea* by Constantine Manasses (of which only fragments survive), and *Drosilla and*

Fig. 24 *Back in prison. After her wonderful salvation from the stake Chariclea is again put in irons and brought to Theagenes' cell. This is the special punishment which the jealous Arsace has devised: by seeing each other tormented the two lovers will suffer all the more. But she makes a miscalculation, as is clearly shown also by our illustration of 1626. To Theagenes and Chariclea it is instead a comfort to go through the same sufferings. Neither of them wants to suffer less than the other and be thus deprived of the possibility of displaying the strength of their love.*

Charicles by Nicetas Eugenianus. The very titles reveal their close kinship to the ancient novels.

The godfathers of the new generation are in the first place Achilles Tatius and Heliodorus. For other reasons as well we know that these two were much read and esteemed in the Byzantine age. They have survived in a number of manuscripts (while Chariton and Xenophon Ephesius were preserved in one only), and they are mentioned, compared, and interpreted (sometimes allegorically) by leading Byzantine intellectuals of different centuries. The Patriarch Photius of the ninth century, whom we have already met as a reader of Iamblichus, prefers the dignified and pious Heliodorus to the scabrous Achilles, but none the less praises the latter for his style: it is aphoristic, clear and pleasant, a feast for the ear. Michael Psellus (eleventh century) tells us that many, even highly educated, people quarrel about whether Heliodorus or Achilles is the better, the one being extolled at the other's expense. Psellus himself prefers to be less categorical — both authors have their strong points — but after a thorough and serious analysis he too rates Heliodorus the higher. The four Comnenian writers show their preferences in practice: Macrembolites prefers to follow closely in the footsteps of Achilles Tatius, with first-person narrative, dreams, descriptions of gardens, *ecphrases* of works of art, and analyses of mental processes; whereas Prodromus and his successors imitate with varying degrees of skill Heliodorus' compositional technique.

Like their models, the Byzantine novels are set in a pagan, nonspecific ancient or late-antique world. The gods are the same, with Eros and Tyche as the predominant forces in human life. Chastity and fidelity are idealized, against a background of violence and cruelty, preferably in oriental surroundings. In some respects however the authors also demonstrate a desire to renew the genre. This is most conspicuous in their approach to form: as previously mentioned, three of the novels are in verse — the Byzantine twelve-syllable verse, or, in the case of Manasses, the fifteen-syllable, so-called 'political' verse. This is a definite break with the ancient tradition, where prose reigned supreme.

However, some Byzantine traits can also be observed in their content. These may possibly be unconscious or, as Herbert Hunger in particular has maintained, the result of a genuine striving for contemporary appeal. In Prodromus' work Hunger points to reflections of Byzantine diplomacy and court ceremonial. The way of life and code of honour of the Byzantine military nobility is also apparent: to be worthy of the hand of his beloved the hero has to possess not only beauty and noble birth, but also the particular knowledge of the martial arts which the times required. Moreover, it is true for all the novels that motifs such as battle, capture by pirates, banquets, however traditional they may be, are sometimes embroidered with details from the contemporary world, which thus constitute more or less successfully camouflaged anachronisms.

The Byzantine novels seem to have been much read, in spite of the fact that the learned language in which they were written must have made them inaccessible to a general audience. From later critics and philologists they have won only utter contempt — no disparaging term has been spared — and have consequently not been subject to very much serious analysis. A certain change of attitude has been noticeable in recent decades, but up till now only *Hysmine and Hysminias* has been thoroughly analysed from a more positive point of view, with the aim of explaining and understanding precisely those peculiarities which were previously categorized as stupidity and artificiality, tastelessness and barbarous pedantry. I shall here mainly follow this new interpretation, presented by Margaret Alexiou, though with the reservation that perhaps this time the pendulum has swung a bit too far in the positive direction.

The novel contains comparatively few external events, the emphasis being on the inner processes. Everything is considered from the point of view of the narrator hero: this is a first-person narrative from beginning to end, without the initial introduction of the narrator — the 'epic situation' — that we find in Achilles Tatius. In contrast to Achilles, Macrembolites succeeds in sustaining his restricted narrative perspective all the way through. The action may be summarized as follows: Hysminias is sent as a herald from his native town Eurycomis to the town of Aulicomis (fictitious names — the last trace of historiography has been thrown overboard!). His host, Sosthenes, has a beautiful daughter by the name of Hysmine, who serves the wine at the evening's banquet. She flirts wildly with Hysminias, who for his part remains relatively indifferent. On the following day Hysminias, in the company of his friend Cratisthenes, inspects the garden and looks at the cycle of paintings put on display there, representing among other things Eros in full armour. In the evening the events of the previous day are repeated, but that night Hysminias is visited in his dreams by the Eros of the paintings. Love for Hysmine is awakened in him, and in a state between dream and waking he imagines Hysmine visiting him in his room:

And I see Hysmine by my bed. Shamelessly I stretch out my hand and draw her to me and sit her on my bed — Love is the father of shamelessness. She is shy, being a maiden, and at first acts reluctantly; but she gives in, as a maiden does to a man, because she has been overcome by love even before I touch her.

She kept her eyes on the ground, but I kept mine firmly fixed on the girl's face; it was full of light, full of grace, full of pleasure. Her eyebrows were black, shaped like rainbows or the crescent moon. Her eyes were dark and lively, and shone brightly: their circle was partly flattened — her eyes were cone-shaped, rather than round. Her eyelashes were quite black. The girl's eyes were the very mirror of love.

Her cheeks are white — pure white except where they are rosy; they are rosy in the middle, but as it were dappled, with the red unevenly distributed, not as if by hand, or painted by art, or faded by night, or washed off by water. Her mouth is open symmetrically; her lips full-fleshed, and both red; you would think the girl had crushed a rose between her lips. . . .

I touch her hand, and she tries to withdraw it and hide it in her dress; but I win in this too. I bring her hand to my lip, I kiss it, I bite it time and time again; she draws it away and shrinks from me. I embrace her; I assault her neck, her lips, with my lips. I fill them with kisses, I let my love trickle over her. Pretending to close her mouth, she gives my lip a love-bite and steals a kiss.

I kissed her eyes and drew love up into my soul — the eye is the fount of love. I busy myself with the girl's bosom too; she resists nobly, shrinks from me, with her whole body she defends her breast as a fortress defends a city; with hands and neck and chin she protects, fortifies her breasts. From below she draws up her knees, she shoots tears from her head like arrows from a fortress, practically saying 'If you love me, yield to my tears: if you don't love me, don't start a war.' But I am more afraid of defeat; I resist forcefully, and just manage to win. And my victory is a defeat; I lose all my aggressiveness; for as my hand engulfed the girl's breast, impotence engulfed my heart.

I was in pain, I was despondent. I trembled with a strange trembling, my sight dimmed, my soul softened, my strength ebbed, my body grew sluggish, my breathing was checked, my heart palpitated violently, a sweet pain ran right through my limbs as if tickling them, I was totally in the grip of an indescribable, unspeakable, ineffable love; and, by love itself! I felt as I had never felt before.

Well, the girl flew at once from my arms, or to speak more properly my arms fell sluggishly and feebly from the girl. And sleep fled at once from my eyes, and by Love! I was annoyed to lose such a lovely dream and be torn away from my dear Hysmine. (3.5.7–7.7)

A new day, another walk in the garden, another banquet: now Hysminias is more than willing to return Hysmine's advances. The subsequent development of the love-affair is likewise narrated in alternation between day and night scenes, between reality and dream. Most of the sex is enacted in the hero's dreams. In the middle of the novel there is a shift of setting: the whole company sails from Aulicomis to Eurycomis, Hysminias' home town. The heroine, who had the initiative to begin with, is now totally on the defensive and refuses to sacrifice her innocence. Then comes a threat from outside: Hysmine's father wants to marry her to another man. There is feasting, sacrificing, evil omens, and more sacrificing. This gives Cratisthenes an opportunity to arrange the escape of hero and heroine. All three flee from Eurycomis by boat, but a storm blows up and the captain throws Hysmine overboard as a propitiatory sacrifice to the sea god. Desolate, Hysminias is put ashore at the next harbour; he is captured by Ethiopian pirates and later sold as a slave in the town of Daphnepolis. His master is appointed a herald for a religious festival, as Hysminias himself was at the beginning of the novel, and at a banquet the hero recognizes his beloved in the guise of a servant. After some further complications it is time for the great recognition scene, when Hysmine and Hysminias are reunited with their parents and released from slavery. In the eleventh and last 'book' Hysmine has to go through an ordeal to prove her virginity — one of the many motifs Macrembolites takes over directly from Achilles Tatius (figure 25) — and then they all return to Aulicomis to celebrate the marriage.

The most interesting thing about this novel is not its close adherence to Achilles Tatius, which is obvious, but some new features, and their interpretation. The style is generally regarded as overdone, as our sample may have suggested. But does this mean that the novel is the product of 'an Achilles Tatius who has gone out of his mind', as Erwin Rohde had it? 'A vast flood of words [*Redeschwall*] is meant to be made more attractive by the most far-fetched puns and the most meaningless, alliterative accumulations of words, by silly antitheses, classic passages inserted from numerous older authors (especially Homer and Euripides), and the like; and yet the result is only a tangle of words [*Wortgekräusel*], which out-does even Achilles, and painful quibbles dressed up in piteously pretentious phrases. . . .' Margaret Alexiou admits that there is a core of truth in Rohde's characterization of the novel, but she interprets the state of affairs in the opposite way: the accumulation of rhetorical effects is quite deliberate, and intended as parody. The over-obvious use of the genre's motivic and plot clichés may be similarly explained. The captain of the ship, who in exaggeratedly

solemn words and with a whole arsenal of classical allusions, performs the sacrifice of Hysmine to the sea god, in this reading becomes the central character in an extremely funny scene.

Even the anti-heroic appearance of hero and heroine can be fitted into this pattern. The heroine's shameless way of courting the hero at the beginning of the novel can now be seen as a comic reversal of the conventional assignment of roles. But this does not mean, to Alexiou, that we are finished with Macrembolites' novel. It is not intended only as an amusing parody, but also offers new elements with more serious intent. In the first place, the psychological dimension has been deepened. The long dream sequences are superficially a grotesque inflation of Achilles' use of dreams; but there is a new content, a bold attempt to present the unconscious, the awakening sexuality of a pubertal youth. 'It is the kind of material deliberately explored by twentieth-century novelists to penetrate the inner complexities of an individual's *psyche*, but not usually associated with Byzantine learned romances of the twelfth century' (Alexiou). Several of the basic types of dreams — upon which modern psychologists confer various special terms — are represented, and their insertion into the surrounding 'reality' of the novel is not just directed forwards, as foreshadowings: the content of the dreams also relates to Hysminias' earlier experiences, all in a psychologically reasonable way.

The first-person point of view, so persistently maintained, is used to account for the blending of dream and reality, as well as for some aspects of the depiction of the heroine. It has been considered an inconsistency that Hysmine tries to arouse Hysminias' desire with all the means at her disposal, only to change suddenly, and apparently without cause, to a more negative attitude, once she has succeeded. Alexiou maintains that this reflects female behaviour as viewed by

Fig. 25 *The chastity ordeal. This illustration (of 1796) belongs to Achilles Tatius' novel — Leucippe triumphantly steps out of the cave in which her chastity has been tried — but the same motif occurs also in Heliodorus and in the Byzantine novel of Eustathius Macrembolites. To preserve her chastity no less in her relationship with the beloved than under attack from other admirers is the heroine's principal ambition in the sophistic and Byzantine novels. The happy ending is not possible until her chastity has been publicly proved, and the same is demanded, at least in principle, from the hero as well. Macrembolites by a flash of genius combines the traditional chastity ideal with advanced erotic descriptions: he lets his hero* **dream** *of the premarital intimacy which the conventions of the novel would otherwise deny him.*

men. At the same time it allows the heroine's virtue to be preserved to the very last page, as the convention of the sophistic novel demands.

Thus on closer inspection what Macrembolites has accomplished is not a 'slavish imitation' of the ancient novels. He is a learned author — witness the number and variety of his classical allusions — who deliberately combines the old clichés to form a new whole. In contrast to his contemporary colleagues he has chosen prose as his medium and is therefore able to switch freely between levels of style, between rhetorical loftiness and everyday dialogue, though all within the compass of a learned language. He plays with the genre, but at the same time he has essential insights into the human mind to convey.

The Comnenian quartet marks the end of the ancient novel, but not of the Byzantine novel. In the fourteenth century we again meet a number of novels with titles of a similar kind: *Callimachus and Chrysorrhoe*, *Libystrus and Rhodamne*, *Phlorius and Platzia Phlore*. . . . Even a quick glance at their content, however, shows that here we have something new. The setting is still the ancient, or at least non-Christian, world, but new ingredients have been mixed in with the old motifs. The folk-tale motifs — the king who has three sons, the virgin who is guarded by a terrifying dragon, the magic apple — immediately catch the eye. Some of the novels are still essentially Greek, even if contemporary contact with the Franks (in the West, or as crusaders) has left its mark, while others can be traced directly to western models: *Florio e Biancifiore*! The relationships and the degree of dependency between East and West have been much discussed, with national feelings a powerful motive on both sides of the argument; but these few comments will have to suffice here.

Even those fourteenth-century novels that are regarded as genuinely Greek belong to a new tradition. This can be seen most obviously in their diction. The Atticist language which had been the mark of the Greek novel since the Second Sophistic is now replaced by a popular language — not the language spoken by the broad masses, but a literary language built on contemporary cultivated speech. The ancient sophistic novel has joined with popular medieval tradition, in which the epic of Digenis Acritas is central, and has at the same time been confronted with the western romance of chivalry. It is in that state, not at the hour of its death but in the midst of its transformation into something new, that we find the Greek novel some 1500 years after its birth.

CHAPTER III

The Social Background and the First Readers of the Novel

The Greek novels can still be read and easily understood without the aid of a heavy academic apparatus, as I hope the quotations in the preceding chapter have demonstrated. Moreover, in many respects they make an amazingly modern and lively impression, especially if one is otherwise accustomed to associate 'Greek' with marble statues and lofty thoughts, with Pericles and the Parthenon, Sophocles and Plato. But the classical age, 480–330 BC, is only a short — though uniquely rich — period in the long history of Greek literature; and other ages too have produced things of worth and interest. In the novels we meet not heroes or mythical figures but private individuals, perhaps divinely beautiful, but with feelings and problems familiar to us. We must ask ourselves: to which period of Greek history does this genre originally belong, who were its first readers, and in what kind of society did they live?

With these questions we have touched on one of the more intensely discussed problems of ancient literary history, the origins of the Greek novel — of special interest since this means at the same time the beginnings of the western novel in general. To be frank, this aspect of the Greek novel was for a long time the only one to be considered worthy of serious study. The genre in itself was of no interest: simple in form, lacking deep and original ideas, obviously aimed at a popular audience; but the problem of its origins fascinated scholars. Many tried to solve it within a literary context: which genre grew, or 'developed', into the novel, or from what combination of existing genres did the new one emanate? Recently the sociological aspect has come more to the fore: the genesis of the novel is regarded as the response to a new social structure and new demands from the reading public.

The debate itself will not be pursued here. It has partly lost relevance since newer finds of papyri have made it clear that we are

81

obliged to seek the genre's origins in the Hellenistic period. (The Roman imperial period had previously been the favourite candidate.) But both the restricted literary approach and the sociological one are fruitful if we wish to reach a deeper understanding of the Greek novel. In the next chapter we shall look more closely at the literary genres that preceded the novel, and from which the novelists took motifs or formal elements; we shall also consider the related genres which existed side by side with the novel in Hellenistic and imperial times. But at present we shall concentrate on society, first and in greatest detail on Hellenistic society. It is true that very little survives of the earliest novels. But a literary genre is generally marked by the time and milieu in which it was first formed. The Greek novel originated in the Hellenistic cultural milieu and in essential respects carries the marks of that period far into imperial times, even, as we have seen, into the middle and late Byzantine periods — but then of course as relics from a distant age, combined with new elements that have been picked up on the way.

Hellenistic Society

'Hellenistic' is the conventional name for the period of Greek history extending from the conquests of Alexander the Great until the last Hellenistic state, Egypt, was swallowed by Rome — that is, in round figures, 330–30 BC. The break between classical and Hellenistic times is unusually sharp. Before Alexander, Greece consisted of a number of small city states around the Aegean, bound together by a common language and culture but politically divided into varying constellations. After Alexander, Greek civilization is spread over large parts of the Orient, and political power has passed to big new monarchies with their centres in Macedonia/Asia Minor, Syria/ Mesopotamia, and Egypt. The corresponding borderline between Hellenistic and Roman times is much more arbitrarily drawn: on the one hand, the Roman conquest of the Hellenistic states begins long before 30 BC; on the other, 'Hellenistic' culture and the Greek language live on in the Eastern Mediterranean region independent of the fact that the states have lost their political autonomy and have been made part of the Roman Empire.

Philip II, King of Macedonia, the northern neighbour of Greece, and his son and successor Alexander had by the use of force brought about the unification of Greece which native idealists had long preached in vain, and quickly assumed the role of bearers of Greek civilization. Under Alexander's command Macedonians and Greeks marched east to inflict the final blow on the Persian great king, the hereditary foe of Hellas. The result was a new world empire, bordering on India in the East, an empire which was soon broken down politically into smaller units but which turned out to be more tenacious as far as language and culture were concerned. The map is covered with newly founded 'Greek' cities; Greeks are to be found in most key positions; the ruling dynasties are Greek. At the same time it is self-evident that the majority of the people in the new kingdoms, especially in the countryside, keep their own culture and language. But from contact and interaction between the Greek newcomers and the old dominant classes there arises what is known as Hellenistic culture, neither Greek nor oriental, but a mixture of both. Greek is the common language, the means of communication and the carrier of culture, though a Greek which has been 'levelled out' and simplified in relation to pure Attic — it is now to be used both by Greeks of different native dialects and by foreigners who learn it as their second language.

For the old Greek mother country this rapid development means no immediately visible revolution. The political freedom of the city states is gone, but everyday life continues in its usual way, as does cultural life. The schools of philosophy flourish in Athens; the people are entertained by Menander and other writers of New Comedy. But taking a long view, one can see a difference: the cultural initiative has passed from Athens to the big new cities at the eastern end of the Mediterranean, in particular to Alexandria in Ptolemaic Egypt. This is where poets like Theocritus, Callimachus, and Apollonius Rhodius settle, and where the first great library is created in the third century BC. This is where the money is. The mother country slowly becomes impoverished materially and culturally.

Hellenistic society is Protean, difficult to grasp and impossible to summarize in a single formula, in contrast to the more homogeneous classical city state, which so readily lends itself to synthesis. This is quite natural: its geographical diffusion is enormous, the Greek element has been mixed with different indigenous cultures in different regions; there is no indisputable centre, either political or cultural. The milieux that are most often described, the literary circle of Alexandria and the creative scientific milieu there and elsewhere, are simply small and not quite representative sectors of cultural life. In addition, we are concerned with a development over three hundred years, with different phases succeeding each other. Late Hellenism shows a face radically dissimilar to that of the early period. The generalizations to be attempted here, in spite of all this, try to pin down some few traits that seem fairly constant and at the same time relevant to a consideration of the novel.

Hellenistic culture was a city culture; the country simply was not Hellenized. In its most typical form it was even a big-city culture. As counterparts, on a smaller scale, of the mastodontic Alexandria we find in the Seleucid Kingdom Antioch (on the Orontes) and Seleucia (on the Tigris), in Asia Minor Pergamum. Between the Greek top stratum of the cities, chiefly consisting of high officials and officers, and the large indigenous mass of workers and farmers, free or slaves, there was the comparatively well-to-do middle class which is of most interest to us in this context: merchants, civil servants (bureaucracy developed rapidly), lawyers, teachers, doctors, engineers, and so forth, either Greeks and Hellenized Macedonians or (in increasing numbers) Hellenized orientals. A Greek school education was a matter of course in this class, it was the very prerequisite for being accepted as 'Greek'. You could find them sitting by the waters of the Euphrates and the Tigris, of the Orontes and of the Nile, grinding away at their Homer.

Political conditions were far from stable. Wars, occupations, and internal struggles for power within the kingdoms followed one upon another. Enormous city walls and other Hellenistic means of defence are witness in their own way to the insecurity of the age. Moreover, there were certain tensions built into the system itself. The 'Greek' cities tried to maintain their status of 'city states', and accordingly their independence in relation to king and central government. Different ethnic groups could easily come into opposition with each other, all the more so since ethnic divisions ran parallel to class divisions. The society had sharp boundaries between the classes, even if 'Hellenization' was possible for orientals of good birth and, on the other hand, poor Greeks might pass on downwards in the system. In the big cities there was a proletariat which had had no counterpart in the classical city state. Riots and revolts of the suppressed lower classes were not uncommon, especially in the second century BC when the grip of the central power had begun to slacken.

The world was widened, new routes were opened for trade, towards China in the East, towards Russia in the North, to the regions south of the Sahara. The Mediterranean and the Near East were traversed by trade routes by land and sea. It became easier to travel, and popular — not just as an explorer, merchant, mercenary, or emigrant hunting for a new home, but also as a tourist, with the intention of seeing and exploring new places and bringing the experiences home. At sea it was possible to get a passage on any of the numerous merchant vessels that used the harbours around the Mediterranean and Black Sea. Travelling that way was not quick — the delays for unloading, loading, and taking provisions on board were many and long — but there was all the more time for sightseeing. To go by land was more laborious, but then the many Greek cities provided welcome opportunities for rest: the Greek or Hellenized traveller could feel at home wherever he went; he could make himself understood in his own language; refresh body and soul in the gymnasium of the place, and make his thank-offering for a successful journey in a Greek sanctuary.

And thank-offerings were indeed called for. Between the harbours and the cities travelling was risky: on the sea storms and pirates, along the roads professional gangs of robbers or half-wild native tribes. Piracy in particular reached grotesque proportions in the Hellenistic period. Bases for organized piracy were first of all Crete, then in late Hellenistic times Cilicia (in SE Asia Minor), whose rocky, rugged coast gave shelter to a veritable pirate state. This business was permitted to continue without too much hindrance thanks to the rivalry of the Hellenistic states. The pirates were even secretly supported in order to harm the other party, and pirates were hired to commit acts of war for which governments did not want to assume responsibility, such as attacks on neutral states. Not only did the pirates terrorize shipping, but they also made unexpected raids inland. Only in the sixties of the first century BC did the Romans under Pompey succeed to some extent in clearing the Eastern Mediterranean of pirates: earlier they too had been only half-hearted in taking measures against piracy, since it weakened their enemies, the Hellenistic monarchies, and at the same time provided the Romans themselves with slaves.

Slaves were in fact the pirates' most important booty and source of income. The old Greek regions, like western Asia Minor, were dependent on slaves for running the large country estates. Mining implied slaves, as did public building work. House slaves and personal servants were a matter of course in the higher strata of society. Besides prisoners of war it was the victims of pirate and robber attacks and kidnappings that satisfied the demands of the slave market. Greeks, Syrians, and other orientals were quicker to learn and easier to handle than barbarians from the West and the North and were consequently in greater demand, not least in Rome. Thus, the activity of pirates and robbers was not just a marginal problem, acute only for merchants and their economic considerations. It meant a real and frightening insecurity for all who travelled and for people of all classes who lived in exposed districts like coasts and islands. Personal liberty was transient, the wheel of fortune could turn instantly: today free, tomorrow a slave.

The insecurity of the individual in the new society, an insecurity on several levels and arising for different reasons, some of which we have specified, is mirrored in the spiritual currents of the Hellenistic period. The problem is attacked most ambitiously by the philosophers: instead of searching for the basic substances of the universe or the idea of beauty, they now tend to concentrate on ethical problems. The individual is the focus of interest: how can he find personal satisfaction and a purpose in his life? There are different answers: Happiness is freedom from all needs (the Cynics); Happiness is freedom from fear and other emotions (the Epicureans); Happiness is virtue and the fulfilment of one's duties (the Stoics).

Political thinking in this period often turns in utopian directions. The reformers sketch — and in some cases even try to bring into being — communities distinguished by all that their own age lacks: a classless social structure, common ownership of property, equality of the sexes, a simple way of life in harmony with nature, without all the degenerate varieties of civilization. Men of practical politics too are well aware of what is missing, as can be inferred from the slogans used in political propaganda: what the Hellenistic kings proclaim as their virtues are 'philanthropy', charity, and concern!

But the mass of security hunters travelled along broader roads than those of moral philosophy, heading for astrology (imported from Mesopotamia), other varieties of belief in fate, or the mystery religions, which promised individual salvation. Tyche or Fortuna, personified chance, a mighty but capricious goddess, is among the most frequently invoked — and most frequently abused — deities of this time (see figure 2). A belief in fate of a still more frightening kind assumes power in late Hellenism: fatalism, the conviction that the same implacable force that directs the stars and planets has also predestined the life of every human being. The flight from this terrifying perspective often led to one of the new salvationist faiths.

Of the old Olympian gods many had definitely been transferred to the waxworks museum of mythology. Some, however, lived on in their own right: Zeus, who was able to catch the monotheist movements of the time, Apollo with his oracles, Dionysus, who of old had his mystery cult. In addition, several of the Greek gods could live on, in name at least, as they were identified with other gods: Zeus himself with the Roman Jupiter, the Syrian Baal, and the Egyptian Amon-Re, Artemis with the Great Mother of Asia Minor, and so on. The fusion of religions, syncretism, was along with the flourishing mystery cults the most typical phenomenon of religious life in Hellenistic times. To some extent it may be viewed as the natural consequence of increased mobility and mingling of peoples: instead of attacking the religion and gods of the newcomers you assimilate them with your own; your own god receives an additional epithet, his cult admits new elements.

Among the mystery religions, most of them of oriental origin, the Egyptian Isis cult is most successful. In late Hellenistic times it spreads epidemically throughout the Mediterranean world. Isis is the greatest goddess, she is identified with all, she has innumerable epithets and functions. As a young woman, with an attractive coiffure and dress and adorned with jewels, she has a great appeal for men (see figure 10). As a wife and mother she is the goddess of women, a precursor of the Holy Virgin. But what attracts a whole army of devoted believers is above all, as in the other mystery religions, the message of salvation. A *mysterion* is, in the definition of A. D. Nock, 'a secret rite, in which the individual participates of his own free choice, and by which he is put into closer relation with the deity honoured; normally he must undergo ceremonies of initiation . . . conferring a new and indelible spiritual condition and commonly giving assurance of happiness hereafter'. As Osiris, Isis' husband, in the myth dies and then rises again, in the same way everyone who is initiated into the mysteries dies to his old life and emerges in a new form. His soul is saved and assured of an eternal life — in the centuries round the birth of Christ this hope drives countless suppressed, insecure, mentally and physically suffering people into the mystery cults.

The Birth of the Novel

There is no doubt that the novel fits well into this Hellenistic milieu, as far as externals go: travel by land and sea; pirates and brigands; kidnapping and slavery; the ravages of chance; religious syncretism. Chariton dwells with relish and inside knowledge on the country-squire life in western Asia Minor, Achilles Tatius on the big city of Alexandria: the city was greater than a whole continent, the people more numerous than a whole nation. . . . Other milieux may have a more distinct flavour of literary borrowings: Chariton's Syracuse, Xenophon's Ephesus, Heliodorus' Delphi. But however much the novelist strives to locate the action in classical times, the characteristics of the Hellenistic period peep through; and even if, on the other hand, most of the surviving novels belong to the middle of the imperial period, the original surroundings make their living presence felt in motifs and spirit. Pirates still maraud freely on the Mediterranean Sea; the Romans are never mentioned by name.

But also in a deeper sense the novel is a product of the Hellenistic period. That the literary genre of the novel was born in this particular time and place is not accidental. The circumstances surrounding this 'birth' have been investigated by the American scholar Ben Edwin Perry in his great work *The Ancient Romances: A Literary–Historical Account of their Origins*, and we shall accompany him part of the way.

Perry maintains that new literary forms may respond to needs of very different types. They vary with time, place, readership, and the personality of the author. Sometimes they may characterize a whole community during a certain period of time, or a whole class of society. In other cases they are limited to a small clique, or are even unique to the author himself. But as far as the really important and lasting genres, such as tragedy and the novel, are concerned, they must have been created in concord with a continuous and widespread demand.

To Perry epic and novel are one and the same genre, though belonging to different types of society. A 'national warrior-epic' like the *Iliad* reflects a simple tribal community, characterized by cultural homogeneity and uniform patterns of thought and action. It is a small, closed world, which permits the individual in the poem to be represented as great and heroic; his experience and fate may be seen as symbolic of humanity as a whole. The audience instinctively experiences this as something with a deeper meaning than the adventures of a private person. The hero represents ideal values that no one questions. This is possible only in a closed society where custom, tradition, and identical experience have moulded the common outlook on life. The epic satisfies all the literary needs of this society, ethical, aesthetic, religious; it teaches history and imparts concrete knowledge in many fields.

When society passes on into a new phase, becoming more complex and sophisticated, the epic is no longer enough. In the Greek city state of the classical period the epic is no longer a living literary form — the *Iliad* and *Odyssey* have stiffened into monuments — but a multitude of genres have assumed its different functions: lyric poetry and drama, philosophic, historical, and scientific prose.

But society is still comparatively closed, with a widespread community of values. Tragedy is the product of a society in which life can still be conceived as a self-evident and well-defined whole and the poet can devote himself to what is behind, what governs human life. But already Euripides points towards a new time. When this cultural solidarity begins to be broken down in a world-wide, big-city culture like the Hellenistic one, and the fixed norms are questioned and replaced by a general eclecticism, then epic flourishes again. But now in a new form: the novel.

Hellenistic society, Perry points out, has fundamental traits in common with modern Western society after the French Revolution. In place of stable traditions and fixed values there enters a vast multitude of conflicting desires and centrifugal tendencies. Common ideals and interests exist only locally or artificially. Small isolated groups may, for a while, keep to the old cultural and literary patterns, witness Callimachus and his Alexandrian circle who cultivated their exclusive poetic style. Anything that has high quality — morally, aesthetically, or intellectually — is understood by a small minority only. Within the community of values prevailing in the closed tribal society it was possible to spread quality; not so now, when anything that hopes to reach and attract a broad and heterogeneous audience must be diluted and adapted. Literature becomes superficial, mechanical, aiming at cruder and cruder effects. At the same time it is open to influences from all sides; in its formlessness it is capable of adjustment to all the wishes of the 'spiritual and intellectual nomads' (as Perry has it) whom it has in view. The novel, he says, is the least defined, the least concentrated, the least organic, and the most formless of all the so-called literary forms. It is the open form for the open society. This 'latter-day epic for Everyman' has everything for everybody, exactly as did the old heroic epic; only the difference now is that 'everybody' and 'everything' have become infinitely more varied entities.

So far Perry. His picture has been supplemented and deepened by B. P. Reardon, who draws the religious aspect as well into the debate. The bigger the world grows, the smaller the individual feels. He feels his helplessness before the immensity of things, he grows passive and feels himself being arbitrarily tossed about by fate. The novel may be looked upon as the *myth* of late Hellenism: with its central theme of the lonely traveller searching for his beloved, it is an expression of the individual's sense of isolation in the world. The search is a search for security, in God or in some other human being. The escape from isolation, the way to salvation, is to find the God or human being who cares about you as an individual. In this way only can you find your social identity; the time has passed when the individual felt he had a meaningful position in society as a 'citizen'.

The need is there: the answer — the novel — we have already come to know. We do not know who wrote the first novel, only that he obviously hit the right note and had many successors. Perry formulates what happened in the following way, in marked opposition to all those who have viewed the genesis of the novel as the almost automatic result of a gradual, literary development: 'The first romance was deliberately planned and written by an individual author, its inventor. He conceived it on a Tuesday afternoon in July. . . .'

The First Readers

Rootless, at a loss, restlessly searching — the people who needed and welcomed the novel are the same as those who were attracted by the mystery religions and Christianity: the people of Alexandria and other big cities round the Eastern Mediterranean. But a prerequisite for the genesis and flourishing of this genre, here as in eighteenth-century England, was of course an increased level of literacy in the population. New Comedy had been the early Hellenistic platform for a romantic and easy entertainment. Menander, and even Euripides, continued to be in the repertoire, but theatrical performances of that kind were naturally rare, available only on special occasions for a privileged city audience. The popular drama, the mime, developed towards an increased coarseness and towards a pure, wordless pantomime. When in the last part of the second century BC literacy had become more widespread, the possibility of satisfying other needs was there as well. The population outside the big cities, the women, people looking for romanticism and idealism — all now had the opportunity to have their wishes fulfilled.

Of course we must not be led to believe that increased literacy at this time meant anything approaching a general ability to read and write, let alone the desire to read for pleasure and relaxation. We are still dealing only with a small proportion of the population, the comparatively well-to-do stratum of Greek or Hellenized citizens working in the administration, in the professions, or in commerce, and their families; and this is probably an important point in dealing with the novel. This stratum expanded during the Hellenistic period, and literacy seems to have increased within it, notably to include the women. Still one may legitimately ask how many attained such proficiency in reading that they took pleasure in it; it is one thing to be able to function in a society which demands an elementary knowledge of reading and writing for economic and legal transactions and for certain kinds of communication, quite another thing to turn to a book for entertainment in one's leisure.

We have already touched on some of the possible motivating forces for taking such a step. One is the implantation of certain cultural ideals through the schools, through reading Homer and other classics. When Chariton alludes to the classical historians, in his style as well as in his subject-matter, and mixes lines from Homer into his prose narrative, he is obviously appealing to his readers' sense of familiarity. At the same time, his novel makes easier reading than the classical models. It entertains, and it provides an escape from the mundane. This is the second, more essential motivation: the fulfilment of certain demands typical of the time, already discussed above. From this we may in turn draw some inferences about the readers. A novel like Chariton's *Chaereas and Callirhoe* presupposes an audience with a taste for sentimentality; certain fragments, on the other hand, such as those from Lollianus' *Phoenicica* (figure 26), indicate that others demanded sexually titillating reading and got their share; violence and exoticism are offered to prospective readers by Xenophon and Iamblichus, and so on.

These are however rather general characteristics of the readers, defining only their psychological condition. It is clearly not permissible to equate this description of the readership with a certain social class. Gareth Schmeling, revising his earlier view of a 'middle-class audience', now more cautiously speaks of 'a sentimental group, that is, one which suspends its intellectual judgements and appreciation for reality and adopts a view that events in life are simple'. Such readers may obviously be looked for both in the top stratum of society and in the Hellenized middle class; the prerequisite is only true literacy, or membership in a group where such literacy is represented. In that connection, we may speculate about one special craft which may have had a crucial role in spreading this kind of literature further down the social scale. I refer to those who made their living by reading and writing for others, the scribes and secretaries, either in public or private service or working in their own employ. In the bureaucracy of the Hellenistic kingdoms citizens were forced in certain situations to have documents drafted for them; laws and edicts of various kinds were conveyed to the public in writing; increased mobility among the population made messages by letter necessary. For such purposes the illiterate had to use professionals, and these artisans of the written word may reasonably be assumed to have possessed more than a formal ability to read. At the

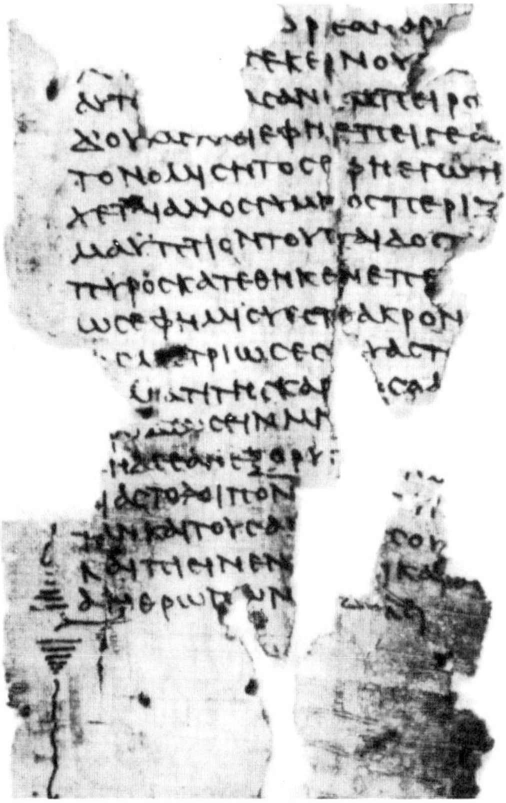

Fig. 26 *A papyrus fragment of Lollianus'* **Phoenician Tale**. *This novel saw its modern* **editio princeps** *as late as 1972. It belongs to Roman imperial times and survives only in fragments in a Cologne papyrus. In the fragments there appears a ritual murder, performed by Egyptian robbers in the Nile delta; we are reminded of the scene in Achilles Tatius quoted above (p. 43). The papyrus was written about AD 200; note that the text, as usual in antiquity, runs along without spaces between the words, which of course made quick silent reading less easily practicable (reading aloud was usual, even when on one's own). The ornamental sign (bottom left) is a so-called* **coronis**, *which marks the end of a larger section (here of one of the novel's books).*

same time they were not necessarily literary highbrows, but belonged to a social level far beneath the top (with the exception of those who held special 'scribe' appointments in Egypt). Chariton, the lawyer's secretary, wrote a novel himself, and we may well suspect that many of his colleagues in still humbler positions belonged to his most devoted readers.

If this was so, one further consequence naturally follows. The ability to read, and read easily and for pleasure, in a milieu where true literacy was not common, no doubt carried with it the obligation to read aloud to members of the household, to a circle of friends, perhaps even to a wider audience. This would mean that the novel could reach not only below the ruling classes, but also outside the towns and beyond the households of the rich landowners: each village would have had a scribe, in function if not in office. This remains a hypothesis, which however to my mind accounts for the wider circulation of the novel better than the assumption that it was due to professional, itinerant story-tellers. It does not seem very probable that these included in their repertoire such extensive, literary works as the novel. The novel is very different in structure from the wonder-stories, or their profane counterparts, which the story-tellers purveyed, and its dissemination is likely to have been different too.

The spread of literacy in itself, quite apart from the key role possibly played by the scribes, must have meant that by means of a chain reaction the opportunities for attending recitations in private circles multiplied. The analysis of the narrative technique of the non-sophistic novels seems to confirm that the authors had precisely that kind of literary consumption in mind. Particularly revealing in this respect are various kinds of repetition and instances of excessive clarity. There are also elements resembling the technique of the serial story, such as foreshadowings and regular plot summaries. Some of these features are inherited from the epic, another genre originally composed for an audience; the techniques will be discussed in somewhat greater detail in the next chapter.

What remains to us of ancient book illustration indicates that the novels were sometimes illustrated in a way reminiscent of modern cartoons, or perhaps rather of the picture-book editions of adventure stories (figures 27–8). This introduction of pictures into novels must have meant that reading was encouraged and facilitated for those who had the formal ability, but not yet the habit. There are also other conclusions to be drawn from the physical remains of the ancient novels, the papyrus fragments unearthed at various places in the Egyptian countryside. It must be remembered, though, that they all belong to the Roman imperial period and thus strictly speaking do not tell us anything of the very first generations of readers. But they do tell us something about the continued reading of the first generations of *novels*; of the later, sophistic novels only Achilles Tatius is represented among the papyri. Some of the fragments are written in a fine script, on new and costly material, while in contrast a comparatively high proportion reuses papyri that had previously been employed for accounts or the like. We may conclude that there were both well-to-do readers who could order or themselves write elegant copies of the novels and others who had to rely on less expensive ways of obtaining the writing material for their light reading. It is also an interesting fact that by the second and third centuries AD the codex form — a *book* instead of a roll — was used quite frequently for the novel (see figure 26). The old

Fig. 27 *An illustrated novel papyrus? In this fragment of an ancient book-roll (second century AD) several columns of text may be distinguished, each illustrated with a simple drawing. The text has not been identified, but it has been suggested that this is a fragment of an unknown novel. The technique of illustration reminds one of modern cartoons more than of book illumination proper: the series of simple pictures will have helped and encouraged inexperienced readers. This tradition continued into the middle ages (see figures 42−3).*

prestigious literary forms continued to prefer the roll, while in early imperial times the more handy codex came into use for non-literary purposes and also for the writings of the emerging Christian church. Though the material is not of a character to be statistically significant, it tends to confirm what we are able to infer from other kinds of evidence about both the literary status of the novel and the social status of its readers, or some of them. Moreover, the connection with early Christian literature is not limited to the physical appearance of the books, as will be clear when we arrive at the apocryphal Acts of the Apostles (chapter VI).

There are some further conclusions to be drawn, at least tentatively, from the internal characteristics of the novels. It is tempting to think of the novel as the first great literary form to have had its main support among women. Heroic epic was a typically masculine form. The theatrical performances of classical Athens were directed primarily towards men. The novel could reach far out into society, into people's homes, and was meant for reading, individually or in groups. If we examine the ideals it expresses, we shall find our

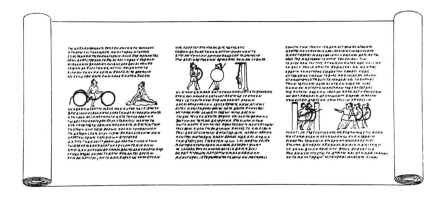

Fig. 28 Reconstruction of an illustrated book-roll. On the basis of existing papyrus fragments Kurt Weitzmann has reconstructed a Hellenistic book-roll containing the twenty-second book of the **Odyssey** *(vv. 169–232). Each book required one roll of about thirty columns, with perhaps as many illustrations. Works in prose were normally contained in considerably larger rolls. The division of ancient literary works into 'books' derives from the physical necessity of having the text accommodated in handy papyrus rolls. In the first centuries AD there is a successive transition from roll to codex, that is to our form of book; but the sub-division of the text into the same smaller units lives on. The Lollianus papyrus (figure 26) belongs to such an early codex.*

theory of a predominantly female audience at least partly confirmed. In several of the novels it is the heroine who is really the main character. Chariton's hero, Chaereas, is a pale and insignificant person in comparison to Callirhoe; he is rather like the young men of New Comedy. One of the most impressively characterized figures of the novels is Melite, the woman in Achilles Tatius who tempts and in fact succeeds in seducing Clitophon in Ephesus.

It has even been suggested that behind some of the pseudonyms — if some authors' names are such — there may hide female writers (figure 29). This remains an unproven hypothesis. As modern parallels show, the circumstance that the novels seem to aim primarily at a female audience does not necessarily imply that the authors themselves were women, and we may well ask whether the image of Woman which the novels idealize — the beautiful, chaste, and faithful-unto-death kind — is not rather a typically male product. On the other hand, the novels, with some exceptions, set the same high moral requirements for the hero as for the heroine. There is room for a closer analysis of the Greek novels from the point of view of sex roles; possibly such an analysis could also shed some more light on the question of female authorship.

Others, less convincingly to my mind, have viewed the novels as directed primarily at young people. Ben Edwin Perry classes them as 'juvenile literature', pointing to the nature of their idealism, and Gilbert Highet finds that even the style, with devices such as antithesis and oxymoron, 'reflects youth'. He finds another indication in the fact that 'all the leading characters in them are about eighteen years old, and think almost exclusively about their emotions'. One might as well assume that all the readers were divinely beautiful. Highet is surely nearer to the truth in his second alternative: the novels 'are meant for the young, or for those who wish they were still young'. So we are back to defining a mental condition rather than a certain age or sex or social position.

Discussion of the social identity of the novel's first readership easily leads to another question: can we identify the birthplace of the novel in geographical terms? Several features of the surviving novels themselves seem to point toward Egypt, and then, in the first place, toward Alexandria. In most of them Egypt is an unavoidable scene for at least some part of the action. B. P. Reardon has suggested, following a hint from the Egyptologist J. W. B. Barns, that the very first (but no longer surviving) novels were written under the influence of Egyptian demotic stories circulating in Greek translations. These would have provided the Greek with the impetus to start writing fictitious narrative *in prose*, the literary medium earlier used primarily for factual, informative writing. One such story translated from the Egyptian, the *Dream of Nectanebus*, survives in fragments in a papyrus of the second century BC. In type it may have resembled the *Ninus Romance* (above, p. 17), a piece of romanticized history, or perhaps the later *Alexander Romance*

Fig. 29 *The cover girl — a woman novelist in her hour of inspiration? Traditionally this young girl on a Pompeian wall painting passes under the name 'Sappho', the poetess of Lesbos (c. 600 BC); but with her thoughtful expression, the pen to her lip and a book of joined wax tablets in her hand, she is more probably a literate woman of the first century AD. We are reminded that the Greek novel will have appealed especially to women, and that some of the writers may even have been women.*

(below, chapter V). Other Egyptian narratives, known only in the original language, are said to show still closer resemblances to the Greek novel of love, and it is of course quite possible that they too were available in Greek.

Yet there are, in my view, strong arguments against this idea. Chariton's novel, the oldest one which we are in a position to judge in full, has no part of its action placed in Egypt. On the whole it is in its very nature the most Greek, the least 'oriental' of all the novels. There can be no serious doubt that it really was written in Asia Minor, in Carian Aphrodisias if we are to believe the introductory sentence. The Parthenope fragment (above, p. 18) seems to belong in roughly similar surroundings. At present — new finds of papyri may at any moment change the picture — to my mind the most probable assumption is that the first novels were aimed at the educated classes of the Hellenistic cities of Asia Minor, to people who looked back with a certain nostalgia to the fifth and fourth centuries (see figure 1). These novels served to perpetuate classical values, in a way some of their successors did not. With the great mobility characteristic of this period and with the fundamental community of culture between all the Greek cities of the Near East, it did not take long before the new genre reached Alexandria. And once there, its real flourishing and its movement down the social scale started. The port and great city of Alexandria was a melting-pot of cultures, a place where East and West really did meet; what existed here was rapidly spread in all directions. For all time, Alexandria put its mark on the genre (figure 30).

But there is still the problem of form to face. The traditional medium for fiction in Greek had been poetry, whereas the novelists from the very start use prose. It is perhaps not so much a matter of going against theoretical precepts; Aristotle himself, with his usual insight, rapidly brushes away those who believe that such a super-

Fig. 30 Mummy portrait of a young woman richly adorned with jewels. From Hawara in the Fayum district, Egypt. c. AD 100 – 150. The mummy portraits, of which some 150 have been found in the cemetery of Hawara alone, are a product of the Hellenistic mixed culture: the mummification itself was an indigenous Egyptian custom, whereas the realistic portrait belongs to the Greco-Roman tradition. The social stratum we meet in these portraits is the privileged, Hellenized middle class of Egypt, administrators and others with a Greek education but of mixed ethnic origins — the very group who will have been the main supporters of the novel.

ficial phenomenon as metre defines the genre. To him, the inner form is the main thing: Empedocles is a scientific writer, not a poet, though he happens to write in the same metre as Homer (*Poetics* 1447b9 ff.), and Herodotus' work would be history, even if it were turned into verse (1451b1−3). It would seem that Aristotle was giving *carte blanche* to the novelists of later centuries.

However, even if there were no formal rules against using prose for fiction, there was undoubtedly the tradition. It is true that already in the classical period imaginative story-telling did occur also in prose, but then it was always within a historiographical, ethnographical, or some other 'serious' framework (see chapter IV). And there is the sub-literary domain, of which admittedly we know very little, but where prose will have been used for popular legends and the like. Nevertheless it seems reasonable to suppose that for an educated person, as Chariton and the unknown author of the *Ninus Romance* certainly were, there would still in the fourth century BC have been a psychological barrier to cross before he could use prose for an extended narrative of his own invention, designed for entertainment. Not so many generations later things were obviously fundamentally different.

If we try to explain this shift of mentality without having recourse to the supposition of direct imitation of, say, Egyptian prose narratives in Greek translation, a look back at an earlier period of Greek history and another area of artistic creativity may prove helpful. The so-called orientalizing period (*c.* 750−650 BC) was one of rapid change and innovation in Greek art and literature, brought about largely through contacts with the East. Oswyn Murray has recently extended the ideas expressed in Gombrich's *Art and Illusion* about conventionalism in art to illuminate the mechanisms of this change within a traditional society, where artistic changes will normally be slow. He concludes: '. . . it is the meeting of two different artistic traditions which is most likely to have a revolutionary impact, partly in substituting a new set of conventions for the old, but also by at least partially *freeing men's vision from the unconscious tyranny of inherited schemata*, and so enabling them to see for themselves' (my italics). Besides the direct imitation of oriental motifs, which is less interesting to us, there is also as a result the creative use of new techniques for genuinely Greek subjects. This parallel may help to explain how in *our* 'orientalizing' period of Greek culture, the Hellenistic, an author like Chariton can treat a typically Greek theme in a very Greek way, but in a new medium. Instead of only one tradition, there was now a variety of traditions available. The individual author could view the system of literary genres with a freer eye: change was possible, if it served his purpose (for instance, a wider diffusion). So, even if Egyptian and other oriental literature is not directly imitated, its mere existence means both an inspiration and, perhaps still more, a liberation, which in due time results in the emergence of the new Greek genre.

The Novels as Mysterientexte?

That the novel was a profane form of literature from the start, a literary response to the Hellenistic city-dweller's need for romanticism and an escape from reality, has, to my mind, been convincingly demonstrated by Perry and Reardon. If one accepts their view, there is no room for the other recent hypothesis which suggests that the novel — like epic, lyric poetry, and drama — has its roots in religion, more particularly in the Hellenistic mystery religions. Reinhold Merkelbach, the scholar who has recently defended this view most consistently, even goes a stage further than his predecessors: he maintains that all the surviving novels, except that of Chariton, are in fact *Mysterientexte*, a kind of ancient *romans-à-clef*, meant to be fully intelligible only to those properly initiated into the mysteries. According to Merkelbach, the *Metamorphoses* of Apuleius (below chapter VII), as well as the novels of Xenophon and Achilles Tatius, glorify Isis, while Iamblichus belongs to the Persian cult of Mithras, Longus to the Dionysus cult, Heliodorus to the sun cult.

Even if we cannot follow Merkelbach all the way, it is rewarding to dwell briefly on his analysis, before passing on to the fortunes of the genre in the imperial period. The similarities of structure between myth and mystery ritual on the one hand and the novel on the other can hardly be explained as the simple relation between cause and effect, but this does not mean that they are accidental or without interest. By looking at Merkelbach's arguments and interpretations we shall acquaint ourselves with ways of thinking that may be unfamiliar to us but were more natural to the ancient readers of the novels.

In the stereotyped plots of the early novels Merkelbach sees different variations of one and the same theme, the Egyptian myth of Isis and Osiris. The separation, wanderings, trials, apparent deaths, and final reunion of the two lovers reflect the pattern of the myth: Isis wanders about all over the world searching for her dead husband Osiris, at last finds him and brings him back to life. In the Isis mysteries the myth of Isis searching for Osiris symbolized man's voyage through life, through dangers and tribulations to final salvation.

In the interpretation of details much depends on the identification of one god with another. The action of Xenophon's novel takes place under the protection of the Ephesian Artemis. This, Merkelbach maintains, is only a cover name for Isis: those not initiated into the mysteries were not to understand the text if it fell into their hands. An oracle of Apollo sends the lovers on a sea voyage. This means that for each human being God has decided his wanderings through life. No hero of an Isis novel is spared a shipwreck, that is, no human life passes without misfortune.

In Achilles Tatius' novel one is particularly to note the scene in which the heroine is apparently executed by robbers but through an ingenious trick escapes unhurt (above, p. 43). This scene is worked out in a way that resembles the Egyptian mummification ritual, the purpose of which is to transform the dead person into Osiris and in that way secure him eternal life. Leucippe's apparent death, Merkelbach says, also corresponds to the death of the initiate: it is a propitiatory sacrifice for the sins the candidate committed in his former life. The scene between Clitophon and Melite, the seductress, correspondingly builds on the holy marriage, *hieros gamos*, of Isis and Osiris, while at the same time it describes a constituent of the initiation ritual of the Isis mysteries.

In the same vein, Heliodorus' novel reflects the otherwise practically unknown Helius mysteries. As the sun cult syncretistically combined in itself the other pagan cults, Heliodorus in his novel combined all that the earlier Isis and Mithras novels had offered. Charicleia, in the introductory scene weeping and embracing her beloved on the shore (above, p. 55), is an image of Isis, who with her embraces awakens the dead Osiris. That the heroine is sentenced to the pyre (above, p. 67) is an ordeal of a type known from both the Isis and the Mithras cults. Her rescue, when the crowd cries out in astonishment, 'Great are the gods!', is a divine wonder.

The whole structure of the *Ethiopica* is shown to be strictly symbolic. Charicleia is a descendant of the sun, and Ethiopia is her true homeland: in the same way the human soul is divine by nature and descends from the realms of the sun. But the soul has fallen down into matter: Charicleia as an infant is exposed and carried away abroad, into the world. Her task will be to escape from the world and return to her true home. Each stage on this journey, from Delphi to Zacynthus, to the mouth of the Nile, to Memphis, and further up the river, brings her one step further south, towards Ethiopia, apparently by chance but in reality under the protection of the sun god: life is the wandering through which man returns to his father in heaven.

If Merkelbach's hypothesis were right, it would mean a revolution not only as far as our understanding of the ancient novels is concerned; at a stroke we would also have acquired essential new knowledge about the mysteries themselves, a subject about which our other sources, naturally enough, generally observe a strict reticence. But experts of the history of religion have rejected the hypothesis with weighty arguments, and simply on the commonsense level there are objections to it. The parallels between life, myth, mystery ritual, and novel are explicable in a simpler way: human life and man's experience of life provide the basic pattern of myth and ritual as well as the novel.

More specifically, the pattern of 'love–separation–reunion' is almost a matter of course for an exciting love story with a happy ending; the 'searching' motif follows logically from the 'separation' motif, and the author could draw upon real life for the erotic hazards and their consequences without having to make a detour through Egyptian myths. Shipwreck and capture by pirates were, as we have already seen, realities in the Mediterranean of Hellenistic times, even if the frequency is, for obvious reasons, unrealistically high in the novels. Even apparent death and 'resurrection' had profane parallels in a time and a climate in which the funeral followed as quickly as possible on the death.

However, as already stated, this does not in any way mean that the religious component of the novels is without significance. Even on the surface religion plays a remarkably important role. Gods, oracles, cults of different kinds are organically integrated into the course of events. In Xenophon, apparently the least profound of these writers, there is hardly any important stage in the action that is not accompanied by an invocation, a prayer, a sacrifice, or a hint at the involvement of some god. And in Heliodorus the missionary tendency in favour of the Helius cult is unmistakable. Nor is it inconceivable that an ancient reader of the *Ethiopica* might have read the novel in the same way as Merkelbach: allegorical interpretation of literary works, however profane, was much practised in late antiquity, Homer of course being its main object. It is also quite possible that direct allusions to mystery rituals, to be understood only by those initiated, were hidden in the texts — for instance in Achilles Tatius — but it does not necessarily follow that the novel as

a whole carried any subtextual secret message. Novels and mystery
religions flourished at the same time and in the same milieu; the
same people were the basis of existence for both.

The Greek Cultural Revival of the Imperial Period

Hellenism does not, of course, cease to exist in 30 BC. The picture of
the social, cultural, and religious milieu of the Hellenistic period
which I have attempted to give above retains its relevance in many
respects for several centuries into the Roman imperial period. Greek
continues to be the predominant language in the Eastern
Mediterranean world, Latin there is at the most the language of the
army and the central administration. The big cities grow, the
mystery religions thrive, and a new salvation creed, Christianity,
enters into competition with them. But there are also new trends,
notably within cultural life. We shall have a closer look at one
particular movement which was to have decisive importance for all
literary activities in Greek, and also for the novels. The movement
referred to is the Greek cultural revival which goes under the name
of 'Second Sophistic'.

Classicism — the striving to return to the spiritual and formal
ideals of the classical period — is not an invention of the imperial
age. A strain of classicism already runs through the later centuries of
the Hellenistic period: that is why, for instance, there need not be too
much hesitation about placing Chariton, with his nostalgic look
backwards, as early as the first century BC. But not until the second
century AD does this movement break through with full force. To
give an entirely satisfactory explanation of why this happened at
that precise time is hardly possible; the causes of 'renaissance'
periods are generally complex and difficult to pin down. In this case
two important, concurrent forces have often been singled out: the
active support of a philhellenic Roman government and the
awakening of Greek nationalism after the humiliations of the
Hellenistic period, which had culminated in the Romans' brutal
crushing of all vestiges of Greek independence in the middle of the
second century BC, notably with the destruction of Corinth in 146
BC. Repeated reminders of the fact that power was now lodged in
the West were given when, in the eighties of the first century BC,
Sulla put down the revolt of Mithridates, which began in Asia Minor
but later spread to Athens, and when Octavian/Augustus defeated
his rival Antonius at Actium in 31 BC.

The Roman government's adoption of a philhellenic attitude may be traced back to the first century AD. A first sign of what was to come is the Emperor Nero's Greek tour and his declaration of liberty for the Greek states in AD 67. It may be that this declaration had no lasting political significance, but among the Greeks themselves the gesture will have functioned as a signal for something of a national revival. Half a century later the capricious gesture has turned into a consistent attitude: from Hadrian (AD 117–38) onwards a strong philhellenic atmosphere prevails at the Roman court, and consequently also among the emperor's official representatives in the Greek-speaking parts of the empire. Greek education is now considered the crown of all education, Greek authors and artists are materially encouraged. For Greek rhetoric, the very basis of education, special professorial chairs are established. The emperors themselves sit at the feet of the professors of rhetoric. The title 'sophist', which in the fifth century BC designated the professional teachers of 'wisdom' who, thanks to the dialogues of Plato, have enjoyed a not very flattering posthumous reputation, was now borne by the highly esteemed teachers of rhetoric; hence the label 'Second Sophistic'. Besides their school teaching, mainly concentrated in Rome, Athens, and the big cities on the west coast of Asia Minor, especially in Ephesus and Smyrna, the sophists also make extended tours throughout the Greek-speaking world. Their performances consist of skilfully composed and delivered speeches which are greeted with storms of cheering from their audiences; they have aptly been called *Konzertredner*, 'concert artists of the spoken word'. They are often honoured with high offices in the Greek cities and act as the ambassadors of their home towns, especially on missions to the emperor.

Thus literary education and literary activity enjoyed an almost unparalleled prestige during this period. The ultimate reason for the central position of culture is of course the long period of tranquillity within the Roman frontiers, the *pax Romana*, and the resultant material prosperity. Rhetoric, which in the heyday of the Greek city state in the fifth and fourth centuries BC had been an important political factor, as it had been in late republican Rome, now flourished in imperial times under quite different conditions: deprived of its political function, rhetoric assumed a value in its own right and became a status symbol for educated people and an obligatory part of all official occasions, such as political and religious ceremonies, festivals of the gods, and athletic contests.

It goes without saying that Greek national pride was nourished by this official recognition of the superiority of Greek education. It was a nationalism, however, which never seems to have found any important political outlet, but rather was confined to the cultural sphere. Parentheses were placed around the Hellenistic period, which meant lack of political liberty, the ravages of civil and foreign wars, and the impoverishment of the mother country. As we have already seen, Greek culture had been kept alive in other places: in Alexandria, Pergamum, Antioch, and the many other cities in the East. It was a culture that used the Greek language, but it was different from the culture of which Athens had been the centre. An affected, 'Asian' rhetoric had succeeded the natural, functional diction of the Attic stamp. A prose for everyday, non-poetical use and a more and more entangled 'officialese' (*Kanzleiprosa*) with no artistic aspiration, 'formless' by Attic standards, had both gained ground. At least, this is how things came to be viewed when classicism gained ground during the imperial period.

The new national pride quite naturally looked back to the political and economic acme of Athens, with its unique cultural achievements. The literature of the classical period was regarded as the model for all literary creativity, that of the Hellenistic period was despised and forgotten. Only words and expressions recorded in the classical authors were admissible for a true 'Atticist'. Not only should the form be Attic, but so should the frame of reference and pattern of thought. The result was a rich literary output, reactionary in word and thought, artistic but at the same time artificial. It is easy to make unfavourable comparisons between this literature and that of the genuine Attic writers, but its historical significance is indisputable. It is the primary expression of the newly awakened national consciousness after centuries of passivity, and it is thanks to its adherents — authors and audience alike — that the classical ideals were passed on to subsequent generations, and to us.

Of central importance in the rebirth of the classical spirit were the schools, which had concentrated more and more on rhetoric. 'Rhetoric' was as necessary and prestigious a part of a good education as the 'humanities' were until recently in our own educational tradition. Rhetoric forms and cultivates the mind: the parallel with Latin in the 'grammar school' of post-medieval Europe is striking. It is to the soul what gymnastics and medicine are to the body. The sophist was responsible for the formal training offered by the schools, but at the same time he also taught philosophy and morals.

The curriculum of the sophists' schools shows interesting similarities with some modern forms of training in 'creative writing'. The students are trained to compose upon a given subject, for instance to embroider one of the animal fables of Aesop or to write a petition to a court. First they are required to analyse in detail classical models, then tackle special training pieces prepared by the teacher, and finally launch on their own attempts. In this way they are supposed gradually to acquire a theoretical knowledge of the whole spectrum of literary devices as well as a practical command of them. Their skill is given the final polish and tested in more and more independent writing exercises.

Extempore speech was another element in the programme, as was the systematic training of the memory. The aim of education was not the storing of as much knowledge as possible but the purely formal training of the intellect; this was regarded as the best preparation for all the higher professions. It follows that this kind of education was not intended to produce only or even primarily professional orators and writers: it was the natural training for future officials, judges, teachers, civil servants, in short for the entire leading stratum of society.

Erwin Rohde, it has turned out, was incorrect in assuming that the Greek novel was born in these very classrooms; but no doubt it was here that the later, more 'sophisticated' novel found its readers — and its authors! Thanks to the school teaching and to the place of honour accorded to rhetoric in most official contexts, every educated person must have been imbued with these classicizing ideals. Whoever devoted himself to literary writing in Greek, be he Syrian, Egyptian, or a Greek from Asia Minor, he could hardly escape embracing the same ideals. It is another question whether he was capable of transforming them into creative literary work, or whether he just applied Atticism as a thin layer of varnish over his natural way of expressing himself.

Even a Hellenistic genre like the novel, aiming originally at a broader audience which made no strenuous demands on literature, inevitably came under the influence of the same linguistic and stylistic rules as the established genres, that is, the rules as they were formulated by the classicists. In the case of Xenophon Ephesius, that thin layer of varnish was applied: Atticism covers a non-classicizing diction, rhetoric is put into a frame of popular narrative. Achilles Tatius, Longus, and Heliodorus are different. The basic structure is still that of the Hellenistic novel, but the language is a studied *Kunstsprache*, artistic prose, and into the open form of the novel have streamed motifs characteristic of the time: digressions and *ecphrases*, speeches and subtleties, many of them certainly over the heads of a broader audience.

Strictly speaking, most of the 'new' constituents were not entirely new: they had been present in a rudimentary form in the Hellenistic novel. But now they were blown up to dimensions hitherto un-dreamt of, cleaned and polished to a brilliant shine. The goal was originality, not in content but in execution. The mentality was the same as in the school of rhetoric: the great sophists made their display speeches extempore on subjects proposed by the audience, but these subjects were in fact taken from a limited repertoire, and the main thing was how the speaker performed his task, whether he was asked to impersonate Xerxes before crossing the Hellespont or to lend words to the lament of a violated virgin.

The novel had thus been raised to a higher literary level, had cer-tainly lost much of its broad popularity, but instead had won new readers in highbrow circles. For its later fortunes this elevation was decisive: it was the sophistic novels that the literarily conscious Byzantines — who in principle embraced the same Atticist ideals as the Second Sophistic — read and preserved. And it was the sophistic triad, with its almost classical form, that won its triumphs in Western Europe during the sixteenth and seventeenth centuries (see chapter VIII), before rhetoric had become a negative concept and before the classical period had again become the only accept-able period of Greek culture.

CHAPTER IV

The Literary Pedigree
of the Novel

Whoever wrote the first Greek novel did not create it out of nothing.
Like his successors within the new genre, he was strongly influenced
by what he had read and heard: by epic, historiography, and tales of
travel, by drama and erotic poetry, by the rhetoric of his time. In
order to define more closely the distinctive literary nature of the
novel, we shall now view it against just that background: its
ancestors and contemporary relatives.

This can be done all the more easily because so much of the
earlier research into the origins of the Greek novel concentrated on
its literary ancestry. Two names should be mentioned. About a hundred years ago Erwin Rohde published the still unsuperseded standard work on the Greek novel: *Der griechische Roman und seine
Vorläufer* (1876). According to him, the novel is a combination of
Hellenistic tales of travel and the erotic poetry of the same period.
The place where the two genres fused was the school of rhetoric of
the imperial period: the novel was a fruit of its exercises in 'creative
writing' (above, p. 106). As we have already seen, this hypothesis of
Rohde's is untenable, not least for chronological reasons; but his
brilliant analyses of travel tales, erotic poetry, and the practice and
products of the school of rhetoric are all useful to our present purpose. As regards historiography, I shall also adduce Eduard
Schwartz's *Fünf Vorträge über den griechischen Roman* (1896), in
which creative story-telling in Greek literature is traced from
Homer, by way of the historians, to the novel (which is itself hardly
treated in the book, despite its title). Again we may ignore the main
hypothesis — that the novel 'developed' out of historiography
— and take advantage of the inspiring descriptive and
interpretative sections.

The Epic

The novel is the genuine heir of epic — in function, in structure, and also from a historical and chronological point of view. The *Odyssey* is the prototype of the Greek novel, and as such is simply the first novel of love, travel, and adventure in Greek. It is true that the basic pattern of the *Odyssey* is not as uncomplicated as that of the novels, with their separation, quest, and reunion of two lovers; but Odysseus' long wanderings between Troy and Ithaca, his fantastic adventures, the women he meets and is tempted by before being reunited with his wife, and Telemachus' quest for his father — all these have their counterparts in the novels. Naturally the connection is often deliberate. Community of genre and direct imitation are complementary explanations for the similarities. In all periods of Greek literature, from the archaic to the Byzantine period, Homer is the natural point of departure for all literary work. Lyric poetry, drama, historiography, the novel, each genre rests on a Homeric foundation in some respect, and is nourished on the 'scraps from Homer's banquet'.

The novelists take some of their motifs from Homer and often allude to epic characters or situations. They also borrow elements of narrative technique from the epic. We have seen how Chariton ends his novel by letting Chaereas and his father-in-law retell the main plot in some detail, just as Odysseus recounts his adventures to Penelope in the twenty-third book of the *Odyssey*. In Achilles Tatius' novel the hero himself is responsible for narrating the whole story — the literary prototype of the first-person narrative is of course Odysseus' account to the Phaeacians of his fantastic adventures among the lotus-eaters and cyclopes. Heliodorus absolutely excels in imitation of Homer. The *in-medias-res* technique is consciously adopted, and developed with ingenuity (above, p. 55). His method of delegating parts of the narration to some of the characters also has simpler counterparts in epic.

Parallel action sets its stamp on the narrative structure of both genres. As Xenophon Ephesius switches back and forth between the adventures of hero and heroine, Homer in the *Iliad* shifts the perspective between the world of the gods and that of the mortals, or between the Greek and Trojan camps. The problem is the same: how to convey in a narrative, which runs along in one single stream, continuously and always in the same direction, several different, though 'in reality' simultaneous, courses of events? In epic, as in the novel, the problem is often solved simply by ignoring the simultaneity: the events at the different places of action are narrated successively, and the listener or reader seldom notices that the narrator leaves gaps in one line of action while attention is concentrated on the other.

The use of oracles, omens, dreams, and other types of foreshadowing also belongs to the epic apparatus assimilated by the novel. Like epic, the Greek novel displays a suspense technique which in some respects is very different from that of modern light novels or films. Often the narrator states in advance — in epic, in a regular *prooemium* — what is going to happen and how things will end. The feeling of suspense raised in the reader thus applies not so much to *what* will happen as to *how* it will happen; his attention is drawn to the actual course of events rather than to the outcome. This technique has met with a surprising lack of understanding from some modern critics, who have argued that the intrigues of the ancient novel are constructed in an amateur or 'primitive' way, since they 'lack suspense'. As a matter of fact, the merest glance at ancient drama should have been enough to demonstrate that ignorance of the story's main elements and outcome is by no means a prerequisite for the audience to feel suspense and engage itself emotionally in the vicissitudes of the characters. On the contrary, in both epic and drama we are concerned with a particularly refined technique of creating suspense, and some of the novelists too, especially Achilles Tatius, skilfully exploit the keen sensitivity to such elements of narration which contemporary readers no doubt possessed (above, p. 49). The whole finely meshed net of foreshadowings sharpens the reader's attention, carries him over digressions and occasional dull passages, and lends homogeneity to the work, in spite of its length and episodic structure. The same effect is achieved by the epic recapitulations — retrospective summaries of longer or shorter sequences of events — which abound in some of the novels; likewise by the repetitions and the simple references to earlier events. These are not lifeless hereditary features taken over mechanically from epic ancestors, but highly functional elements meant to make it easier for the readers, or listeners, to take in the narrative.

Historiography

The novel is thus the epic of the Hellenistic period, fulfilling the functions of epic in a new age, and assuming some of its techniques. But it is not only society that has changed: within the literary system as well, much has happened that will affect the literary form of the novel. The deepest influence comes from historiography, the earliest prose genre to flourish among the Greeks. But the Greek *historia* should not be understood only as 'history' in our narrower sense of the word, but also as the exploration of the world in all its aspects and the reporting of what has been seen and heard. Travel description with a geographic and ethnographic bent naturally belongs here. Nor should we understand the term 'history' as the opposite of myth. Our distinction between myth and history is not shared by the Greeks; for earlier times the two flow together, and there is to the Greek mind no difference in principle between such subject-matter as may fill an epic like the *Odyssey* and what a historian like Herodotus may narrate. The demand for 'truth' in the broad outlines and the freedom to embroider the details in one's own way apply to both. The epic poet or dramatist who builds on myth cannot change its fundamental features: Agamemnon must be murdered on his arrival home from Troy. On the other hand the historian too has his freedom, within the bounds of the established historical framework, to invent things of his own, in so far as his inventions keep to the *credible*. The credible, of course, varies with distance in time and space: beyond the limits of the known world men with dog's heads are possible; in the earliest times gods walked on earth. Creative story-telling within the bounds of credibility, and with prose as its medium, is the novel's inheritance from the classical historians, above all Herodotus, Xenophon, and Ctesias.

Herodotus' gift for story-telling needs no special demonstration. His *History* is arranged as a broad epic of the struggle between East and West, culminating in the wars between the Persians and the Greeks during the first decades of the fifth century BC. Into this historical frame are inserted not only extensive and vivid descriptions of peoples and places, but also extended passages of legendary narrative matter, which Herodotus had gathered on his journeys in the Orient. The story of the master builder's sons who outwitted Pharaoh himself may be cited as a typical example of such elements in the *History*. Here popular story-telling has been taken up and cast in a literary mould. This literary form, which retains and artistically exploits specific traits of oral narrative, is imitated with varying success by later narrative literature in Greek. Herodotus' diction is unmistakable in the stereotyped form it assumes in, for instance, Xenophon Ephesius: a straightforward paratactic sentence structure (that is, mostly co-ordinated main clauses), repetition of words instead of the use of pronouns, standardized transitional phrases and frame-phrases for direct speech — all may directly or indirectly be traced back to the 'father of history'.

The novelist's older namesake, Xenophon of Athens — the disciple of Socrates who let himself be recruited for a daring expedition far into the Persian Empire and then reported his adventures in the *Anabasis* — in later years also wrote a romanticized biography of the founder of the Persian Empire, Cyrus the Great, the so-called *Cyropaedia* or 'Education of Cyrus'. His intention was not primarily to impart Persian local colouring or to reconstruct a historical course of events. The book is a mirror for princes in which Cyrus embodies Xenophon's own moral and political ideals, which were in their turn more Spartan and aristocratic than Athenian and democratic. The *Cyropaedia* is sometimes characterized as a historical novel, for want of any really adequate designation: the amount of pure fiction is too great to allow it to be called history or biography, in the modern sense. If we leave the terminological question open, we note it as particularly interesting in our context that Xenophon inserts into the *Cyropaedia* a romantic and tragic love story, which agrees in tone and setting as well as in some specific details with the later Greek novels, in particular Chariton's. But what is the main thing in the novels is in Xenophon just one constituent of a whole which has quite different aims.

It is no coincidence that so much of the story-telling in Herodotus and Xenophon deals with oriental themes. Ionia, the province on Asia Minor's west coast where *historia* was born, was a borderland between East and West. Its Greek cities were for long periods of time politically under Persian rule, which at least had the advantage that Ionians could move comparatively unhindered within the Persian Empire. The combination of Greek curiosity and oriental tradition constitutes the basis of Ionian historiography, in a wide sense, which was in some ways incarnated by Herodotus, even though he himself was not an Ionian by birth. However, a still more typical representative is Ctesias of Cnidus, who spent a good many years as personal physician to the great king. Back home again, he wrote in the nineties of the fourth century BC a voluminous *History of Persia*, which in its detailed final part, was an eye-witness account.

Ctesias' work has not survived in its original form, but from imitations, fragments, and a summary in the *Bibliotheca* of Photius its character can be fairly well surmised. The local colouring has been applied with broad strokes of the brush: the description, in Eduard Schwartz's words, 'breathes seraglio and eunuch perfumes, mixed with a disgusting stench of blood'. Genuine tradition has combined in a most peculiar way with Ctesias' own fantasies; historical facts fight a losing battle with the desire to shock, move, excite and dazzle. For Hellenistic historiography this virtuoso striving for effect becomes an ideal, to a far greater extent than the billowing verbosity of Herodotus or the scholarly ambitions and intellectual style of Thucydides. Ctesias' direct influence on the novelists is therefore hard to distinguish from what might have come from Ionic and Hellenistic historiography in general; note, for instance, Chariton's lingering on the Persian court milieu, or the macabre sensationalism to which Achilles Tatius sometimes and Iamblichus often yield. On the other hand it is obvious that oriental matter in the Greek novels does not have to be explained at all costs as borrowings from the Greek literary tradition; several of the novelists were themselves Hellenized 'barbarians', with free access to oriental traditions and 'local colour' (above, p. 34).

The same issue may be approached from another point of view: were the novelists perhaps influenced by the theoretical superstructure of Hellenistic historiography, that is, by the rules guiding the choice of stylistic means which had been formalized by Aristotle and his successors? Among other things, Aristotle demanded that style should not only serve as decoration but also characterize, be graphic and sensuous. His school, the Peripatetic, devoted much attention to historiography. Schwartz describes the Peripatetic ideals in the following way: 'The main thing was that the historian was given a task similar to that of the tragic poet, that is, the tragic poet according to Aristotelian theory: he is to move, awaken fear and pity through the artistic structure and the plastic description of shocking events: the place of the gods is taken, characteristically in this godless age and this godless philosophy, by the blind, cruel, persecuting ravagings of Tyche (Fate).' The theoretical background of the novel might well be formulated in a similar way, and the opinion has been advanced that Chariton, the first novelist whose writing we can judge directly, deliberately followed these rules for Hellenistic historiography, in composition as well as in style. In a corresponding way also his characterization, which avoids labels and instead graphically describes the characters' modes of action and reaction, is said to derive from Aristotelian principles. Possibly this means overestimating the author's theoretical grounding or consciousness: the similarities may also be due to imitation of those Hellenistic histories which really were shaped according to such patterns.

Biography

Another Greek novel, different in kind from the novel of love, is directly dependent on Hellenistic historiography of this sensational type: the pseudo-historical *Alexander Romance*, which will be treated in more detail in the next chapter. It was composed in the imperial period but is based on several different Hellenistic components, among others a biography of Alexander. Alexander's expedition to the East gave rise to a whole flood of 'histories' of all kinds, from sober accounts to wild legends. The Alexander historian whose work the novel incorporated obviously exploited to the full the sensational style; he certainly showed little concern for historical fact. The outer form seems to have been that of a biography, a *Vita Alexandri*. However, the ancient genre of biography should, no more than its cognate 'history', be understood in the modern sense of a documentary account of a person's life. In antiquity biography is a literary product which may serve quite different purposes: it may be a laudatory memorial, or an idealizing programme piece like the *Cyropaedia* (above, p. 113), or simply be meant for entertainment, as this Alexander biography probably was.

A special, very popular form was the life of a philosopher: some include this type of biography in the category of 'ancient novel'. Pythagoras — the legendary philosopher, mathematician, and founder of a religion (sixth century BC) — was its first and most cherished subject. There we find the travel motif and the taste for the exotic. In later times, at the beginning of the third century AD, novel and biography meet in a remarkable and influential work, Philostratus' *Life of Apollonius*, the sage from Tyana (figure 31). Apollonius, who lived in the first century AD, is in Philostratus' version a kind of Christ figure, but a travelling one, with the whole Mediterranean world and the Orient as far as India in the East and Ethiopia in the South as his field of action. He is a Pythagorean, a vegetarian, a pacifist, and a magician; he cures the sick, awakens the dead, and is able to predict the future. He prevails over death also on his own behalf, rises to heaven to the accompaniment of a choir of virgins, and some time later appears to his disciples in order to prove his immortality.

In writing his *Life of Apollonius* Philostratus was no doubt strongly influenced by the sophistic novels; the historical core almost disappears in the romantic pulp. Philosophic conversations and geographic, ethnographic, and biological digressions focusing on

Fig. 31   *The sage Apollonius of Tyana on a Roman contorniate medallion (latter half of the fourth century AD). That Apollonius was depicted on this kind of medallion, with a laurel wreath and a philosopher's beard, is not surprising. The stamping of contorniate medallions was a means of propaganda used by the pagan reaction in Rome against Christianity, which had during the fourth century been promoted to the state religion in New Rome, Constantinople. In this context Apollonius of Tyana, a younger contemporary of Jesus of Nazareth, could take on the role of a counter-Christ; he was honoured as an ascetic, a miracle-worker, and a teacher of wisdom, just as Philostratus had portrayed him in his biography (written at the beginning of the third century AD). For centuries Philostratus' **Vita Apollonii** remained a dangerous book in the eyes of the Christians, a book which was taken in deadly earnest and refuted with apologetic works.*

paradoxical phenomena in animal and plant life are to be found in proportions similar to, for instance, those in Achilles Tatius. But influences in the opposite direction have also been noticed: Heliodorus seems to have borrowed from Philostratus' biography.

It should be kept in mind, however, that these are instances of the interchange of external matter between separate genres. In a corresponding way, no doubt, the early biographies and the early novels mutually inspired each other. In the Hellenistic period both were new genres under construction: for both the captivating narration, adapted to the taste of the time, was a vital necessity. The edifying purpose which characterized the lives of philosophers at least was not alien to the 'ideal' novel either.

Fantastic Travel Tales

Another genre typical of the Hellenistic period is *Reisefabulistik*, fantastic tales of travel and adventure. Behind these ethnographic and paradoxographical stories of strange peoples and places we may discern Greek seafarers' tales told to the home audience about their fabulous adventures in far-off countries. Odysseus' account to the Phaeacians of lotus-eaters, cyclopes, and other strange creatures is built up of such matter, likewise the stories attached to the voyage of the Argonauts, featuring hybrids like long-heads and half-hounds, or pygmies and hyperboreans (people of the far North). As we have already seen, these fantasies came later, in Ctesias for instance, to be combined with reports of the scientific exploration of distant countries in the North and East, India in particular. The boundary between the factual and the fabulous was fluid. Plato's account of the fairy island of Atlantis is a traveller's tale subordinate to another purpose, the description of a political utopia. The real impetus was given to the genre by Alexander's expedition. There are typical examples of fabulous matter in the *Alexander Romance*, some of which will be quoted below (p. 133). Euhemerus (*c.* 300 BC) wrapped his doctrine about the origins of the worship of gods — they were originally particularly prominent men — in just such a fantastic tale, and Iambulus (*c.* 100 BC) tells of the utopian life on a group of islands in the Indian Ocean near the equator, a veritable Cockaigne, where the inhabitants live without family ties in an almost communistic labour-sharing society.

Both Euhemerus and Iambulus survive only in the summaries provided by the historian Diodorus Siculus (first century BC), and thus the most vivid picture we can get of this genre comes to us indirectly, in a parody by Lucian, the satirist and moralist (second century AD), entitled *The True Story*. It tells of fights between the inhabitants of the sun and the moon, of how reproduction is arranged on the moon where even the word woman is unknown, of life in the belly of the whale and on the Islands of the Blest. Lucian himself says that it is all modelled on Ctesias, Iambulus, and others, Homer included; his aim in writing the satire was hardly to torpedo the genre itself, which was obviously still extremely popular in the imperial period, but to surpass his predecessors in the art of telling a good story.

The travel motif is thus to be found both in the tales of travel and in the novels, though in different forms. In the novels travelling is above all movement between places of action, and it is confined to the Mediterranean Sea and adjacent countries, with Mesopotamia as the eastern and Ethiopia as the southern terminal point. The dangers threatening the travellers are weather, pirates, and brigands — no sea monsters or men with dogs' heads. It is true that there are descriptions of paradoxical natural phenomena in the later novels, but as digressions and with parallels in other imperial literature, not as an integral part of the plot. In the earliest novels, those of Chariton and Xenophon, travelling is realistic and trivial. But there is one book which is situated somewhere on the borderline between tales of travel and novel: *The Marvels beyond Thule* by Antonius Diogenes, probably written about AD 100.

The Marvels beyond Thule

The work of Antonius Diogenes, like Iamblichus' novel surviving only in Photius' summary (and some papyrus scraps), originally consisted of no less than twenty-four books, which means that it was presumably at least double the size of Heliodorus' *Ethiopica*. Its structure is complicated, with one first-person narrative within the other, like a set of Chinese boxes. Unfortunately Photius' summary, which is less than ten pages in all, does not permit of any exact reconstruction of the work, but something can be said.

The primary first-person narrative is delivered by an old man, Deinias of Arcadia, who sits in Tyre in Phoenicia telling a fellow countryman of his wide, adventurous travels. His account is written down in two copies: one is to be taken to his native country, where people are eager to share in his knowledge, the other will be placed in his grave. This latter copy is the one which Antonius Diogenes pretends to rely on: it was brought to light when Alexander the

Great conquered Tyre! This calls to mind the fact that several of the Greek novels end with the deposition in a temple archive of a written account of the fortunes of the two lovers. As is well known, the same type of fiction, or 'pseudo-documentarism' — the author has found an authentic report which he simply passes on to his readers — frequently recurs in the later history of the novel.

The old Deinias relates that at one time he left Arcadia together with his son 'in order to search for knowledge (*historia*)'. Thus the same urge that inspired the actual Greek voyages of discovery is adduced as a motive for his fictitious travelling. In the novels proper, on the other hand, fate in one form or other *forces* the principal characters out on to the sea: kidnap, flight, or obedience to an oracle. No hero in the novels is inspired from the beginning by any active desire to widen his knowledge of the world; the 'searching' always has a definite object, the beloved, in whose tracks the hero crosses land and sea; and the tourist activities, as can be observed especially in Achilles Tatius, are secondary padding for the main plot.

Crossing the Black Sea and the Caspian, Deinias travels with his son north into the cold. They make a wide sweep eastwards but arrive at last, after a long time and many adventures, on the Island of Thule, where they stop. Deinias becomes involved in an affair with a woman of noble birth, Dercyllis of Tyre, who is staying in Thule with her brother. From Dercyllis Deinias hears of the adventures of the brother and sister, how they were forced to leave their native country to wander the Mediterranean world; how they even caught a glimpse of the underworld, as befits travellers in the wake of Odysseus; and how, after a long period of separation, they have finally landed up in Thule. What Dercyllis told Deinias at that time is now retold by the same Deinias in Tyre, in the autumn of his life. But that is not all: within Dercyllis' story there is another story, which she in her turn had heard from a man whom she met on her journey; and *this* man, in his turn, recounts what he has heard from somebody else. Later on, Dercyllis' brother tells her yet more stories of a fantastic kind to pass on to Deinias. This is a type of composition which reminds us of the later novels, Heliodorus' in particular, although Antonius carries the technique to an extreme.

Rather than follow all the further vagaries of the action we shall limit ourselves to some glimpses of the fantastic material offered within this complicated frame. In one country Dercyllis meets human beings who can see by night but are blind in the daytime, in another she finds matriarchy practised: while the women take the field, the men sit at home engaged in 'female' occupations. Paapis, the cruel pursuer of the brother and sister, transforms them by spitting in their faces, so that they are dead during the day but wake again when night falls. Their tombstones thus eventually carry peculiar inscriptions like: 'Dercyllis, daughter of Mnason, lived 39 years and 760 nights'!

The last of the twenty-four books contains what the title promises, Deinias' marvellous experiences *beyond* Thule. He arrives in Arctic regions, where the night may last a month, six months, or even a whole year (!), and the day is of the same length. At last he gets so far north that he reaches the moon, but at this stage Photius' patience runs out: he simply refuses to report what fabulous things Antonius Diogenes has to tell of this visit. During his sleep Deinias is miraculously transferred to Tyre, where Dercyllis and her brother have arrived too. A happy ending, then, but no wedding, nor anything else that would indicate that this was a love story: *The Marvels beyond Thule* could never have been entitled *Deinias and Dercyllis*.

It is true that there are many similarities between Antonius Diogenes' book and the novels: those parts of the travelling pattern that are restricted to the Mediterranean region; the role played by surprising incidents, oracles, and cruel pursuers (as in Iamblichus) in determining these travels; some of the acts of violence; the motifs of apparent death and resurrection and of separation and reunion (although here applied to brother and sister). But the differences carry greater weight. The erotic motif seems to have been of secondary importance in Antonius Diogenes (love-affairs are mentioned two or three times, in passing, in Photius' summary). In the novels the tone is mostly serious and idealistic, in Antonius it was in all probability light, possibly even parodic as in Lucian's *True Story*; otherwise it is difficult to imagine how the most fantastic details could have been presented as part of the main characters' own experiences. The relative realism of the novels, with known geographic surroundings and few supernatural incidents, is in strong contrast to the overtly fabulous contents of this traveller's tale.

If Antonius Diogenes is to be categorized, the safest choice would be to view him as a successor of the other writers of travel tales, whose primary intention was to entertain. Whether there was in addition a serious Pythagorean tendency, as has been asserted, cannot be deduced from the summary. Antonius achieved his aim of entertainment partly by incorporating elements from the novel of love, which was already flourishing in the first century AD. The most important influence from that quarter is his device of letting the adventures and personal relations of private individuals be the frame into which the predominantly fabulous matter is inserted. By contrast, the *Alexander Romance* provided a *historical* frame for the same kind of material. Antonius could draw this fabulous matter from (pseudo-) historical and geographical accounts, from utopias, and from earlier tales of travel of varying authenticity. A good deal might of course be ascribed to the inventiveness of the author himself: this genre 'snowballed'. The complicated pattern of intrigue woven round the principal characters made it possible for him to combine within one and the same tale all the conceivable routes across the known world as well as beyond its frontiers — a sort of sum, then, of the whole genre: the ultimate snowball. So long and comprehensive a tale could not conceivably have consisted of the adventures of one single traveller — the genre's basic pattern — without becoming excessively monotonous. The filtering of the experiences through several characters, who stand in various kinds of relationship to each other, and the excessive use of the story-within-a-story technique, were Antonius' solution to the problem of creating at the same time variety and unity.

Erotic Poetry

After all these related prose genres it is high time to look at a branch of poetry. The erotic poetry of the Hellenistic period, which got much of its subject-matter from local legends and tales, was a creation of the Alexandrian poets, Callimachus and others, who were active in the first half of the third century BC. Greek poetry of the archaic and classical periods was bound to the world and the forms of myth, even as far as the expression of purely human feelings was concerned. Now, as the old Greek cultural community had been dissolved and had given way to an individualistic and cosmopolitan one, myth was useless, dead. It is true that the learned Alexandrian poets devoted their attention to the old gods and heroes as well, but often the result was antiquarian exercises without the strength of a living tradition or the response of a larger audience. The *Argonautica*, the epic poem by Apollonius Rhodius, was a heroic venture by a single poet and enjoyed neither immediate success nor imitation (until Virgil combined Homer and Apollonius in the *Aeneid*).

Instead of the great, panhellenic themes which classical poetry had untiringly treated, poets now turned to local legendary material tied to individual places or provinces. Such matter was available in summary records by local historians or other collectors with anti- quarian interests. This was the mine where writers could find fresh subjects for the short, precious poems favoured by contemporary taste. Among other things, poets were attracted by the popular legends about the changing fortunes of young lovers; these they transformed into sentimental poems. A collection of such stories in a concentrated form, intended for use and embroidery in poetry, has actually survived and provides us with an interesting insight into the working methods of Hellenistic poets; I refer to the *Erotica pathemata*, or *Amatory Tales*, of Parthenius, who lived in the first century BC and himself wrote elegiac poems.

Some of these motifs, and also the shape they actually assumed in Alexandrian poetry, show a striking resemblance to the love stories of the novels: the superhuman beauty of the young hero and heroine, their first meeting at a religious festival (figure 32), love violently erupting and manifesting itself physically, and so on. It is quite possible that some of the novelists were directly or indirectly influenced by the treatment of the motifs in poems of this kind, but it must be remembered that this is not a necessary conclusion: access to the motifs was not exclusively through the poems. The same variety of local legends that provided the Alexandrian poets with their subject-matter must also have been available to the early novelists, and there is no way of knowing the exact amount of decorative detail already to be found in the sources. Side by side, perhaps inspiring each other mutually, both genres explored and utilized the same popular sources; and the inclination towards the individual and the personal, as well as the sentimentality which characterizes both, in contrast to classical poetry, is the mark of their origin in a common milieu.

Much more could be said. In fact it would be possible to write a history of almost the whole of Greek literature from the point of view of the novel, so eagerly did the novelists gather their flowers in the most widely different localities. The most important omissions in the present survey are, in the domain of prose, rhetoric — the court- room orators in particular practised the art of the graphic descrip- tion of a dramatic course of events with great skill — and short- story writing, which burgeoned in the Hellenistic period: some glimpses of the 'novella' will be given in the chapter on the Roman novels. Drama too is important. Euripides did not exclusively write

Fig. 32 *A whirling dance in Apollo's honour, represented on a South Italian vase of c. 410 BC. The girl wears a **kalathiskos**, a wide basketlike hat. The Greek religious feasts, often celebrated continuously for several days and nights, offered the only opportunity for young people of both sexes to be together without their parents supervising them. What could happen in the nightly frenzy is mirrored in literature: in Menander's comedy **The Woman from Samos** the young girl of good family is seduced by the boy next door during an Adonis feast, and in Hellenistic erotic poetry, as in the novels, a religious festival regularly provides the background for 'love at first sight'.*

plays of the kind which earned him the addition 'most tragic' of poets; during one short period of his career he also produced what Gilbert Murray called his 'romantic dramas', in which adventurous intrigues in foreign surroundings, romantic love, female beauty (Helen!), and happy endings inevitably make one think of the novel. The New Comedy of Menander, though keeping to the local Athenian setting, in many other ways follows in Euripides' footsteps: New Comedy, with its intrigues, characterization, and function of entertainment is the nobler half-sister of the novel. But rather than pursuing any of these lines further we shall return to the *Alexander Romance* — next to the New Testament the most successful work of Greek literature, bar none, if success is to be judged by diffusion.

CHAPTER V

From Historical Novel to Medieval 'Popular Book'

It would not be altogether unreasonable to call some of the Greek novels of love, travel, and adventure 'historical novels'. Chariton sets out to transport his readers back to an earlier historical period; he provides local colour by attaching the action to familiar figures and events from Greek history as well as by adopting the style of classical historians. And the last novelist of antiquity, Heliodorus, sets his novel in a period when the Persians are ruling over Egypt, that is before Alexander the Great. Anachronisms and inconsistencies abound in the historical fictions of the novels, but this does not prevent the authors from having *intended* to describe a period of time other than their own — with the exception of Achilles Tatius, who prefers another means of providing authenticity: that of claiming to have met his hero. On the other hand, private individuals unburdened by historicity stand at the centre, and therefore it may be more correct to reserve the designation 'historical' for those novels that really do follow a historical course of events, in however imaginative a way. The *Cyropaedia* of Xenophon (above, p. 113) makes a start; the *Ninus Romance* (p. 17) is unfortunately, through the whims of textual history, hardly more than a question mark for us. Not until the *Alexander Romance* do we find a complete living specimen of the genre.

The Alexander Romance of Pseudo-Callisthenes

In the form we know it, the *Alexander Romance* is a creation of late antiquity (*c*. AD 300). In some medieval manuscripts it is ascribed to Callisthenes, Alexander's court historiographer, but it has nothing to do with him; hence the prefix 'Pseudo-'. According to Reinhold Merkelbach, who is the last to have tried to unravel this tangled skein, whoever composed the novel built on at least three distinct sources, all belonging to the Hellenistic period. The main source was the 'biography' of Alexander which I have already described briefly (p. 115). The aim of its author was to arouse fear and pity, like a tragic poet; he collected sensations rather than facts, and from a modern point of view we should perhaps call his work a 'romanticized biography' rather than, at this early stage, a 'historical novel'. But our means of passing a fair judgement on it are limited, since the compiler of the *Alexander Romance* treated his main source in a highly cavalier fashion.

His most important innovation was to incorporate letters into the narrative framework. Most of them are short and originate from something which Merkelbach identifies as a continuous 'novel-in-letters' of the late Hellenistic age. Their origin was presumably the historical report of an actual exchange of letters between Alexander and Darius III, the Persian king; from this idea someone seems to have developed the novel. The main lines of the historical course of events are mirrored in fictitious letters exchanged between the persons involved. Fabricated letters of famous statesmen, poets, and philosophers were a flourishing genre in late Hellenistic and early imperial times, and Alexander was a natural choice for such a composition. The purpose was not only to tell a story from different points of view, but also to have the letter-writers' differing characters emerge from their ways of writing and of interpreting events. So the more accidental collection of letters gives way to the epistolary novel proper. It is in the nature of things that such a novel should be anonymous. The charming little *Chion Novel* (first century AD) about a young well-born man of Xenophon's and Plato's generation is the best example to have survived in its original form. The epistolary *Alexander Novel*, on the other hand, must be reconstructed chiefly from the remains included in the *Alexander Romance*, even though there also exist some papyri, the oldest dating from the first century BC, that contain fictitious letters to and from Alexander — some of which are identical with those in the *Romance*, and thus provide clues for the reconstruction.

The third source is a number of longer separate letters, which have supplied some of the most interesting subject-matter of the whole novel, or at least what secured its great popularity in the middle ages. These letters, addressed to Olympias, Alexander's mother, and to Aristotle, his teacher, deal with the hero's wonderful adventures in the fairyland of India and his drive towards the ends of the world. They are filled with the most fantastic reports of fabulous animals, men in animal guise, and other things of the kind which the fantastic travel tales, or *Reisefabulistik*, loved (above, p. 117). Alexander reaches the Land of the Blest, with the help of birds he flies into the sky, and he descends to the bottom of the sea in a glass diving-bell. Here the aim is no longer to indicate the character of the correspondent; the fabulous material pours forth without restraint.

A life of Alexander, an epistolary novel, and letters describing marvels — these three main constituents combine in Pseudo-Callisthenes' novel (figures 33–4). It is a confusing mixture: to fuse the biography and the epistolary novel, which Pseudo-Callisthenes probably regarded as a collection of authentic letters, presented problems which the author did not fully master. The mixture and the internal contradictions earlier led scholars to the view that the novel was the accidental outcome of an oral tradition, a Legend of Alexander which in the course of the centuries had absorbed all sorts of peculiar elements from various quarters. Merkelbach, however, convincingly shows how most of the matter derives from the purely literary sources mentioned. But there is a remainder which the author must have found elsewhere, or invented himself. The conspicuous role of Egyptian material makes it a natural supposition that behind the label 'Pseudo-Callisthenes' hides an Alexandrian: among other things, the story of the foundation of Alexandria has a prominent position in the novel.

The book teems with chronological and geographical associations of the most absurd nature. The Euphrates and Tigris debouch into the Nile; Plataea (in reality lying in ruins since the Peloponnesian War) and Antioch (not founded until 300 BC) both appear in the account. Having quickly subdued Asia Minor, Alexander makes a small detour to Sicily, Italy (where he graciously accepts the surrender of the Romans), and Carthage! Whether the author was ignorant of the actual facts or just did not care about them is not clear. However that may be, the aim and effect of the novel remains the same, the strangely potent depiction of the invincible hero, conqueror of the world, and explorer of the unknown.

In the novel Egypt takes its revenge, rather late, on its Macedonian conqueror: Alexander is not the son of Philip, as 'most people' believe, but of the Egyptian Pharaoh Nectanebus! The latter has been forced to flee from his country and has arrived in Pella, the capital of Macedonia, where he appears in the guise of an Egyptian prophet and astrologer. While King Philip is away during a war, Queen Olympias sends for Nectanebus: 'Seeing that she was very beautiful, Nectanebus was seized with desire for her beauty.' His

Figs. 33–34 *Contemporary illustrations of the **Alexander Romance**: obverse and reverse of two Roman contorniate medallions (latter half of fourth century AD).*

*In figure 33 Alexander is dressed as the young Heracles, with the lion's jaws over his head. The legend reads: Alexander Magnus Macedon, 'Alexander the Great of Macedon'. The reverse shows Alexander's mother Olympias on a **kline**, a couch with a dolphin-shaped back. The snake, by which, according to the novel, she conceived Alexander, approaches from the left. Legend: Olympias Regina, 'Queen Olympias'.*

This beautiful head (figure 34) reflects the representations of Alexander in Hellenistic art, with his eyes fixed on the far distance. The reverse shows Alexander on horseback killing a barbarian; the defeated enemy's shield is to be seen between the horse's legs. Legend: Alexander Magnus Macedon.

Alexander is the favourite motif on the contorniate medallions (see figure 31). This shows the currency which the Alexander figure enjoyed in the fourth century AD; the **Alexander Romance** *is dated to the beginning of the same century. Some of the motifs, like Olympias and the snake, are clearly influenced by the novel (or possibly by the legends which the novel assimilated).*

magic equipment impresses her, and she asks him to cast the horoscope of the royal couple, because there is a rumour that Philip after his homecoming is going to repudiate her in favour of another woman:

Nectanebus said to her 'Tell me your birthday and Philip's.' And what did Nectanebus do then? He put his own birthday along with that of Olympias. He made a calculation and said to her 'The rumour you heard about yourself is not false. But I can help you, for I am an Egyptian prophet, so that you are not set aside by Philip.' 'How can you do that?' she said. He said 'You should lie with a god who lives in the world, and conceive and bear and rear a son by him, and have him as your means of revenging the wrongs Philip has done you.' Olympias said to him 'What god?' 'Libyan Ammon,' he said. 'And what is this god like?' she asked. 'A middle-aged man,' he replied, 'with golden hair and beard; he has horns on his forehead, and they too are like gold. So you must get yourself ready like a queen for him, for today in a dream you will see this god coming to you.' 'If I see this dream,' she said, 'I shall honour you not as a prophet but as a god.'

So Nectanebus left the queen, and in a lonely place he picked some plants which he knew to induce dreams, and extracted their juice. Then he made a wax figure of a woman and wrote Olympias' name on it. Then he lit lamps and poured the juice from the plants into them, and with oaths invoked the spirits appointed to this function, so that Olympias had a vision. She saw the god Ammon embracing her that night and saying as he rose to leave her 'Woman, you have a male child in your womb, who is your avenger.'

When Olympias awoke from sleep she was in wonder, and at once sent for Nectanebus and said to him 'I have had the dream and seen the god Ammon whom you told me about. I beg you, prophet, to bring me together with him again. And find out when he is going to come to me, so that I can be better prepared for my bridegroom.' 'To start with, my lady,' said Nectanebus, 'what you saw was a dream. When he comes into your sight in his own person, he will do what is necessary. But if your highness approves, give me a room to sleep in, so that I can intercede with him on your behalf.' 'Why,' said the queen, 'you shall have a room by my bedchamber. And if I become pregnant by this god, I shall honour you greatly, as befits a queen, and treat you as the child's father.' Nectanebus said to her, 'For your instruction, my lady, the sign announcing that the god is coming in will be if you see a snake gliding towards you when you are sitting in your room in the evening [see figure 33]. Tell everyone to go out. But do not put out the lamps which by my knowledge I have got ready for lighting in the god's honour, and which I now give to you. Get into your royal bed and be ready, and cover your face, and give only a glance at the god, whom you saw coming to you in your dream.' With these words

Nectanebus left, and the next day Olympias gave him a room very close to her own bedroom.

Nectanebus prepared for himself the soft fleece of a ram with horns on its temples, and the horns like gold, and an ebony sceptre and a white garment and a very clean cloak the colour of dragon's blood. He went into the bedroom, where Olympias lay on the bed, covered up. She glanced out of the corner of her eye and saw him coming in; she was not frightened, because she was expecting him as she saw him in her dream. The lamps lit up and Olympias covered her face. Nectanebus put aside his sceptre and got into her bed and lay with her [figure 35]. And he said to her, 'Be still, woman, you have a male child in your womb who is your avenger and king and sovereign of the whole world [*kosmokrator*].' And Nectanebus took his sceptre and left the bedroom and hid all the implements of his deception. (1.4.7–7.3)

This story of Nectanebus' deceit belongs to the more 'novelistic' or 'romantic' elements of Pseudo-Callisthenes. We shall take a big step forward and look at a passage which by contrast distinctly smacks of pathetic Hellenistic historiography. Alexander has grown up, killed his real father Nectanebus, tamed the wild horse Bucephalus, won the quadriga race in the Olympic Games, and avenged the murder of his official father, Philip. He has marched out to war against Darius and conquered many towns and countries; and he is now on his way to meet the Persian king himself, who after a defeat in battle has retreated to his palace. But two of the king's own satraps, anticipating the natural course of events, stab Darius with a sword:

So the Macedonians found the river Stranga frozen over and crossed it, and Alexander entered Darius' palace. When the criminals learned that Alexander had arrived they fled, leaving Darius half-dead. Alexander reached King Darius and found him half-dead, his blood pouring out of his wounds; he raised a cry of sorrow over him in keeping with his grief, shed tears over him, and covered Darius' body with his cloak. Laying his hands on Darius' breast, he spoke words full of grief over him: 'Get up, King Darius, rule your land and be master of what is yours! Take the crown as ruler of the Persian people, grasp your great power! I swear to you by Providence above, I am speaking truly and not in pretence. Who are they who struck you? Tell me who they were, so that I can give you satisfaction.'

Darius groaned at Alexander's words, stretched out his hands and drew Alexander to him. Embracing him he said 'King Alexander, never exult in your royal position! When you achieve a godlike success and want to grasp heaven in your hands, think of the future. For Chance [Tyche] knows no king, be he never so powerful; Chance sways mindlessly this way or that [see figure 2]. You see what I was and what I am now. Alexander, when I

am dead, bury me with your own hands. The Macedonians and Persians
must conduct my funeral. Let Darius' and Alexander's family be one! I en-
trust my mother to you as if she were your own mother. Have pity on my
wife as you would your sister! My daughter Roxana I give to you as wife,
that you may leave children in everlasting memory of you: glory in them as
we gloried in our children, and keep our memories alive, you Philip's,
Roxana that of Darius, as you grow old together.' So said Darius, and with
his arms round Alexander's neck he died. (2.20.4−9)

These are strains familiar from tragedy. Alexander's noble-
mindedness on this occasion does not accord with his deceitful and

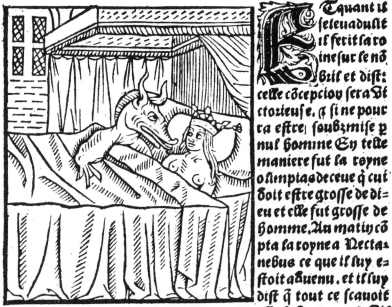

Fig. 35 *The snake, or dragon, goes to bed with Queen Olympias,
Alexander's mother. This picture of the conception of Alexander the Great
is to be found in the first printed edition of a French prose version of the*
Alexander Romance, *called* **Alixandre le Grant**, *(Paris, 1506). It was
illustrated with some thirty woodcuts, only a few of which were cut
especially for this book; the others were freely reused by the publishers in
novel after novel!*

cruel way of acting in other situations. Incidentally, it is the death of the great king that is the subject of Alexander's own report later on in the novel, in a letter to Olympias and Aristotle (figure 36). He states that he had the murderers of Darius crucified on the king's grave, and then continues — and now once more we find ourselves in a quite different kind of narrative:

Leaving there I subdued the realm of Areiobarzan and Manazaces. I brought under my control Media and Armenia, Ebesia and all of Persia that Darius had ruled. From there I took guides and wanted to penetrate the remoter parts of the desert, towards the direction of the Wain, and they advised me not to go there because of the number of wild animals in those parts. But I disregarded what they said and set out on the journey. So we came to a region full of ravines, where the road through the ravines was very narrow; we travelled along it for eight days. In that region we saw animals of various kinds such as we had never seen before. When we had passed through those parts we came to another, yet more dismal region. There we found a great forest of trees called 'anaphanda', which bear a strange, rare fruit — enormous apples like big pumpkins. And there were men too in that wood called 'Phyti', twenty-four cubits tall, with long necks of about a cubit and a half, and likewise long feet. Their forearms and hands were rather like saws. When they saw us they rushed at the army. I was very frightened at the sight, and gave orders to capture one of them. When we rushed at them with cries and the sound of trumpets they ran away. We killed thirty-two of them, but they slew a hundred of our soldiers. We stayed there, eating the fruit of the trees.

Moving from there we came to a green land in which there were wild men like giants, round in shape, with flame-coloured countenances — they looked like lions. There were others with them called 'Ochlites', who had no hair at all; they were four cubits tall and as broad as a spear is long. . . .

The next day I decided to visit their caves. We found wild animals chained to their entrances — they were like lions, but had three eyes. We saw fleas jumping there, the size of our frogs. Leaving there we came to a place where a copious spring gushed out of the ground. I gave orders to pitch camp there, and we stayed there two months.

We moved from there and came to the land of the Apple-eaters. There we saw a man whose whole body was covered with hair, a very big man, and we were frightened. I gave the order to seize him, and when he was seized he looked at us with a savage expression. I gave orders for a naked woman to be brought to him; he seized hold of her and began to eat her. When the soldiers rushed in a body to snatch her away he babbled something outlandish in his own language. His neighbours heard him and came at us from out of the marsh, about ten thousand of them — but

Figs. 36–39 *These four pictures are illustrations for the **Alexander Romance** taken from a Greek fourteenth-century manuscript, which contained no less than 250 miniatures. The manuscript, now preserved in Venice, was probably copied from a (lost) thirteenth-century manuscript produced in a Syrian or Palestinian studio. The style is Byzantine, with Frankish and Muslim features.*

Figure 36: Letter-writing: the wife, mother, and daughter of Darius, the Persian king, write to Alexander; and Alexander himself (bottom)

*writes a letter to his mother. Letters to and from Alexander form an important part of the **Alexander Romance**; the author seems to have fused a ready-made collection of letters with his main source, a biography of Alexander, both of Hellenistic origin.*

Figure 37: Alexander visits the Gymnosophists, the 'Naked Wise Men' of India. They live on an island, and 'Alexander embarks in the ship with fifty soldiers and goes to the island', says the Greek caption. In the bottom half of the picture we see him conversing with the sages, hearing 'words full of wisdom'. This conversation between the young Greek world-conquerer and the Indian brahmins is one of the constituents of the Alexander legend that has fired the imagination.

Figure 38: Portents forewarning of Alexander's imminent death and his successors' struggle for power. Simultaneously a woman is shown bearing a deformed child and bringing it to Alexander, who calls for prophets to have the sign interpreted.

Figure 39: Alexander on his death-bed. 'There was no one who did not weep when he saw the great king Alexander lying half-dead. When Alexander wept, all the crowd was filled with lamentation and woe. His horse Bucephalus came galloping amongst them all, and drawing up beside Alexander it began to flood his bed with its tears. At the flood of tears from the horse, lamentation arose among them all, both Persians and Macedonians.'

there were forty thousand of us. I gave orders to set fire to the marsh, and they fled when they saw the flames. We chased them and caught three of them. They would not eat any food, and died after eight days. They did not have a human intelligence, but barked like dogs.

Leaving there we came to a river. I gave orders to pitch camp, and for the troops to lay down their arms as usual. There were trees in the river, and at sunrise they started to grow, until the sixth hour; from the seventh hour they grew smaller, until they disappeared completely. They gave off a sap like Persian myrrh, and had a very sweet, noble scent. I gave orders for cuts to be made in the trees and the sap collected with sponges. Suddenly the men collecting the sap were whipped by an invisible divinity. We heard the sound of them being whipped and saw the marks of the lashes appearing on their backs, but we could not see those doing the whipping. A voice was heard which forbade the cutting and the sap-collecting. 'If you don't stop the army will be struck dumb.' So I was frightened and forbade anybody to cut the trees or collect their sap.

There were black stones in the river; anyone who touched them found his flesh turn the same colour as the stones. There were a lot of snakes in the river as well, and many kinds of fish, which were cooked not by means of fire but in cold spring water. So, one of the soldiers caught a fish and washed it and put it in a jar of water — and found the fish cooked. There were also birds in the river very like our birds — but if you touched one, fire came out of it. . . .

Leaving there we reached a place where there were men without heads, who talked like human beings in their own language; they were hairy, wore animal skins, and lived on fish. They caught fish in the nearby sea and brought them to us; others brought mushrooms from the land, twenty-five pounds each in weight. We saw a great many big seals crawling on land. My friends strongly urged me to turn back, but I refused — I wanted to see the end of land.

Going on from there we travelled over a desert and reached the sea. We saw nothing any more, neither bird nor animals, only the sky and the earth. We could not see the sun now; the air was dark for ten days. . . . (2.31.5–38.1)

And so it goes on. Alexander's legendary longing — for what? — drives him farther and farther towards the limits of the world and of human knowledge. Not only do the marvels of nature fascinate him, he also tries to explore all Man's wisdom. India had long enjoyed a reputation for having attained the highest possible level of wisdom, and therefore Alexander visits the Gymnosophists, the 'naked wise men' (figure 37):

A river ran all round that land; its water was clear, and white as milk, and there were palm-trees in great number, loaded with fruit, and the vines had a thousand clusters of grapes, very beautiful and enticing. And Alexander saw the naked sages themselves living in huts and caves. Far off, at a great distance from them, he saw their wives and children with the cattle, grazing them.

Alexander questioned them. 'Do you not have graves?' he said. 'This patch of land we live on', they said, 'is our grave as well. For we take our rest here on earth when we bury ourselves in sleep. The earth gives birth to us, the earth rears us, and when we die we lie under the earth in our everlasting sleep.'

Next he asked 'Who are more numerous, the living or the dead?', and they said, 'The dead are more numerous, but since they do not exist any longer they are not to be reckoned. The visible are more numerous than the invisible.'

His next question was 'Which is stronger, death or life?' They answered, 'Life, because the sun shines brightly when it is rising but is weaker to the sight when it is sinking.'

Then he asked 'Which is greater, the land or the sea?' 'The land,' they said, 'for the sea is itself embraced by the land.'

His next question was 'Which is the most dangerous of all animals?' 'Man,' they said. 'How?' he asked. 'You can see that from your own case,' they said: 'you are an animal — look how many animals you have with you, so that you alone can rob the other animals of life.' He did not become angry but smiled.

Next he said 'What is empire?' 'Unjust power of superiority over others, courage helped by the luck of the moment, a golden burden.'

His next question was 'What came first, night or day?' 'Night', they said; 'for what is born grows in the darkness of the womb, then the womb brings it out to receive the light of day.'

His next question was 'Which side is better, right or left?' 'Right,' they said, 'because the sun itself rises on the right and moves to the left-hand part of the sky; and a woman suckles with her right breast first.' (3.5.4–6.8)

This encounter, with its intricate questions and sometimes witty, sometimes merely strained (or incomprehensible) answers, makes a strange impression. The explanation is given in other sources, in which the scene is reproduced in something nearer to its original form. Alexander obviously put these questions not out of any desire for wisdom, but as a macabre game before the intended execution of ten captured Gymnosophists, who had supported their own king in his struggle against Alexander. The artful questions, originally ten in all, were meant to be impossible to answer 'correctly', and an 'incorrect' answer was to be punished by death — a well-known folk-tale motif. The Indians, however, surpassed their Greek interrogator in cunning, and Alexander at last, to his great mortification, was forced to spare their lives. Pseudo-Callisthenes recast this episode, basically hostile to Alexander, to suit his own purpose. He changed the sequence of the questions and sometimes also the wording of the answers; he replaced some questions with new ones, and missed several points. His Alexander was to appear superior in all respects; to wind up the episode, Alexander is shown lecturing to the Gymnosophists about his own role as the instrument of the gods.

Alexander returns to the old world, to Babylon. He is only thirty-two, but the moment of his departure from human life is already near. Several portents are reported. A woman of the people gives birth to a child the upper part of whose body is human, but dead, whereas the lower part consists of the living heads of lions and wild dogs (figure 38). The woman shows her child to Alexander, who calls for soothsayers and magicians. Various interpretations are offered, but the most prominent prophet gives the solution: the human half symbolizes Alexander himself, who is soon to die. The animal heads are his closest followers, who will survive him. They lack reason, and they are wild and hostile towards him.

Sure enough, a conspiracy against Alexander's life is being plotted. His cupbearer becomes the conspirators' instrument: at a banquet he administers a cup of poison to Alexander, who drinks it and falls ill. By his own orders his death-bed is placed so that the whole army can march past it and see him. Moving scenes take place when the ordinary soldiers say farewell to their adored leader (figure 39). He dictates his last will and a letter of consolation to his mother; and then:

A mist formed in the air and a big star appeared, falling from the sky towards the sea, and an eagle along with it, and the statue in Babylon called the statue of Zeus moved. The star rose again into the sky, followed by the eagle. When the star disappeared into the sky Alexander at once fell into his everlasting sleep. (3.33.5)

King Alexander in the Middle Ages

The explanation of how the *Alexander Romance* came into being may seem complicated enough, yet it is straightforward and easy to grasp in comparison with what happened thereafter. The tradition is already widely ramified in Greek. The novel was meant for entertainment, and it was anonymous. Consequently it did not meet with the respect which was due to a literary work belonging to any of the 'higher' genres, and which guaranteed a certain degree of faithfulness in the transcription process. Whoever copied and thereby (consciously or not) preserved a work like the *Alexander Romance* for posterity, felt free to delete passages of the text at his own discretion, to remodel it, or to make additions. Some exercised this right to a greater extent than others and created their own versions, in textual criticism often called 'redactions' or 'recensions'. (Textual transmission is examined in greater detail in the Appendix.) Five such 'recensions' of Pseudo-Callisthenes' novel have been identified; none of them, however, survives in its original form, but each is represented by late medieval manuscripts which are derived from the original but are not literally exact copies of it. The different 'redactors' emphasized what they themselves thought essential in the Alexander tradition, often by adding matter from sources other than the novel, and they suppressed other, original elements. The passages translated above are taken from a fifteenth-century manuscript, which in turn goes back to a recension thought to belong to the fifth century; this particular recension lays stress on the historical aspects of the story.

However, the internal Greek tradition is just one part of the medieval life of the *Alexander Romance*, and not the most interesting one at that. If copies could be free, translations were even more so, and the *Alexander Romance* was translated into at least thirty-five different languages, in some cases more than once. In the West the translations were generally made by way of one of the Latin versions, while in the East the Greek text, in one of its five 'redactions', was the usual point of departure. Even by the beginning of the fourth century AD, that is, shortly after its first appearance, the novel had already been translated into Latin by Iulius Valerius; in the fifth century an Armenian version came into being; in the sixth we find a Syriac one which was based on a Middle Persian translation which is now lost. Other eastern languages follow during the middle ages: Arabic, Hebrew, Georgian, Ethiopic. Around 1600 the novel reaches Java via Arabic! A Bulgarian adaptation is dated to the tenth or eleventh century, and Russian, Serbian, Ukrainian, and Romanian renderings are added before the end of the middle ages.

In the West there is a great variety of medieval versions in the vernacular, originating in some cases from an epitome of Iulius Valerius' Latin translation, but mostly from a new rendering into medieval Latin which had been produced in the tenth century by the Archpriest Leo of Naples. To his translation was later added other subject-matter, and in that form — conventionally called *Historia de preliis*, 'The Story of [Alexander's] Combats' — it became the spiritual father of a long series of verse or prose versions in French, in Spanish and Italian, in German and English, in Czech, Polish, Hungarian and many other languages.

As a concrete example we may choose the Old Swedish *Konung Alexander*, 'King Alexander', composed about 1380 on commission from a member of the aristocracy, Bo Jonsson Grip, at that time the most powerful man in the country. The poem consists of no less than 10,584 doggerel verses. The translator himself is unknown, but from his work it is obvious that he should be counted among the more talented and original poets of the period. He followed the course of events in the *Historia de preliis* reasonably faithfully, but inflated the narrative in various ways — to a much greater degree than could be put down to the mere need for rhymes. In particular the descriptions of fighting are enlarged upon. The style is more concrete than that of the model; vivid and evocative details are added; proverbs and vigorous popular sayings enliven the text, which in its Latin original was rather dry. Antiquity fades away, fourteenth-century Sweden makes its entry into the Alexander legend. In all these respects the Swedish translator appears as a typical representative of the medieval adapters of the novel, in particular of those who put it into verse. A fresh gift for telling stories, combined with a disrespectful attitude towards the original, yields a result no doubt well suited for reading aloud in the banquet hall and on other festive occasions.

The popularity of the *Alexander Romance* was due to a number of concurrent factors. The fabulous oriental content fascinated the medieval audience: the fabulous animals, the oracles, Alexander flying in the air. The narrative frame, the military expedition, was in itself slender, but could easily be padded out at discretion: each century through which the novel passed had the opportunity to see its own favourite themes unfolded there. And the figure of Alexander himself, whose reputation also lived on outside the novel, never ceased to thrill the imagination: the world-conqueror, or the young man who died before his time; the representative of the Divine on earth, or rather a warning of man's insatiability and the vanity of all human aspirations? Alexander could thus be used in the preaching of the church as well as in political propaganda: he is presented as the feudal master who leads his men to victory, or becomes, as he sometimes does in the Swedish version, the mouthpiece of political wisdom.

In the more advanced poetic versions such tendencies can often be discerned, in addition to the desire to entertain. Many other versions, however, especially the prose translations of the late middle ages, are more deserving of the designation 'popular books', or 'folkbooks': they have no observable literary ambition or political content, but depend entirely on the drawing power of the subject-matter. They may be stylistically poor, but the plain narrative nevertheless possesses a captivating force. They belong to those products which the art of printing picks up in the last decades of the fifteenth century, and so their continued success is assured. In simply designed booklets, sometimes decorated with woodcuts (see figure 35), they are circulated among the people for reading, or reading aloud.

It may be added that illustrations are part of the *Alexander Romance* from its very beginnings. Several medieval manuscripts are abundantly and exquisitely illuminated (see figures 36–9), and a comparison of the iconography of some of the finest manuscripts has led to the conclusion that they have a common point of departure in an ancient pictorial cycle that may have been added to the novel in Alexandria as early as the fourth century AD (see figures 33–4). Certain scenes of the novel are favoured for the illustration of the medieval vernacular versions: for instance, Alexander's descent to the bottom of the sea and his flying in the air (figure 40). Alexander carried to the sky by griffins is also a wide-spread motif outside the realm of books; one famous example is the relief on the north wall of San Marco in Venice; a less well-known piece decorates a portal in Fardhem Church on Gotland in the Baltic Sea (figure 41).

The Troy Romances of Dictys and Dares

Just as the medieval picture of Alexander, in the East as well as the West, originated more often with Pseudo-Callisthenes than with ancient historians, so too knowledge of the Trojan War was usually not derived from its proper source, Homer. Dante could not read Homer, but he could meet the Homeric heroes elsewhere: in the late antique *Troy Romances* attributed to Dictys of Crete and Dares of Phrygia, or in their medieval offshoots.

Dictys' description is presented as a 'Diary of the Trojan War', *Ephemeris belli Troiani*, written by one who was there himself. According to the prologue it was found, written in Phoenician characters on lime-wood tablets, in Dictys' tomb at Cnossus; the

Figs. 40–1 *Ancient science fiction: his urge to 'try the impossible' forces Alexander up into the air. Two white birds are yoked together by their necks, and a basket of oxhide is attached under the yoke. The birds are starved for three days, then Alexander steps into the basket with a long spear in his hand, at the point of which a piece of horse-liver is fastened. The starving birds fly for the liver, Alexander steers with his spear. Having arrived high up in colder strata of air he meets a flying being who warns*

him not to continue, and as he looks down at the small earth, he becomes
frightened and turns the spear downwards.

Figure 40, from a German manuscript of the late middle ages, gives a
less realistic picture of Alexander's flying machine than the novel.

The stone relief (figure 41) in Fardhem church, Gotland (twelfth
century), is more true to the text: it shows Alexander standing in his
gondola.

tomb had opened in an earthquake in AD 66. Of course this is a fiction of the kind we have already encountered in *The Marvels beyond Thule* (above, p. 118). What remains of the novel is a fourth-century Latin rendering and a couple of papyrus fragments of the Greek original, which was possibly one or two hundred years older. The first half of the novel tells of the war itself; the second half, which has been heavily abbreviated by the Latin translator, describes the return journeys and homecomings of the heroes. The whole account, prosaic in a double sense, thus covers the themes of both the *Iliad* and the *Odyssey*.

Dares' 'Story of the Destruction of Troy', *De excidio Troiae historia*, also purports to derive from a contemporary eyewitness account. It survives in a sixth-century Latin translation only, and is more original, insofar as it views the war from the point of view of the Trojans, correcting and criticizing Homer's pro-Greek account. This anti-Homeric aspect was well suited to the West. Through Aeneas the Romans traced their ancestry back to Troy, and consequently so also did the Franks and Britons of the middle ages. Aeneas was not the only Trojan in exile from whom one could derive one's ruling dynasty, and the similarity between the names Frangia and Phrygia sufficed to couple the two countries together.

To begin with, the verse romances which were written from 1150 onwards in France favoured ancient topics: Alexander, Aeneas, the Argive expedition against Thebes (typically inspired not by the Attic tragedies but by the Roman poet Statius' *Thebais*), and the Trojan War. The extensive *Roman de Troie* by Benoît de Sainte-More uses Dares of Phrygia as its main source, and Dictys as a secondary one: the *Troy Romances* offered raw material that called for processing. This French verse romance became influential. An epic poem by Boccaccio builds on it, inspiring Chaucer too to compose an epic, which in turn inspired Shakespeare to write his *Troilus and Cressida*. . . . But after this literary progress there is not much left of Dares; not even the loving couple is his. More of him survived on the more popular level to which the *Troy Romance* soon returned — via the French verse romance! At the end of the thirteenth century the latter was translated back into Latin prose by an Italian, Guido delle Colonne, and from that again into different vernaculars. In the company of many other novels with ancient or national themes it eventually reaches the printing press as a folkbook.

From the translator's preface to a Swedish version of 1529 — a version written in a clumsy and bombastic style, with the Latin sentence structure shining through — we can catch a glimpse of the motivation for publishing this kind of literature. The attitude is one of condescension to genre and audience alike: when people are gathered together with nothing very useful to do, it may be of more benefit than harm to listen to someone reading aloud about what once happened at Troy, so the translator tells us; and he adds: at least this is better than indulging in rude language, slandering, scorn and derision, quarrelling and fighting, or other such ungodly activities, that thrive in the ale-houses!

King Apollonius of Tyre

The fate of the *Alexander* and *Troy Romances* was shared by another ancient text, which does not however build on history or myth, but is fictitious through and through: *Historia Apollonii regis Tyri*, or 'The Story of Apollonius King of Tyre'; it too attained its greatest importance as a widely circulated 'popular book' during the middle ages and the beginning of modern times. Besides several free Latin versions, some in verse, it appears in Old English, Old French, Italian, Byzantine Greek, Middle High German, and several different Slavic renderings, just to mention the older and more important ones. As usual with this kind of diffusion, the novel goes through the most violent metamorphoses, as regards both form and content. A late offshoot of the same tradition is Shakespeare's *Pericles, Prince of Tyre*.

But let us return to the original, or more exactly to the oldest surviving version, which is in Latin and dates from the fifth or sixth century. At that time Christian elements had already been inserted into the originally pagan framework. Some hold that the earlier, third-century version which has been postulated was an original work in Latin, others that it was an adaptation of a Greek original. However that may be, the story strongly resembles the Greek novels, especially Xenophon's *Ephesiaca*. The main lines of the plot are as follows:

Once upon a time there lived a King Antiochus of Antioch, who was a widower and had a daughter old enough to marry. He was himself seized with a violent passion for his beautiful daughter, raped her and then secretly lived with her in an incestuous relationship. The suitors who asked for her hand had to answer a riddle; anyone who gave the wrong answer was to lose his head, and he who gave the right one was to have the princess as his wife — but was in reality beheaded too! Now young Apollonius of Tyre arrives. He gives the correct answer to the riddle (which refers to the king's relationship with his daughter), but even so for some reason or other the king allows him to go back to Tyre in order to continue brooding on the solution. Apollonius finds that his first answer was the right one. Realizing that the king will try to kill him, he flees from his native town, and Antiochus puts a price on his head. For a while Apollonius finds a place of refuge in Tarsus (in Cilicia, SE Asia Minor); but on his continued flight towards Africa he is shipwrecked. A fisherman gives him shelter and kind treatment — compare the fisherman episode in Xenophon Ephesius (above, p. 21) — before he journeys on to the King of Cyrene (on the north coast of Africa), whose daughter falls in love with him. Having dismissed her ordinary suitors her father gives his consent to the marriage.

Some time after his wedding to the princess Apollonius receives the message that King Antiochus and his daughter are dead, struck by lightning, and that Apollonius himself has been appointed to succeed the king. Together with his wife, who is pregnant, he sets out for Antioch, but his wife dies during the voyage and is buried at sea, having first given birth to a little girl. The coffin is carried to land at Ephesus, and it turns out that the woman was only apparently dead; she becomes a priestess in the shrine of Artemis. Simultaneously Apollonius, mourning his wife's death, gives up his plan of going to Antioch, leaves the baby and a large amount of money with friends in Tarsus, and himself spends fourteen years as a merchant in Egypt. His daughter Tarsia, who has grown up with her foster-parents, is kidnapped by pirates and goes to meet the same fate as Antheia in Xenophon's novel:

And so Tarsia's kidnappers made their way to the city of Mytilene [on Lesbos]. She was put on the auction block along with various other slaves. Hearing of this, a notorious brothel-keeper wanted to buy no other man or woman except the young Tarsia, and he began a struggle to purchase her. But a leading citizen of this very municipality, Athenagora by name, realizing that a high-born, intelligent, and very beautiful virgin was up for sale, offered ten thousand sesterces in gold. The brothel-keeper, however, was ready to bid twice the amount. Athenagora offered thirty thousand; the brothel-keeper forty; Athenagora fifty; the brothel-keeper sixty; Athenagora seventy; the brothel-keeper eighty; Athenagora ninety. The brothel-keeper on the spot puts up one hundred thousand in gold and says, 'If anyone makes a better offer, I'll put up an additional ten thousand.' Athenagora then says, 'If I take on the fight with this brothel-keeper just to buy one woman, I'll be selling several women. However, I'll allow him to buy her and when he puts her up for prostitution, I'll be the first to go in for her and I'll break her virginal knot at a cheap rate, and it'll be the same for me as if I'd bought her.'

What more is there to say? The virgin was knocked down to the brothel-keeper and she was taken by him into his entrance hall, where he had a golden statue of Priapus decked out with jewels and more gold, and he says to her, 'Bow down to the deity who has been my greatest help.' The girl says, 'Are you from Lampsacus then?'[7] The brothel-keeper says, 'Don't you realize, you miserable creature, that you have entered the house of a money-grabbing brothel-keeper?' The girl, however, on hearing this, trembled all over, and throwing herself at his feet, said, 'Have pity on me, my lord, and save my virginity! And I implore you, don't put this poor body up for such a sordid sale!'

The brothel-keeper says to her, 'Pick yourself up, you miserable creature. You don't realize that with a brothel-keeper or a torturer neither prayers nor tears have any effect.' And he called over the manager of his girls and said to him, 'The room should be carefully furnished and the notice written above it should be: "Whoever wishes to take the virginal Tarsia, will pay half a pound of gold; thereafter she will be available to the public for a single gold piece."' The manager did what his master, the brothel-keeper, had told him to do.

Two days later, she was led into the brothel, following a large crowd and accompanying musicians. Athenagora, however, was there earlier and enters the brothel with his head covered. But once he had entered, he sat down. And in came Tarsia; she threw herself at his feet and said, 'Have pity on me! I beg you — you're young — don't let yourself violate me under that sordid notice. Restrain your indecent lust and listen to the accidents that brought me to my present miserable state or consider my family background.' When she had told him of all the accidents that had happened to her, the prince was distressed; indeed, because of his sense of decency, he was dumbfounded, and said to her: 'Get up! We know the quirks of fortune; we're human also. I myself have a daughter who's a virgin, and for her I can be anxious about a similar mischance.' Saying this, he pulled out forty gold pieces and put them in her virginal hand and he said to her, 'Tarsia, dear lady, look, you have more than your virginity called for. Do the same with the next customers until you get yourself freed.' The girl, of course, with flowing tears, said, 'I am most grateful for your decent behaviour.'

When he came out, a colleague of his came up to him and said, 'Athenagora, how did you make out with this new slave?' Athenagora replied, 'It couldn't have been better; enough to make you cry!' After saying this, he trailed him. As the friend went in, he lay in wait to see how

---

[7] Priapus, the fertility god often represented in phallic form, was venerated especially at Lampsacus on the Hellespont and was depicted on the coins of that town, though in a less indecent shape.

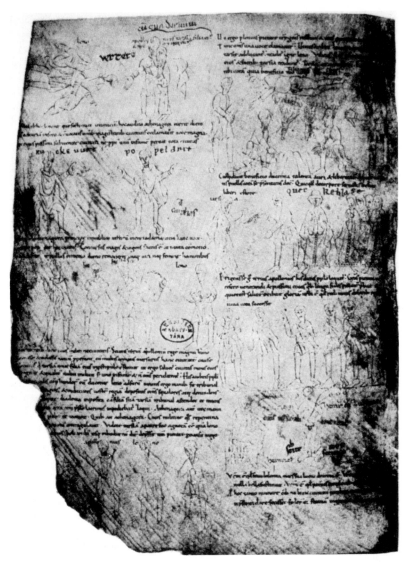

Figs. 42–3 King Apollonius of Tyre *in a comic strip. In a medieval manuscript, dated c. 1000, the Latin text was illustrated in this way all through, though only four leaves have survived. The text is shortened and divided into small units, each illustrated with a simple drawing. For ancient precedents, see figures 27–8.*

*Figure 42 shows a page containing some of the later chapters of the tale: (top left) Apollonius is reunited with his daughter Tarsia (the figure lying before them is not the brothel-keeper [**leno**], as somebody has written above the figure, but the nobleman Athenagora, prostrated to ask for Tarsia's hand); (bottom right) the inhabitants of Mytilene have erected a golden statue of their benefactor Apollonius, who is represented with his foot on the head of the executed brothel-keeper.*

Figure 43 is of a detail from the same page showing the brothel-keeper's punishment — he was burnt over an open fire — and how Tarsia rewarded her friends: the good manager of the brothel receives 200 gold coins, the prostitutes are set free and inherit the brothel-keeper's wealth. The drawings have had extra details and scribbles added to them at a later date.

things would turn out. Once the friend had entered, Athenagora waited in front. In the usual way, the girl closed her door. The young man said to her, 'If you're in good shape, tell me how much the young man who just came in to you gave you.' The girl replied, 'He gave me forty gold pieces.' The young man said, 'Damn him! What would it have been to him, since he's so rich, if he'd given you a whole pound of gold? Just so you'll know that I'm the better man, take a whole pound of gold.' But Athenagora, waiting outside, said, 'The more you give, the more you'll grieve!' The girl, however, threw herself at the friend's feet and, in the same way, told him of her mishaps; this disturbed the fellow and diverted his mind from his sexual urges. So he said to her, 'Get up, dear lady! We too are human and subject to misfortunes.' The girl said, 'I am most grateful for your decent behaviour.'

On leaving the place, he found Athenagora laughing and said, 'You're a great man! You didn't have anyone to offer your tears to!' And swearing themselves to mutual secrecy, they began watching for others to emerge. What more is there to be said? As they watched from their secret observation post, they found that all those who entered, paying each a gold piece, left with tears in their eyes. (Chapters 33–5)

The brothel-keeper gets his money, but all the same flies into a rage on hearing that Tarsia is still a virgin. He orders the manager personally to rob her of her virginity, but he turns out to be as soft-hearted as the customers when faced with the girl's entreaties. The end of the story is that Tarsia, thanks to the assistance of Athenagora, is reunited with her father, who had believed her to be dead. The greedy brothel-keeper is sentenced to death and burnt alive; while the manager is spared and the former prostitutes set free and allowed to share in the fortune which the brothel-keeper left behind and which they had themselves amassed through plying their trade (figures 42–3). Apollonius marries his daughter to Athenagora and is himself reunited with his wife in Ephesus. He punishes all the villains of the piece one by one, remunerates his helpers, and ends up as King of Antioch, Tyre, and Cyrene.

The mixture of folk-tale and Greek novel of love, travel, and adventure is evident. The story is only partly worked out in detail; it often rushes along rapidly and summarily, as does the *Ephesiaca*. Both novels within their short compass contain astonishingly rich narrative material; in both there prevails an unashamed negligence of motivation and consistency. Athenagora is, for instance, at the same time a 'youth' who is quite logically later married to Tarsia and the father of a virgin of Tarsia's age: the motifs of 'elderly, fatherly benefactor' and 'young, suitable bridegroom' have been confounded, 'contaminated'. Consequently both the *Historia Apollonii*

and the *Ephesiaca* have now and then been taken as unskilful ab-
breviations of originally homogeneous and well-written novels. To
me, however, this seems about as well founded as it would be to
maintain that modern detective stories or adventure films which are
lacking in logic and characterization are really cut versions of more
accomplished representatives of those genres.

Moreover the *Historia Apollonii* is the best proof that weaknesses
of this kind do not necessarily diminish the attraction of a book. Its
enormous popularity in the middle ages may give us some idea of the
success of the non-sophistic novel with the general public of late
Hellenistic and early imperial times. They both offered the opportunity, typical of trivial literature, to identify with a beautiful and
noble, but in other respects rather vaguely defined, hero or heroine,
who is exposed to the most horrible misfortunes but who nevertheless finally reaches a safe haven, unscathed and happy, and
receives the rewards reserved for virtue.

CHAPTER VI

The New Heroes: Apostles, Martyrs and Saints

Paul and Thecla

It is said of the Apostle Paul that having escaped from Antioch in Pisidia he came to Iconium in central Asia Minor. Even before he entered the town he was met by a man called Onesiphorus, who had got the Apostle's description in advance: 'Small of stature, bare-headed, bow-legged, of healthy complexion; eyebrows meeting, nose rather long; he is full of grace — sometimes looking like a man, sometimes having the countenance of an angel. . . '. There could be no mistake, so Onesiphorus brought Paul to his home, where Paul preached to the circle of believers. His sermon emphasized chastity and its reward in Heaven:

'Blessed are the pure in heart, for they shall see God.
'Blessed are those who keep the flesh holy, for they shall be God's temple.
'Blessed are the chaste, for God shall speak to them.
'Blessed are those who renounce this world, for they shall please God.
'Blessed are those who have wives but are as though they had them not, for they shall inherit God. . . .
'Blessed are the bodies of virgins, for they shall please God and they shall not lose the reward of their chastity. . . .'
When Paul said this in the meeting at Onesiphorus' house, a virgin named Thecla, the daughter of Theocleia, betrothed to a man called Thamyris, sat at the window of the house nearby and listened night and day to what Paul was saying about chastity [figure 44]. And she did not turn from the window, but was encouraged in her faith, with great joy. And seeing many women and girls going in to Paul, she too longed to be thought worthy to stand beside Paul and hear the word of Christ, because she had not yet seen what Paul looked like, but could only hear him speaking.

And when she did not leave the window, her mother sent for Thamyris. He came with great joy, thinking that he was now going to take her as his wife. So Thamyris said to Theocleia 'Where is my Thecla?', and Theocleia said 'I have a strange thing to tell you, Thamyris. For three days and three nights Thecla has not stirred from the window, neither to eat nor to drink. . .Thamyris, this man is stirring up the city of Iconium, and your Thecla as well: all the women and young men are going to him and being told by him that they should fear one god only, as he says, and live in chastity. And what is more, my daughter, caught like a spider in the window in the web of his words, is overcome by a new desire, a frightening passion. . . .' (5–9)

Fiancé, mother, and servants try to recall Thecla to order with prayers and tears, but in vain. From some disloyal members of the congregation Thamyris has his worst apprehensions confirmed: Paul is preaching in favour of virginity and against marriage, he is robbing women of their bridegrooms and men of their brides by proclaiming: 'You will not share in the Resurrection, unless you remain pure, not defiling your flesh, but keeping it pure.'

Thamyris' jealousy is awakened: Thecla is no doubt in love with the stranger and he himself will be robbed of his bride. Now Thamyris is not just anybody: he is the leading citizen of Iconium. At the head of a furious crowd he fetches the 'wizard', drags him before the governor of the province, and loudly accuses him of not

Fig. 44 *Paul and Thecla in an Egyptian ivory relief (fifth century AD). The left half shows St Paul sitting with a book roll in his hands. He reads or preaches, and Thecla listens thoughtfully from her position inside a house with a tower. Perhaps it is their first meeting in Iconium that is visualized in this way. To the right St Paul is threatened with stoning: the standing man lifts a stone in his right hand, in the fold of his garment he holds more ammunition.*

permitting young girls to marry. Paul in his defence states that he is
only following the commandments of God, and is put in prison.

At night, Thecla took off her bracelets and gave them to the gatekeeper,
and when the door was opened for her she went into the prison. She gave
the warden a silver mirror and went in to Paul, and sat at his feet and
heard of God's mighty deeds. And Paul was not afraid at all, but talked
with her in the freedom of God's word. And her faith grew, and she kissed
his chains. (18)

Thecla's relatives search for her; she is eventually found in the
prison, 'a kind of co-prisoner [of Paul] through her love'. Paul is
again brought before the court; Thecla rolls in the dust at the place
where Paul had been sitting preaching in prison. She is also summoned into court, and goes there happy and proud. Paul is flogged
and driven out of town, Thecla is sentenced to be burnt at the stake
in the theatre before the governor and all the people. Her eyes
search for Paul, 'like a lamb in the desert looking around for its
shepherd'. She discovers the Lord sitting among the spectators in the
guise of Paul and takes courage.

The boys and girls brought wood and dry grass to burn Thecla. When she
was brought in, naked, the governor wept and wondered at the strength in
her. The executioners spread out the wood and told her to get up on the
pyre. She made the sign of the cross and climbed up on the wood, and they
lit the fire. And great flames blazed up; but the fire did not touch her,
because God in His pity caused a rumbling under the ground, and a cloud
came in the sky, full of rain and hail, and the whole theatre was flooded, so
that many people were endangered and lost their lives, and the fire was put
out and Thecla was saved.(22)

In the meantime Paul dwells in an open grave outside Iconium. He
sighs over Thecla and prays to God that the fire shall not harm her.
Thecla searches for him and after six days finds him there. She
bursts into prayers of thanksgiving to God for having saved her from
death, so that she may see Paul. The reunion is celebrated with five
loaves of bread, vegetables, water, and salt.

And Thecla said to Paul 'I shall cut off my hair and follow you wherever
you go.' And Paul said 'These are bad times, and you are beautiful; I hope
you are not caught in some other trial, worse than the first, and cannot en-
dure it but turn coward.' And Thecla said 'Only mark me with the sign of
Christ, and trials shall not touch me.' And Paul said 'Thecla, be of good
courage, and you shall be baptized.' (25)

Paul brings Thecla with him to Antioch in Pisidia. A high official by the name of Alexander sees Thecla and immediately falls in love with her. He wants to buy her from Paul, but Paul denies her: 'I do not know that woman. . .'. Alexander embraces Thecla in the middle of the street; she cries out shrilly that he must not use violence against a servant of God, rips his clothes to pieces, and tears off the wreath he is wearing on his head. She is again dragged into court, admits her guilt, and is sentenced to be thrown to the beasts. Women among the audience protest, shouting: 'An unjust sentence, a godless sentence!', but Thecla's only request is to be allowed to remain virgin till the execution. A rich widow, Tryphaena, whose daughter has recently died, takes care of her and comforts her. The dead daughter appears in a dream, urging her mother to regard Thecla as her own daughter; through Thecla's intercession the dead daughter herself will be transferred to the dwellings of the righteous. When the day appointed arrives, Tryphaena prevents Alexander's men from dragging Thecla away and herself conducts her to the place of execution.

Thecla was stripped, and seized a cloth to cover herself. She was thrown into the arena, and lions and bears were let loose on her. A fierce lioness bounded towards her and lay down at her feet; and the crowd of women cried out loudly. And a bear ran at her; but the lioness ran to face the bear and ripped it apart. Then a lion belonging to Alexander, that had been trained to attack humans, rushed at her; and the lioness grappled with the lion and both were killed. The women cried more loudly in grief now that the lioness that had helped her was dead.

Then they sent in many wild beasts; she stood with outstretched arms, praying (figure 45). And when she had finished praying, she turned and saw a great artificial lake, filled with water, and said 'Now it is time for my bath.' And she jumped in, saying 'I am baptized on my dying day in the name of Jesus Christ.' And when they saw this, the women and the whole crowd wept and cried 'Do not throw yourself into the water', so that even the governor wept, that seals should devour such beauty. So she threw herself into the water in the name of Jesus Christ; and the seals were killed by the sight of a flash of lightning, and floated up to her dead. And there was a cloud of fire round her, so that neither did the beasts touch her nor was she seen naked. (33–4)

More wild animals are set on Thecla, but they become dazed by perfumes and volatile oils thrown into the arena by the women. She is tied to raging bulls, but a flame burns through her fetters. At the sight of this Tryphaena collapses. She is believed to be dead, and people take fright: what if the Emperor, her relative, is informed of the circumstances of her death! The baiting is interrupted, and Thecla testifies before the governor that she is the servant of the living God; that is why the beasts have not touched her. She is dressed and solemnly set free; the women rejoice and thank God so loudly that the whole town vibrates.

Tryphaena, who has regained consciousness, once more takes care of Thecla. 'But Thecla longed for Paul, sent messages all around, and searched for him everywhere.' She hears that he is in Myra on the south coast and goes there, dressed in a man's clothes. He is struck with wonder upon seeing her, and she proudly announces that she has received baptism. Paul takes her hand and leads her to the house in which he is a guest. He listens to her wonderful story. Then Thecla rises, saying: 'I am going to Iconium,'

Fig. 45 *Thecla as a martyr. From Seleucia in Pisidia the cult of Thecla soon spread over much of the Orient and Europe: via Rome and Milan it reached Cologne as early as the third century, and via the Middle East it penetrated into Egypt, as this Coptic lime-stone relief (sixth century?) shows. The victory of faith is represented by simple and expressive means: the wild animals attack Thecla in vain, nor can the flames hurt her, where she stands half-naked, receiving the cross in her lifted arms. Apart from the cross, the picture might as well have illustrated any of the pagan novels, in which hero and heroine suffer similar martyrdoms (see figure 23).*

and Paul answers: 'Go and preach the word of God!'

Thecla returns to her home town. Her ex-fiancé is dead, but her mother is still alive. Thecla bears witness to God at Iconium as well as in nearby Seleucia, at last passing away in a peaceful sleep, 'having enlightened many with the word of God'.

These are the main lines of one of the many versions of the story of *Paul and Thecla* which survive in Greek, Latin, and several oriental and slavic languages. The tradition is of the same 'wild' nature as that of the *Alexander Romance*. Some Greek manuscripts have her stay for many years in a cave high up on a mountain, where she cures sick people on such a scale that the doctors in the district of Seleucia are in danger of becoming unemployed. They come together to discuss the serious situation in the labour market, and the Devil suggests to them the idea that they should hire some unscrupulous men to rape Thecla: if she ceases to be a virgin, her wonderful power will be gone. The plan is carried out, but at the critical moment God intervenes and makes the rock open behind Thecla. She enters, the rock closes again behind her, and only a patch of her veil in the hands of the assailants testifies to what has happened. Underground, Thecla sets out for Rome to see Paul; but he has already died, and shortly afterwards Thecla too, by now ninety years old, passes away and is buried near her master's grave.

All through the middle ages this theme is elaborated in many ways, as is shown not least by the art of the period. In the modern period also Thecla has continued to exercise her charm. An amusing example is a work by the first Swedish novelist, Jacob Mörk, which was published in Stockholm in 1749–58 under the title of *Thecla, Eller Den Bepröfwade Trones Dygd*: 'Thecla, Or the Virtue of Well-Tried Faith'. Here it is the Emperor Nero who falls a victim to the attraction of the maiden, but is of course rebuffed. The jealousy of the empress, military operations, and a number of martyrdoms fill the novel, but Thecla always escapes safe and sound.

There were many stories of this type circulating in antiquity, attached to one apostle or other: Peter and Paul (together, or separately); Thomas (who carries his mission to India and suffers martyrdom there); Andrew (who is crucified for having exercised a harmful influence on Maximilla, the wife of the governor of Achaea); John, Philip, and others. The conventional collective label is 'apocryphal Acts of the Apostles' — 'apocryphal' originally perhaps because their genesis, authors, and true purpose were 'hidden'. In the Greek manuscripts they are called *praxeis*, 'doings', 'acts' ('The Acts of Paul and Thecla', etc.), corresponding to the

Latin *acta*; or sometimes *periodoi*, 'wanderings' or 'tours', which is
no bad description.

From one point of view, however, the designation 'novels of the
apostles' would be more appropriate. Novelistic motifs abound. In
Paul and Thecla we met the beautiful young girl (seventeen years of
age when the story begins), her fiancé of noble birth, who later also
plays the part of a jealous rival, the travel motif, the separation and
search, the summary trial, and the wonderful escape from cruel
punishment. Compare Habrocomes crucified and burnt at the
stake, p. 30, and Charicleia undergoing a similar ordeal, p. 67.
Thecla visits Paul in prison, as Antheia visits Habrocomes. To
rebuff Alexander's advances she refers to her status as 'servant of
God', just as Antheia in a similar situation alleges that she is consecrated to Isis. Thecla is prepared to cut off her hair, and later appears in a man's clothes, like Thelxinoe in the story of the old
fisherman in Xenophon's novel (p. 25). Other motifs reappear in
other 'Acts': storm and shipwreck, the heroine sold to a brothel,
oracles and dreams, poisoned drinks, and so on.

As we have seen, the erotic element lies all the while beneath the
surface: Paul and Thecla do not get married, but eyes, gestures, and
speech indicate that their relationship is not of an exclusively
spiritual kind. Thecla's first reaction when she hears Paul preaching
in the neighbouring house — she does not touch food or drink, she
worries her family by her distracted behaviour — is reminiscent of
the purely physical manifestations of awakening love in, for instance, the *Ephesiaca*. Chastity is a principal motif in the novels as
well; Charicleia in particular constantly sings its praises in the
Ethiopica, and it is preserved at all costs until the final reunion of
the loving couple. The apostle heroine preserves it even unto death:
the final step on the way to asceticism has now been taken.

However, these similarities in narrative structure and motifs do
not imply that the Acts of the Apostles should be regarded as 'novels'
tout court. They have other important elements, for instance those
linking them to 'aretalogy', miracle tales demonstrating the power of
the gods over mankind. And we should not forget the motifs which
the Acts, at least the later of them, have in common with the
fabulous travel stories: Matthew arrives in the country of the man-
eaters, and visits an ideal community of the Iambulus and
Euhemerus type (above, p. 117), dog-headed men and giants appear in the *Acts of Bartholomew*, and so forth. On the whole, it is
inadvisable, as has sometimes been attempted, to press a paternity
suit, categorically proving or disproving that the Acts are

'descended' from one genre or other. The history of the birth of the novel was repeated once again: a new historical situation, with new demands, gave rise to a new literary form, which borrowed freely from predecessors and contemporaries. The novel was perhaps the main source for borrowings, and no doubt its popularity was deliberately used to propagate the new faith.

If, for a moment, we view the matter from the point of view of the novel, one particular circumstance is worth noting. The Acts of the Apostles begin to emerge in the second century and then flourish in the third and throughout late antiquity. The more popular type of Greek novel can be followed, thanks to the papyrus finds, through the second century, but no further; instead come the three sophistic novels with their higher literary ambitions. Should we conclude that the broader audience from the third century on was reduced to reading the old novels, or that they had to do without lighter reading of that kind? Presumably the answer is this: the same readership which provided a market for the Hellenistic novel was now devouring stories about apostles, martyrs, and saints. And these stories, slacker in construction than even the *Historia Apollonii* and with many loose ends, may in turn help us to form a better idea of what the more popular type of novel normally looked like. If our analogy is correct, we may establish as a fact that Chariton is on a level far above the average, and in the light of this comparison even Xenophon — who otherwise has most in common with the Acts — leaves an impression of literary discipline.

Somewhere at the back of the apocryphal stories lie of course the canonical Acts of the Apostles: they relate to each other as does the *Alexander Romance* to the genuine Alexander historians. Evidently a need was felt to supplement the meagre information about the life and travels of Paul and the other apostles given in the canonical Acts and in the Epistles, in much the same way as figures from the Old Testament had appeared in romantic stories in Greek, such as *Joseph and Asenath* (an embellishment of Genesis 41:45). Paul's visit to Iconium is thus rather briefly described — and without Thecla! — in Acts 13:51–14:6. If the Hellenistic novel of love offered its readers romanticism of the kind today provided by the serials and short stories in weekly magazines, the apocryphal apostle stories in addition correspond to the gossip column: meet Paul in private! This, however, is just one aspect of it: primarily these stories had a serious, edifying purpose, containing quantities of Christian preaching put into the mouths of the apostles as sermons on suitable occasions.

The apostle stories thus also gave the different movements the chance to propagate their individual variety of the faith; for instance, the *Acts of Thomas* have a clearly Gnostic bent. And in *Paul and Thecla*, besides the advocacy of an ascetic form of life, we are certainly aware of a feminist tendency. We here meet a Paul who eventually, albeit reluctantly, allows women to speak in the congregation: 'having fought her way through the martyrdoms, she was entrusted with the office of apostle by the holy and respected apostle Paul', says the explicit statement found in one of the manuscripts. Moreover women are throughout on the side of the good in the story — witness the noble widow Tryphaena and the female spectators at the trials and martyrdoms — while the men are usually heathens and brutes. That *Paul and Thecla* was written by a female author — and that women continued adapting and adding to the story in the course of centuries — seems to be the natural inference; though whether the apostle story is an heir to the novel in this particular respect as well (see above, p. 96) is of course less certain.

Tertullian, who in his treatise *On Baptism* (*c*. AD 200) is the first to refer to the existence of the *Acts of Paul*, of which *Paul and Thecla* forms a part, is unhappy with the idea of a woman teaching and baptizing. He reports that the author of these false Acts, a priest in Asia Minor, was properly punished, though claiming in his defence to have written them 'out of love for Paul'. If Tertullian's information is correct, the fact that the author was a man still does not disprove our hypothesis of female authorship for *Paul and Thecla*: this particular part of the *Acts of Paul* is different from the rest, notably in reducing Paul to a minor figure, while Thecla takes the lead. Scholars are inclined to believe that the priest in question was less of a real author than a compiler, who sometimes rather mechanically included in his Acts accounts written by others. In that case, the story of *Paul and Thecla* started as an independent piece of writing, exactly as it later escaped once more from its larger context and led a flourishing life throughout the middle ages as the Legend of Thecla, her life and miracles.

The Pseudo-Clementines, a Christian Novel

The literary and sub-literary landscape around the Apocryphal Acts of the Apostles is covered by a dense, almost impenetrable vegetation: stories of miracles, acts of martyrs, lives of monks. . . . But one distinctive work, *The Pseudo-Clementines*, rises above its surroundings and may rightly claim to be called the first genuine

Christian novel, even though it is built on the remains of a pagan one.

The work's name stems from the fact that its first-person narrator and principal character is Clement, Peter's successor as Bishop of Rome; but he is not the author. Of the oldest versions surviving one, called the *Homilies*, is in Greek, whereas the other is in Latin and bears the name *Recognitiones*, or 'Recognitions', after the well-known novel motif. They both belong to the fourth century, but are derived from a common Greek original of the second or third century, probably circulating under the title *Periodoi Petrou*, 'The Preaching Tours of Peter'. Its content may be reconstructed in the following manner:

The young Roman, Clement, is a seeker after truth. He goes to Palestine in order to hear about Jesus. In Caesarea he meets Peter and accompanies him on a preaching tour in Phoenicia. He is present at a theological debate between Peter and Simon the Magician (who also appears in Acts, 8). Clement tells the story of his life to Peter: when he was a child, his mother left home together with her two elder sons, who were twins, and they have all been missing ever since; later on his father went away to search for them, and he too has not returned; this happened twenty years ago. Now, through Peter's agency, something wonderful takes place: on the island of Aradus — where Chariton too set his recognition scene (above, p. 13) — Clement is reunited to his mother, and in Laodicea in Syria he meets up again his two older brothers; they had been separated from their mother by a shipwreck, sold as slaves by pirates, but then adopted by a rich woman and given a good education. At last they are all reunited with their father, and the complex threads are disentangled.

This typically novelistic intrigue — the *Historia Apollonii* immediately comes to mind — is, however, embedded in a piece of writing in which the preaching is the main content. It is quite conceivable that the author constructed the plot himself on the pattern of the pagan novels, but some specific traits, for instance the entirely unexploited motif of the twins, make it more probable that he simply took over parts of a ready-made story. Using them as the basis he erected the superstructure which was his primary concern: a defence of the Christian faith. The surviving adaptations differ in the emphasis they lay upon the two types of subject-matter: the novelistic intrigue is more developed in the *Recognitiones*, the disputations and sermons of Peter grow more exuberant in the *Homilies*. There are polemics against polytheism, classical mythology, pagan philosophy, and especially against astrology, to which Clement's poor father has become addicted in his despair over the unlucky fate of his family. His sons have a tough job trying to guide him to the right faith.

The original work seems to have been directed at pagans, while the later additions and adaptations took a stand on internal Christian issues. The novelistic form was the means of attracting pagan readers. The aim was, then, rather similar to that of the Apocryphal Acts of the Apostles; but the preaching and argumentation are here on a distinctly higher level. The author obviously had a more intellectual audience in mind, presumably those who read the sophistic novels.

Hagiographic Novels

Hagiography, writings about saints, became one of the most important literary genres of the middle ages. The collective concept covers books of very different kinds, popular or ultra-literary, fictitious or factual; this mirrors the genre's varied background in ancient literature. The life of the saint is generally followed from birth to death: thus the biographies of monks were among the main models. This genre had received its classical form in the fourth century in Athanasius' *Life of St Antony*, the Egyptian monk; a work which itself had been influenced by the pagan lives of philosophers (above, p. 115). The death of the future saint was almost always a martyrdom: thus the ancient Acts of the Martyrs were an important — perhaps the most important — source of inspiration for the hagiographic writers. We could discern elements of this in *Paul and Thecla* as well. The point of departure might have been reports of court proceedings or authentic eye-witness accounts of an execution, but the theme itself irresistibly led to the invention of more and more sensational detail. The hagiographic novel is the life of a saint in which the fictitious element has got the upper hand.

The factual element may consist solely of the name of the saint: the feast of a given saint was sometimes celebrated without anything being known about his or her real achievements, and fantasy was allowed free play. Thus a life was constructed of purely conventional materials, though perhaps an authentic touch was added through the localization of the events to one's own surroundings and by introducing historically known persons into the action; then a dramatic and touching martyrdom was invented as the end of the earthly existence of the saint.

The hagiographic novel which was to become most widely known does not however quite fit into this standard frame. *Barlaam and Joasaph* is the story of the Indian prince Joasaph, who after a sheltered childhood in the royal palace is struck by a sudden awareness of the evil of the world. By the agency of the monk Barlaam he is converted to the Christian faith, founds a Christian kingdom, and eventually spends his last years together with Barlaam as a pious hermit in the desert. Not until the mid-nineteenth century, when Joasaph and Barlaam had been worshipped as Christian saints for a thousand years, was it finally realized that this is in fact the Indian legend of the Buddha in a Christianized version — the form of the name, Joasaph, derives via Arabic from the Indian Bodhisattva. Exactly how the legend wound up in the West and took its Christian form is a matter of dispute: are the Persian and Arabic versions, and the Christian one in Georgian, to be regarded as intermediaries, and who gave the novel its Greek form? The Orthodox theologian John Damascene (*c.* 675–750) and the Georgian abbot Euthymius Iberites (*c.* 955–1028) are the main candidates. Whoever it was, the Greek version is no pure translation, but an adaptation with literary qualities by a learned theologian, who added much subject-matter of his own to the story. This version was then the point of departure for a long series of renderings into various languages. For example, via Latin it reaches northern Scandinavia in an Old Norse version, the *Barlaams ok Josaphats saga* (mid-thirteenth century).

Barlaam and Joasaph is then one more instance of the phenomenon which we have met so many times in the last two chapters: the 'popular book' which, while not originating as any kind of folk-tale or popular composition, being rather the result of deliberate literary creation, during its progress through the centuries and across linguistic frontiers always succeeded in adapting itself to its surroundings and in winning new readers.

CHAPTER VII

The Roman Comic Novel

As we have seen, the Greek novel is mainly serious in tone and purpose, an ideal novel of love and sentiment. Only Achilles Tatius among the surviving five differs from this pattern, with his slightly ironical distance from his hero and the events of his story. By contrast, in Latin two voluminous prose novels exist of a distinctly different kind: the *Satyricon* by Petronius and the *Metamorphoses*, or *The Golden Ass*, by Apuleius. They are realistic and comic, with a strong tendency towards satire and burlesque. The author of the *Satyricon* is in all likelihood identical with the Petronius who was Emperor Nero's *arbiter elegantiae*, 'Arbiter of Taste', and whose character, career, and death are poignantly described by Tacitus in his *Annals*. If this is the case, the novel dates from *c.* AD 65. Apuleius, a hundred years later, was an African by birth and a sophist of the kind we have already encountered (above, p. 105), though his primary language was Latin (figure 46). His *Metamorphoses* has been variously placed in the mid- or late second century AD. Both novels show a sometimes bewildering mixture of high and low elements, of advanced literary exercises and low-comic or pornographic scenes. The authors belonged to the upper stratum of society and evidently did not have to hide behind any pseudonyms. Their books, being from the very beginning intended as sophisticated entertainment for a literarily cultivated audience, have to this day retained a much higher literary reputation than the ideal Greek novel.

Indeed, to appeal to the cultivated was probably their only hope, since there does not seem to have existed in the Latin-speaking part of the empire any really broadly based literate audience to address; there was no counterpart to the comparatively widespread literacy in the Greek Hellenistic world which was the prerequisite of the non-sophistic Greek novel. Nor do the Roman novels bear the mark of having been designed for recital. While Chariton mostly appears before his 'audience' in the role of a *narrator*, it is significant that Apuleius starts by turning to his 'reader': *lector, intende. . .* ('Pay

Fig. 46 *Apuleius on a Roman contorniate medallion (see figure 31). He wears a wreath and has long flowing hair, perhaps indicative of his African origin: he was born c. AD 125 in the Roman colony of Madauros in modern Algeria. It was hardly as a novelist that Apuleius was honoured with a medallion — his fame in late antiquity rested rather on his merits as a philosopher (he was a Neo-Platonist) and as a magician. He was even put on trial for having won a rich widow as his wife by the use of magic. His defence in court, his **Apologia**, which has survived, is an eloquent plea for a philosophical way of life; while the accusation of meddling in the black arts is scornfully repudiated. He was acquitted, and this — it is alleged — only added to his reputation as a miracle-worker.*

attention, dear reader . . .'); and from time to time continues to address him in the second person singular. It is quite another matter that his style is largely built on acoustic effects (rhymes, assonances, alliteration): as a practising sophist he naturally used the tricks of his trade even when writing a novel. Nor should we forget that the ancient reader usually read aloud even in private; in that sense all literature was 'oral', and people were no doubt more sensitive to such devices than we generally are.

For the educated Romans the elevated constituents of the *Satyricon* and the *Metamorphoses* — the allusions to famous poems like the *Aeneid*, the parodic discussion of literature, art, and philosophy — may have served as a kind of justification for at the same time revelling in sex, sadism, and jokes about physical or mental defects. The artistic quality is indeed high: both authors are masters of style, their satire is to the point, and each gives us in his way unique insights into the social conditions of his time. Their importance for the future, as models for the picaresque novel, is at the very least as great as Heliodorus' influence was in his field. Consequently a considerable amount of philological research and literary criticism has been devoted to them, though the present rapid survey can give no more than a few hints of this activity. The primary purpose here is to point out the historical and typological connections between the Roman and the Greek novel, which justify, in spite of all their differences, referring to them together as 'the ancient novel'.

Petronius: Satyricon

The *Satyricon* has survived only in extracts. The most extensive and well-known of them is the 'Cena Trimalchionis', 'Trimalchio's Feast', a crushing satire on an upstart who has assumed a rich man's behaviour: the freedman Trimalchio keeps court like a second Nero, excelling in capriciousness, vulgarity, and in reciting his own poetic trash. The burlesque banquet scene (figure 47) is just one in a

Fig. 47 'Trimalchio's Feast' is the climax of Petronius' novel **Satyricon**, at least of the extant parts of this huge work. Trimalchio, the former slave, is given all the defects of a nouveau-riche upstart: vulgarity mingled with literary dilettantism, and a boisterous jocularity that can tip over into brutality at a moment's notice. The illustration, from a French translation of 1694, shows the feast's magnificent facade, with musicians playing and slaves carrying dishes laden with culinary delights.

series of genre pictures drawn from contemporary Roman life which Petronius had inserted into what was to become, some 1500 years later, the conventional framework of the picaresque: an anti-hero, a comic reversal of Odysseus or Aeneas on his wanderings through the world, meets with a wide variety of people and gets caught up in diverse strange adventures. Petronius' anti-hero and narrator is called Encolpius; he is a Greek student from southern Italy with studies in rhetoric behind him. During his travels he picks up a beautiful slave boy, Giton, with whom he has fallen in love. Another educated youth, Ascyltus, joins with them, and the situation soon develops into a typical *ménage-à-trois*, characterized by solidarity against the outside world and fierce jealousy among themselves. The surviving fragments mostly give only short glimpses of their not very decorous tour from town to town in Italy and Gaul: theft and murder, charlatanism and blasphemy, and above all sex, of both kinds: bisexuality was in vogue in the Roman circles in which Petronius moved.

The original compass of the novel has been a cherished matter of scholarly dispute. To my mind there are no very good reasons to doubt the information given in some, admittedly late, manuscripts to the effect that the 'Cena Trimalchionis' was the fifteenth 'book' of the *Satyricon*, whereas the other, shorter fragments belonged to the immediately preceding and following 'books'. If this is correct, we are concerned with a true mastodon of an ancient novel, comprising maybe twenty books (or twenty-four, as in the *Odyssey*?), the equivalent of something between five hundred and a thousand printed pages (the length of ancient 'books' varies considerably). Several scholars have considered this great size totally unbelievable; in fact, however, similar or even higher figures are reported in the case of two more or less contemporary Greek works of prose fiction, the *Babyloniaca* by Iamblichus (sixteen or thirty-nine books, see p. 32) and *The Marvels beyond Thule* by Antonius Diogenes (twenty-four books, see p. 118). Even such a voluminous *Satyricon* would not measure up to a modern novel like *War and Peace*: J. P. Sullivan estimates the *Satyricon* at 400,000 words, *War and Peace* at 650,000. On the whole it is unwise, as far as episodic works of this kind are concerned, to state categorically that they could not have been much longer than their surviving extracts. 'Trimalchio's Feast', describing a single evening in the roving life of Encolpius fills a complete, lengthy book on its own.

Whether Petronius was able to keep up the same high standard all through the novel is of course another question; usually it is not chance alone that decides what parts of an ancient literary work are to survive, while others fall into oblivion. As far as we know, the *Satyricon* is the only major literary creation by Petronius. In it he invested his whole artistic talent, demonstrating his keen eye for human weaknesses and exploring his facility for widely different styles: lofty (not always parodic) poetry, cultivated spoken language, the vulgarisms and slang of the freedmen. What is left to us, then, is presumably just a small, and perhaps the best, section of a very broad description of Roman society in the time of Nero, seen in a distorting mirror.

The *Satyricon* is above all a *Roman* work. The principal characters are Greek, but it is Roman society that is mirrored, and Roman literary genres — or at least those genres brought to their perfection on Roman soil — that have put their distinctive mark on the product. The first form to come to mind is of course satire, which developed into a great genre in Rome in the hands of Lucilius, Horace, and others, even if this form too had its roots in Greek literature. The Menippean satire, so called after its Greek creator, the Cynic philosopher Menippus (third century BC), was written in a mixture of verse and prose, *prosimetrum*. Its Latin equivalent was developed by Varro, a contemporary of Cicero, and influenced Petronius to break up his prose narrative with passages in verse. At times the purpose is clearly parodic, but as I have already mentioned, there are some places where the tone of elevated poetry is seriously evoked; we may recall Chariton's more naïve manner of weaving quotations from Homer into his narration.

The sort of satire with which we are familiar from Horace is often evident in Petronius' depiction of the different types of characters Encolpius meets on his odyssey. The low-comic elements in turn are taken from the Roman mime, in which sadism and sexual perversion ran riot: Petronius' text is full of direct references to that kind of scenic show, which enjoyed an enormous popularity in Rome. The more refined erotic tales, on the other hand, such as 'The Widow of Ephesus' (figure 48) — the genre which Boccaccio brought to perfection in the *Decameron* — are Greek in origin: they belong to the 'Milesian' tradition, to which I shall return below in connection with Apuleius. Moreover, the narrative frame itself, surrounding this extremely varied collection, was probably inspired by Greek literature, in the first instance by the ideal novel.

That the *Satyricon* should be a parody of the Greek ideal novel may be regarded as a rather obvious supposition. The theme of travel is common to both. The chaste heterosexual love of the Greek novel has its equivalent in the homosexual orgies of the *Satyricon*, the former's moral tone is matched by the latter's total immorality and freedom from established convention. Whereas the chaste Artemis initially guides the course of events in Xenophon's *Ephesiaca* and Aphrodite unites Chaereas and Callirhoe in Chariton's novel, the whole of the *Satyricon* proceeds under the sign of Priapus, the fertility god usually venerated in phallic form. Obvious as the supposition may seem, it has however not been accepted by the majority of Roman scholars. This was only natural as long as the Greek novel was looked on as a product of the imperial age: the idea that Petronius should have had Greek models was rejected as empty speculation, with the exception of the *Satyricon's* self-evident connection with the old epic — for instance, Priapus as the counterpart of Poseidon in the *Odyssey*: subjected to the wrath of each of these gods, anti-hero and hero are driven around the world. But with the dating of the Greek novel to Hellenistic times the situation should now be different, and recently P. G. Walsh in his excellent introduction to the Roman novel has proposed a less rigid view of the concept of 'influence'. Without denying the genuinely Roman character of the *Satyricon* it is possible to admit its structural similarity to the Greek novel and to explain it in historical terms. I shall examine the similar points in rather more detail, mainly following Walsh's exposition.

Fig. 48 'The Widow of Ephesus' is a short story told by one of the characters in Petronius' novel; since then it has wandered through world literature. An Ephesian woman, renowned for her chastity, loses her husband. Her grief is so deep that after the funeral she refuses to leave the burial chamber; she wishes to starve to death at the side of her dead husband, and everyone admires her idealism and love. But nearby lies the place of execution, where some robbers have just been crucified. The soldier who guards their bodies sees a light shining in the burial chamber, approaches, and is enchanted by the widow's beauty. He tempts her first with food and drink, and she eats. Then he lays siege to her chastity and is victorious in this campaign too. They spend three amorous nights together in the grave, with the door shut to encourage passers-by to believe that the chaste widow has died from starvation grieving over her husband's dead body. Meanwhile the parents of one of the executed robbers take the opportunity to steal their son's body to give him an honourable burial. Terrified, the soldier sees his imminent punishment — but the widow solves the problem, as our illustration (of 1694) shows: she lets her husband take the robber's place on the cross. 'Better sacrifice the dead than kill the living'!

LA MATRONE
D'EPHESE.

First of all we have the episodic structure, with the theme of travel
as its backbone. It is of course possible to maintain that this structure is epic in general, or that the Hellenistic tales of travel followed
the same pattern; however, the loving couple travelling from town
to town in the familiar Mediterranean world is something more
specific. Further, the fluctuations in the homosexual relationship
between Encolpius and Giton may well be seen as a burlesque on the
scheme of the early Greek novel of love: hero and heroine fall in
love, get married, are separated by force — though the separation
motif is not so prominent in Petronius (nor in Longus, for that matter) — are afflicted by jealousy when real or supposed rivals appear
on the scene, and so on. Shipwreck threatens the lovers' lives (figure
49), they seek consolation in each other. Attempted suicide,
rhetorical lamentations, elaborate court scenes are further motivic
similarities. Fate (Tyche/Fortuna) interferes in the action, is invoked or cursed. Other gods too have a finger in the pie: for his salvation Encolpius thanks Mercury, the god of thieves! As Walsh
points out, Petronius' satire is directed against hypocrisy in three
areas: religion, learning, and wealth. This serious message is
conveyed in an eminently entertaining form, and one of the
elements in the entertainment is poking fun at the ideal novel and
its, to the *Satyricon's* sophisticated readership, naïve advocacy of
virtues like chastity, fidelity, and piety.

   A papyrus published recently, the so-called *Iolaus* fragment, has
resurrected the discussion about whether the *Satyricon* could even
have had a direct precedent of its own genre, a realistic comic novel
in Greek. The style and spirit of the fragment's exposé of the
mysteries of Cybele, with its erotic accents and vulgar vocabulary,
no doubt remind one of Petronius. Unfortunately, however, the
date of the papyrus (second century AD) does not allow any conclusions about priority; Petronius may well have been the earlier.
Nor is it certain that what we have here is the remains of a full-scale
novel; if the complete work was a short story, the find is less
sensational, as we shall see in the next section.

Fig. 49 *The shipwreck. Encolpius, the narrator and anti-hero of
Petronius' novel, delivers a funeral oration over the captain, Lichas, who
was drowned when his ship went down. The shipwreck is a stock motif in
the ideal Greek novels, in which it is usually framed by passages of pathetic
rhetoric. Petronius misses no opportunity to make fun of such clichés.*

Le
NAUFRAGE
de
LYCAS.

The Greek Story of the Ass

If, then, Petronius' *Satyricon* should be regarded as an original Roman work, borrowing its basic structure from the Greek novel and taking the opportunity to parody its idealizing streak, the *Metamorphoses* of Apuleius on the other hand has demonstrably sprung more organically from a Greek tradition. The tradition, however, is not that of the ideal novel but that of the burlesque short story. Such a story was *Lucius or The Ass*, which Apuleius developed into a novel. His novel preserves the burlesque but at the same time has a serious aim. It is in addition stylistically more refined than its model. In the process, between the states of burlesque and edifying novel, elements of the ideal novel have also been absorbed. But let us take one thing at a time and start with the Greek *Story of the Ass*.

The main outline of the story is as follows. The narrator, a certain Lucius of Patras (N Peloponnese), recounts the story of a business trip he once made to Thessaly. His curiosity about the magic arts for which this province was famous led him near to destruction. The mistress of the house in which he was a guest practised magic, so he seduced the maid in order to get a glimpse of the secret activities of her mistress (figure 50). The maid has been given the eloquent name of Palaestra, 'wrestling-place', and the act of love itself is consistently described as a wrestling-match, hold by hold. As a recompense the maid lets him peep at her mistress when, at night, she turns herself into a bird and flies away to her lover. He asks the maid to rub him with the same ointment, but to his horror he perceives a tail beginning to grow from his back, his fingers and toes becoming hoofs, and his ears and face being elongated — in short, he is turned into an ass (figures 51−2).

Lucius has experienced his metamorphosis. In order to be restored to human form he has to eat roses. The rest of the story is the amusing account of his fortunes as an ass, in the hands of various human and inhuman owners, while he tries constantly though in vain to get hold of his antidote of roses. Bandits assault the house where he had been staying and use the beasts of burden, Lucius included, to carry away the booty; the poor unpractised ass suffers mightily from the hardship of the Thessalian mountain roads and from the cruelty of men. He falls into the hands of villainous mendicant priests, drudges at a miller's, and so on. At last, in the theatre at Thessalonica, where he is to entertain the audience by copulating with a woman sentenced to death for murder by poisoning, he manages to swallow some roses and so regains his human shape (figure 53). On his return home he thanks the gods for his salvation.

The ass's eye view gives a realistic, comic picture of the world, of different types of men and their behaviour. The story has inherited its realistic art of description and the idea of an animal as the observer of human life from popular narrative. At the same time there are a number of literary borrowings. The robbers' rhetorically studied deliberation about what to do with their fugitive ass and with a captured girl has close parallels in Chariton and Xenophon Ephesius. The motif of the young bride who is kidnapped from her bridegroom also smacks of the novel, as does the end of the story with votive gifts after a happy homecoming. The narrative structure too resembles that of the novel: Lucius/the ass travels from Patras

Fig. 50 *'How gracefully, my lovely Palaestra,' said I, 'you move and tilt your bottom in harmony with the pot. The small of your back ripples like liquid to my eyes. Lucky man, whoever dips in there.' She, however, being a very bold little girl as well as a charmer, said: 'Young man, you would get out of here if you have any sense and want to live longer — it's full of fire and the fragrance of hot meat. If you were just to touch it, you'd have a severe burn and you'd be a slave to it, believe me, and no one else, not even a divine doctor, would cure you except myself alone, the one who burnt you.' This is the beginning of the seduction scene between Lucius and the maid in the Greek* **Story of the Ass,** *and Apuleius (to whose novel the illustration of 1872 belongs) takes over the dialogue into Latin almost word for word.*

through Thessaly and Macedonia to Thessalonica, and into the framework of his journey are inserted episodes of great variety.

Yet one hesitates simply to class *The Story of the Ass* with the other Greek novels, or to call it a parody of such a novel. The similarities in structure are after all general; among other things, the splitting up of the action into the different experiences of two lovers, typical of the novel, is missing here. The erotic descriptions are comic and burlesque, and there are no indications of any intention to ridicule the chaste counterparts in the novels. Of course the ass — meeting with attacks by robbers, being near death as a 'propitiatory sacrifice', delivering platitudinous inner monologues or cursing his fate — is in a way a comic equivalent of the novels' heroines, such as Callirhoe or Leucippe. However, the comic effect is more direct than that: an ass in these human situations is something comical enough in itself, without the additional level of literary parody.

Figs. 51–2 *Lucius changing into an ass, in two versions. Figure 51, taken from a French translation of 1584 of Apuleius' novel, by way of a double-exposure technique shows both the process itself (Lucius' ears growing, etc.) and the end result. Figure 52, from 1872, captures the burlesque qualities of the **Story of the Ass**. Shakespeare transferred this*

There are nevertheless good reasons for not being too categorical when trying to define the 'true nature' of *The Story of the Ass*. It survives only in a shortened version, which has come down to us among the writings of Lucian the satirist (above, p. 118). We therefore have no way of knowing the exact compass and nature of the original story, though recent investigation has shown beyond reasonable doubt that the story never was very long: probably less than half of it fell a victim to the epitomizer's blue pencil. The abbreviation affected mainly the descriptive elements and presumably also a certain, limited, number of stories within the story, whereas the primary narrative frame was left intact. This can be established through a minute comparison with Apuleius' novel, such as has recently been carried out by Helmut van Thiel. Apuleius clearly started from the complete Greek version. He worked so much subject-matter of his own into it that it multiplied in length, but it has proved possible to identify, along with his genuinely new

*comic effect to the stage: the ass's head carried by Bottom the Weaver in **A Midsummer Night's Dream** is probably borrowed from Apuleius, whose novel had appeared in William Adlington's English translation in 1566.*

material, certain elements that must have belonged to the original, even though they are missing in the surviving Greek abbreviation.

Apuleius: Metamorphoses

We leave behind the comparatively simple Greek *Story of the Ass*, which in all likelihood was intended chiefly to entertain, and enter the more complex novel structure of the *Metamorphoses*, with its much-debated ambivalence, its blend of seriousness and frivolity. While we meet in Apuleius most of the subject-matter contained in the shortened Greek version of the story, there are also substantial additions of various kinds. On the formal level, one is immediately struck by the extent to which Apuleius pads out the borrowed main story stylistically. This is demonstrated by the following juxtaposition. Of course some allowance must be made for the effects the shortening may have had on the Greek version, but there is every reason to believe that most of the additions in the Latin one are the responsibility of Apuleius the sophist alone:

So he took the girl, seated her upon me, and brought her home in this way. When the villagers saw us, still in the distance, they realized that we were all right, since I had brayed out the good news in advance, and so they came running up, embraced us, and led us inside. (*Lucius or The Ass*, 26.5)

He put the girl on my back and directed his path to his home town. As soon as we arrived the whole city poured out for the long-awaited sight. Up rushed her parents, her relatives, her family dependants, young and old, the household slaves, all with happy faces, all overflowing with joy. You would have been seeing a parade of every age and every sex, a new and, by heavens, unforgettable spectacle: a maiden riding in triumph on an ass. Then I myself, as glad as I could be, but not wishing to appear aloof from what was going on, with ears outstretched and nostrils flared, I brayed

Fig. 53 *The ass's wanderings now approach their conclusion: he becomes the lover of a rich and noble lady; in the light of the full moon he receives Isis' promise that he will be transformed back into a man; and this metamorphosis finally takes place in the prescribed manner — we can watch the ass start to consume a wreath of roses, with an immediate effect on his right hand and left foot! These woodcuts are from a 1516 edition of Apuleius, printed in Venice and containing a commentary by Ph. Beroaldus. The illustrations are more decorative than exact representations of the letter and spirit of the text.*

boldly; in fact, I made a noise like thunder. (*Metamorphoses,*
7.12.5–13.3)

The addition of concrete details and the rhetorical elevation of the
account, simple and bare as it was in Greek, alone produce a considerable increase in length. Moreover, characterization has become
more elaborate in Apuleius' hands, and new episodes have been admitted into the central plot. More important still, a substantial
number of stories with a looser connection with the ass theme has
been added, and there is a brand-new ending: purified by his suffering, Lucius is initiated into the mysteries of Isis (see above, p. 87).
Here the author finally gives up his own ironic distance from his narrator hero and allows him to bear personal witness to the mystery of
salvation. The novel 'undergoes a metamorphosis from comic
romance to moral fable and religious apologia' (P. G. Walsh). Incidentally, in so doing it approaches the Greek ideal novel, which also
has an edifying tendency: there the happy ending may be interpreted as the gods' reward for the preservation of chastity in the face
of threat and temptation.

This transformation of Apuleius' novel, in its eleventh and last
book, into a serious edifying work is however not as unexpected as
has sometimes been suggested. There are several premonitions,
though mostly hidden to the uninitiated reader. Worshippers of Isis
will no doubt already have sensed the symbolic meaning in Lucius'
transformation into an *ass*, even though this is embedded in an
overtly grotesque scene taken directly from the Greek model. In the
Isis cult, the ass is directly associated with Seth-Typhon, the evil
power of the myth of Isis and Osiris. To be turned into an ass and
finally to be delivered from that shape are thus intensely meaningful
events. So Apuleius quite deliberately chose the story of an ass to
convey his message of salvation from human bondage: the amusing
package is organically related to its serious content.

Another premonition of the end, less easy to ignore than the
earlier one, comes right in the middle of the novel: in a break from
the burlesque adventures of the ass, we have the deeply serious tale
of Cupid and Psyche. This long inset story was not inherited from
the Greek model, nor taken over from any other source; it is
Apuleius' own creation, and on it rests much of his literary reputation in later times. It is about the beautiful princess Psyche, who is
object of Venus' wrath. The goddess sends her son Cupid (Amor) to
punish her, but he falls in love with Psyche and makes her his
wife — on one condition: she is never to be allowed to see who he is.

She lives in a fantastic palace and is visited by her winged husband by night (figure 54). Her jealous sisters, however, entice her into breaking the agreement: she lights a lamp in order to see her sleeping husband. A drop of hot oil from her lamp awakens Cupid, and he leaves Psyche in a rage (figure 55). She wanders, suffering, through the world, searching for her husband, until she finally chooses to submit to Venus. The goddess subjects her to a series of trials, one of which is to descend to Hades to fetch a jar that she must not open — a temptation which she of course cannot resist. At last she is saved by Cupid, who succeeds in getting Jupiter's permission to marry her. Psyche is admitted to the ranks of the immortals, and Venus dances at her wedding.

Apuleius, using motifs of the kind of which folk-tales are made, has created something approaching a Platonic myth. In some ways it resembles Plato's description in *Phaedrus* of the pilgrimage of the soul — Apuleius himself was in fact a Neo-Platonist. P. G. Walsh has convincingly shown how Apuleius designed the tale as a kind of mythic projection of the story of Lucius. The same lesson is to be learned from both. *Curiositas*, curiosity about the kind of knowledge which is not for man, leads to destruction: the wanderings and sufferings of Psyche and of the ass. Psyche finally yielding to the will of Venus is meant to prefigure Lucius' final submission and initiation into the mysteries. The actual ceremonies of initiation, as they are described in the eleventh book of the *Metamorphoses*, have been anticipated in the trials Psyche has undergone before being restored to favour.

Looked at from a literary point of view, this tale combines elements from a variety of sources. The folk-tale motifs are easily recognizable: the king's daughter and her wicked sisters; the lover who disappears when his true form has been disclosed; the seemingly impossible tasks imposed on Psyche by Venus/the witch. The burlesque scenes from the life of the gods with which Apuleius intermingles the description of Psyche's fortunes are derived from Alexandrian literature. But what interests us most here is of course the parallels with the Greek novel of love, leaving aside the basic similarity in structure — lovers' separation, searching and reunion — which already existed in the old myths.

The very beginning of the tale with the superhumanly beautiful girl whom people come from all quarters to pay homage to as if she were the goddess of love herself, strikingly resembles the introduction of Chariton's novel. Psyche's parents ask an oracle for advice and then obey its harsh orders with sorrow in their hearts, as

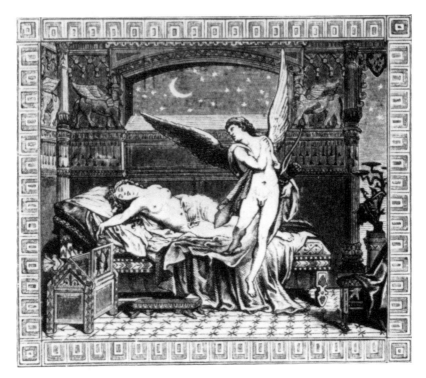

Figs. 54–5 *Cupid and Psyche. The tale of Cupid and Psyche has far surpassed the novel itself in popularity: in the art, literature, and music of
modern times numerous works have been devoted to this Greek fairy
princess and her divine lover. Among the works of art Raphael's ceiling
painting in the Villa Farnesina in Rome and Antonio Canova's statue
groups are perhaps the most well-known. Bertel Thorvaldsen also
perpetuated the motif in a couple of reliefs. In Figure 54, Cupid leaves
Psyche's bed after one of his nightly visits. The 1872 illustration is in the
classicizing spirit of Canova and Thorvaldsen. In Figure 55 Psyche violates
their agreement and lights a lamp to look at her bedfellow; at any moment
a drop of hot oil from her lamp will wake him, and he will fly away in
anger. Our seventeenth-century illustrator is truer to the text than the
classicists in his representation of Cupid, 'the most meek and sweetest beast
of all beasts' (Adlington); under these circumstances it seems indeed quite
reasonable that Psyche is strictly forbidden to see her lover and husband!*

in Xenophon Ephesius. Venus wants to humiliate her beautiful, mortal rival by inspiring in her love for some really miserable, sick and poor man; the same motive drives Manto in the *Ephesiaca* to marrying Antheia to a serf. Detail after detail in the plot has obvious parallels in the novels. It is true that some of the similarities may be explained as common borrowings from the folk-tale; we have already noticed similar influx, in Xenophon Ephesius especially. Yet it seems clear that Apuleius has taken over certain elements directly from the pre-sophistic novel — though of course not necessarily from the few examples available to us. The rich characterization in particular testifies to this; Psyche appears as a heroine of the Callirhoe type. It may be added that the different literary and popular elements combined by Apuleius do not always form a coherent and consistent whole: the contamination of motifs (see p. 152) with its consequent loose ends and abrupt shifts of character is a distinctive feature of the whole novel, not only of this particular tale.

Moreover, Apuleius inserted into *The Story of the Ass* a number of erotic tales that are light in tone. This type of story is generally known as 'Milesian'; the designation derives from the collection of *Milesiaca* compiled by Aristides of Miletus in the second century BC and subsequently translated into Latin. Plutarch tells an anecdote

Fig. 56 *'The Tale of the Tub'. Framed by a series of tableaux from the life of the ass, a well-known novella, told by one of Apuleius' characters, is illustrated in the centre. A man leaves for his work, his wife receives her lover into the house. But the husband happens to return home, finds the door locked, and innocently praises his wife's decency. At his knocking on the door the woman resolutely hides her lover in an empty tub. She receives her husband with reproaches for neglecting his work, while she toils away all day, instead of wallowing with lovers like the wife next door. The man defends himself: he has just earnt them the day's food by selling the empty tub, which is only getting in the way. Now he wants his wife's help to carry it to the buyer. Once more the woman finds a way out: she has herself found a buyer, who will pay a higher price, and he is already inside the tub checking its condition. Jointly the woman and her lover then persuade the husband to enter the tub himself in order to clean it; they themselves resume their interrupted love-making, while the woman simultaneously sets her husband to removing one spot of dirt after the other, 'until both tasks were finished'. This is a tale of typically 'Milesian' stamp, and from Apuleius it progressed to Boccaccio, who embroidered the motif in the* **Decameron** *as the seventh day's second novella.*

about the Parthians, the hereditary foes of the Romans, who having defeated the Roman army under Crassus at Carrhae were horrified to find such salacious reading matter in the baggage of a Roman officer. I have already mentioned the most famous example, 'The Widow of Ephesus', which Petronius retells in the *Satyricon* (above, p. 171, and figure 48) and which has been wandering through world literature ever since. These tales often begin, in a tone reminiscent of the ideal novel, by describing some particular wife's reputation for irreproachable decency, only to puncture the myth quickly and cynically, demonstrating how willingly she allows herself to be seduced by the first man who happens to pay some attention to her (figure 56).

Such scabrous stories — with the moral that 'no man's honesty and no woman's virtue are unassailable' (F. F. Abbott) — were evidently a cherished form of entertainment at banquets and in club meetings in the Hellenistic period. Similarly in the novel a story of this kind may be told by one of the characters in merry company or in order to kill time while waiting or travelling (figure 57). Other recurrent motifs of a popular origin are witchcraft and magic; the title of the book is not without reason 'metamorphoses' in the plural (figure 58). The underlying Greek *Story of the Ass*, with its mixture of sex and magic, itself doubtless has its roots in the Milesian tradition. Apuleius therefore had a double reason for stating in the introduction to his novel that he intended to offer a number of miscellaneous stories in the Milesian style, *sermone isto Milesio*.

However, Apuleius' portraits of women do not always bear the Milesian stamp. He also introduces into his narrative women who appear to be taken directly from a Greek novel of the ideal-sentimental type: beautiful, virtuous and faithful. It is true that he borrowed from his immediate model the motif of the young bride who is snatched away from her bridegroom at the wedding feast itself, and who is later rescued from the robbers by her husband; but

Fig. 57   The witches tear the heart out of Socrates and one of them voids her bladder over his terror-stricken companion Aristomenes. The illustration refers to a blood-curdling horror story which the cheese-monger Aristomenes himself tells Lucius to kill time on their trip through Thessaly. The story exists only in Apuleius but it may also have been part of the Greek Story of the Ass before it was abridged. Like figures 55, 56 and 58, this is taken from a magnificently illustrated French translation of Apuleius' novel (Paris, 1637).

Apuleius filled out these thin contours with additional borrowings from the Greek novel to form a complete romantic story. Here we find the heroine constantly bemoaning her unlucky fate and calling on the gods for aid, without any parodic intention. There is also a dream, and its interpretation, as well as the detailed description of how the hero uses his courage and cunning to save his beloved. And later in the novel, without precedent in *The Story of the Ass*, Apuleius tells about the newly married couple's subsequent adventures, right up to the bitter end when the faithful Charite takes her own life by the tomb of her young husband – an idealistic counterpart to the cynical 'Widow of Ephesus' cliché. Apuleius developed into a romantic sub-plot in its own right what in *The Story of the Ass* was incidental to the main theme.

Apuleius' novel thus belongs to a Greek tradition in a more fundamental way than does that of Petronius: the author takes over a ready-made Greek story and retains Greece as the scene of action; he inserts into this story other motifs and tales of a Greek origin; and, in addition, he allows his Latin prose style to be coloured by Greek rhythms and strains. Apuleius is the creator of a new artistic style, mixing archaisms with newly coined words to produce a very personal blend. He is also a virtuoso in changing from one stylistic level to another: at one moment he parodies inflated rhetoric, at another he effectively reels off a popular tale. And, like Petronius, he has a higher aim than just momentary amusement. The entertaining story is used as an instrument for other purposes: social satire, literary parody, and even, as becomes quite clear at the end, religious edification.

Fig. 58   The first metamorphosis: through a chink in the door Lucius watches how his hostess rubs her whole body with ointment, murmurs an incantation, and then gradually turns into an owl, with wings, plumage, and claws. At the bottom right we can see what happens when Lucius himself, with the maid's help, tries the same trick.

CHAPTER VIII

The Renaissance of the Greek Novel

'What Schole-boy, what apprentice knows not Heliodorus?' This rhetorical question was asked in the early seventeenth century by the satirist, and later bishop, Joseph Hall. We do not know the degree of exaggeration involved. But it seems pretty clear that at this time Heliodorus as well as Longus and Achilles Tatius were part of the conceptual world of educated people, both in England and on the continent. In translation and print they will have acquired a wider readership than ever they did in their own language in antiquity and the Byzantine period. The official recognition which ancient literary critics had denied them was now bestowed upon them in abundance: as 'prose epics' they were models which the literary talents of the time strove to imitate. Some tableaux from this rich *Nachleben*, especially that of Heliodorus, will be presented here, to round off this introduction to a genre which soon passed again into oblivion. Perhaps some samples of the aesthetic judgement of another age may help to put into perspective the indifferent or condescending attitude which has now for so long been predominant.

More, or Less, Faithful Translations

In February 1534, the first printed edition of the *Ethiopica* appeared at Basle, followed in 1552 by the first Latin translation; the translator was a Polish nobleman by the name of Stanislaw Warszewicki. But the true birth-date of Heliodorus Redivivus falls between these two: in 1547. In that year Jacques Amyot presented his congenial French translation of Heliodorus' novel, entitled *L'Histoire aethiopique de Heliodorus, contenant dix livres, traitant des loyales et pudiques amours de Theagenes Thessalien, et Chariclea Aethiopienne* (figure 59). In countless reprints and revised editions it was to hold the market far into the seventeenth century and so establish Heliodorus' image — in some respects an undeservedly flattering image, it might be added. This is Amyot's first success; his later translations of Longus' novel and of Plutarch's *Lives* and *Moralia* meant a similar breakthrough for these authors. In addition, Amyot's translations as a whole effectively contributed to the development of French literary style. According to a modern French critic, Amyot, while often following the meanderings of Heliodorus' Greek, at the same time lent to the language grace, ease, and a seductively rocking tone which was entirely his own. He also succeeded in retaining the original's variations between long, heavy periods and short, lively, sometimes ironic inserts. Thus Heliodorus rapidly came into fashion on Romance soil, in France, Spain, and Italy; and the credit is due to Amyot, even if each language soon had its own *Ethiopica*. In Spanish the novel appeared in 1554, in Italian two years later. As early as the 1550s it had been published in German, and other languages were to follow, although some of the works presented in bibliographies and catalogues as translations of Heliodorus' massive novel turn out on closer inspection to be thin booklets, which retell the story in the vernacular, often following some Latin epitome. This is true, for instance, of the Danish version of 1636 and the Dutch of 1726. Of course these condensed versions too bear witness in their own way to the popularity of the novel (figure 60).

An independent achievement of a high order, comparable to Amyot's, was Thomas Underdowne's 1569 English rendering of *An Aethiopian Historie written in Greeke by Heliodorus, no lesse wittie than pleasaunt*, to quote the title of the second edition of 1587. He based his version on Warszewicki's Latin translation and was also faithful to its mistakes. Against Amyot's relative sympathy with the tone of the Greek original stands Underdowne's lively wilfulness, making an Elizabethan romance out of the late Greek tale. The lyre is turned into a virginal, and the hero is 'Captaine' Theagenes, who occasionally may be seen 'walking about the church and in the cloisters'! An English literary historian, with a low opinion of Heliodorus' own style ('the style of a bookworm, not even remotely poetical') and of Amyot's otherwise highly praised French version ('prolix and tasteless'), concludes that Underdowne transformed the *Ethiopica* 'from the faded experiment of a studious pedant into a fresh and open-aired romance' (Charles Whibley, 1895).

If we insist that a translation should hit the right tone and be strictly accurate, then Underdowne's version is indeed a bad one,

L'HISTOIRE AE-
thiopique de Heliodorus,
CONTENANT DIX LIVRES,

TRAITANT DES LOYALES ET
pudiques amours de Theagenes Theſſalien, & Chari-
clea Aethiopiéne. Nou-
uellement traduite
de Gręc en Fran-
çoys.

Patere, aut abſtine.

Nul ne ſy frote.

Auecq' Priuilege du Roy.
Pour 6 ans.

ſ PARIS.

De l'Imprimerie d'Eſtienne Groulleau demourant
en la rue Neuue noſtre Dame à l'en-
ſeigne ſaint Ian Baptiſte.
1 5 4 7.

but as an independent work of art it had qualities which assured the novel great popularity in England for more than a century. Shakespeare came to know Heliodorus in this guise. There is in the last act of *Twelfth Night* a direct allusion, which the public of that time would probably have been able to catch. The Duke says to Olivia:

> Why should I not, had I the heart to do it,
> Like to th' Egyptian thief at point of death,
> Kill what I love? — a savage jealousy
> That sometimes savours nobly. (V. i. 115 – 18)

'Th' Egyptian thief' is Thyamis, the robber chief in Heliodorus, who loves Charicleia so much that he intends to kill her to prevent her from becoming someone else's bride — by so doing he would be reunited to her after death, according to Egyptian belief. In the darkness of the cave Thyamis plunges his sword into the breast of a girl who speaks Greek and whom he therefore believes to be Charicleia. 'And after this sorrowfull sort, that woman giving up her last, and gastly groane, was slain' (Underdowne). But of course this is one of the novel's scenes of mistaken identity: the murdered girl is not Charicleia but a slave, Thisbe, who thus innocently falls a victim to the robber's blind passion (figure 61).

From Imitation to Emulation

The translations are the first step; when artists like Amyot or Underdowne wield the pen, they contribute to the creation of a usable and enjoyable language for literary prose. New words, stylistic figures, images, patterns of thought are incorporated into the native literary language at a stroke. In addition, they invite imitation within their particular genre. The second step consists in precisely such imitations — a concept without as yet any negative connotation. The line is not always easy to draw; an author may sometimes pretend to give a translation of a Greek original but in fact insert into the text much of his own work — the tag 'Made in Antiquity' was a guarantee of quality. An immense number of novels inspired by or imitating ancient models appeared on the

Fig. 59 Heliodorus Redivivus: the title-page of the first edition of Heliodorus' novel in Amyot's French translation, printed in Paris in 1547.

de Theagenes & de Chariclée. 26

Suitte de la proceſſion, ouChariclée paroiſt,portée ſur vn char traiſné
par des bœufs blancs,ayant des fleſches en vne main & vne torche
en l'autre

La belle Chariclée apres vint à ſon tour,
Portant en ſa main droiĉte vne torche allumée;
Mais de ſes deux beaux yeux la ſplédeur enflamée,
Faiſoit honte aux rayons du clair aſtre du iour.

De l'autre elle portoit, vn arc auec des traiĉts,
Qui ſembloient bien ayder aux charmes de ſa grace
Mais l'Amour qui logeoit au milieu de ſa face,
Faiſoit bien autremẽnt redoutter ſes attraiĉts.

D 2

literary scene, especially in France. *L'Astrée* by Honoré d'Urfé, in which the beautiful heroine is coveted by the handsome shepherd Celadon, is still mentioned with a certain respect by literary historians, but most of the later products in the 'heroic' genre are nowadays considered unreadable. Mlle de Scudéry's mastodon novels are notorious; the longest of them, *Le Grand Cyrus*, numbers 13,000 pages in one edition. This kind of literature and its breeding ground, the Parisian salons, were subjected to the murderous attacks of Molière in *Les Précieuses ridicules* (1659) and of Boileau in *Les Héros de roman* (1666), but this did not prevent its spreading further afield, and abroad as well. The direct line to ancient models is, however, generally broken in the ensuing imitations of imitations.

From the imitation, whose author regards the ancient model as an absolute ideal, a third and decisive step is sometimes taken, to the independent work of art, which stands on ancient ground and emulates the masters of antiquity. The intention is not just to equal, but also to excel. Cervantes' *Persiles and Sigismunda* is a work of this particular kind. But before we reach Spain, we shall stay a while in Elizabethan England. A novel of 1580 might read like this — the spelling has been modernized and the italics are mine:

Thus was their banquet turned to a battle, their winy mirths to bloody rages, and the happy prayers for the duke to monstrous threatening his estate; the solemnizing his birthday tended to the cause of his funerals. But as rage hath (besides his wickedness) that folly that, the more it seeks to hurt, the less it considers how to be able to hurt, they never weighed how to arm themselves, but took up everything for a weapon that fury offered to their hands: some swords and bills; there were other took pitchforks and rakes, converting husbandry to soldiery. Some caught hold of spits, things serviceable for the lives of men, to be the instruments of their deaths; *and there wanted not such which held the same pots wherein they had drunk to the duke's health to use them (as they could) to his mischief.*

Fig. 60   *The beautiful Charicleia leaves Artemis' shrine at Delphi in her carriage drawn by white oxen (see p. 65). One of 120 etchings for Heliodorus' novel executed by Pierre Vallet and dedicated to Louis XIII in 1613. They were published as a book: the novel is rapidly retold in 120 pages of words and pictures, each page containing a short caption above the picture and two four-line stanzas on the same theme beneath it. The existence of condensed versions, with or without pictures, testifies to the novel's popularity at this time, while the royal dedication indicates something of its prestige.*

The description of this rural revolt is from the original version of Sir Philip Sidney's pastoral *Arcadia*. Everyone even slightly acquainted with the Greek sophistic novels will at once recognize the style, over-burdened with antitheses (banquet/battle, prayers/threats, birth-day/funeral etc.), and also the moralizing insertions. Those who remember the first chapters of the *Ethiopica* (quoted above, p. 54) will be familiar with the motif as well, and anyone who happens to have read Heliodorus in Underdowne's version will feel still more at home with Sidney. The passages printed in italics above may be compared with the following quotation from Heliodorus/Underdowne: 'For that sudden mischief wrought new devices, and taught them instead of weapons to use pots . . . brewing blood with wine, joining battle with banqueting.' It comes as no surprise, then, that in his little treatise *An Apology for Poetry*, designed as a speech in defence of poetry's place in society, Sidney mentions the *Ethiopica* on an equal footing with the *Aeneid* and with Xenophon's *Cyropaedia*, which was highly esteemed at this time: '. . . so true a lover as Theagenes . . . so right a prince as Xenophon's Cyrus, so excellent a man every way as Virgil's Aeneas'. 'Theagenes' does not even need to be specified by the author's name! Later in the same treatise Sidney states that the *Cyropaedia* and the *Ethiopica* are to be regarded as 'heroic poems', in spite of the prose:

. . . it is not rhyming and versing that maketh a poet — no more than a long gown maketh an advocate, who though he pleaded in armour should be an advocate and no soldier. But it is that feigning notable images of virtues, vices, or what else, with that delightful teaching, which must be the right describing note to know a poet by. . . .

Through journeys on the continent and in Italy Sidney was person-ally acquainted with the leading personalities of contemporary cultural life, and his literary views are more representative than original. We have already seen how at about the same time in Spain El Pinciano expresses an equally high esteem for Heliodorus (above p. 1). Both the English and the Spanish author of poetics could

Fig. 61   The murder in the cave: the Athenian Cnemon shines his torch on the murdered girl, who turns out not to be the heroine but a poor slave, the innocent victim of the robber chief's sword. Chariclea and Theagenes embrace each other, happily reunited against all the odds, and then fall fainting to the ground. . . . Shakespeare and Calderón are among those who have been attracted by this melodramatic event.

take their stand on that great authority Julius Caesar Scaliger, who in his *Poetices libri septem* (1561) had decreed that the *Ethiopica* should be carefully studied by every epic poet and stand before him as the supreme model.

Sidney put this into practice. When he recast his *Arcadia*, the first (unprinted) version of which he regarded as immature, he gave it a narrative form clearly modelled on Heliodorus' novel. *Old Arcadia* was already influenced in style and motifs by the *Ethiopica*, as the quotation above demonstrates; but it had a straightforward, chronological structure. In *New Arcadia* (1590) the chronological sequence is broken, the reader arrives *in medias res* and is then offered a complicated pattern in which one retrospective narrative is woven into the other. Much material is added that does not belong to the main plot: independent love stories and tales, philosophical and political expositions, descriptions of works of art, of a garden, and so on. The elaboration of these *ecphrases* reveals that not only Heliodorus but also Achilles Tatius was on Sidney's reading list, probably in French, since the English translation of *The Loves of Clitophon and Leucippe* did not appear until 1597. On the other hand, there does not seem to be any direct influence from Longus in *Arcadia*, in spite of the common pastoral setting. For that kind of material Sidney is indebted, rather, to Renaissance precedents: Sannazaro's *Arcadia*, Montemayor's *Diana*, and others. These authors, Montemayor in particular, also borrowed heavily from Heliodorus, and this has rendered the scholarly debate on Sidney's sources somewhat confused: what did Sidney take over directly from the Greek novel, and what indirectly by way of his European colleagues? Since he obviously did read Heliodorus/Underdowne as well as Montemayor, there is no real point pursuing the matter: one influence simply reinforced the other.

Since *Old Arcadia* was finally made available in print at the beginning of this century, criticism has been divided in its appreciation of the two versions. While expressing their respect for Sidney's technical skill in the revised version, most critics seem none the less to regard the less pretentious original as the more enjoyable for a modern reader. But *New Arcadia*, with its Heliodoran structure, was the one that gave Sidney his reputation as a novelist, with no fewer than thirteen editions appearing within a hundred years. Sidney — and therefore, indirectly, the Greek novel — was an active agent in the rise of the modern novel in eighteenth-century Britain. Richardson was strongly influenced by *Sidney's Arcadia Modernized*, which was published in 1725, and he acknowledges his debt by naming his heroine 'Pamela' after the king's daughter in Sidney's novel — a kind of allusion we find in ancient and Byzantine novelists as well.

Cervantes: A Northern Tale

It may seem paradoxical that it is Cervantes who on Romance soil writes the most perfect 'Greek' novel. To us, the author of *Don Quixote* is the genius who broke with tradition and created something quite new. Can *Los trabajos de Persiles y Sigismunda* perhaps be his first attempt at writing a novel, an experiment which he later repudiated? The reverse is true: it is his last novel, published posthumously in 1617, and Cervantes regarded it as the culmination of his literary work. In the introduction to his *Novelas ejemplares* he mentions the forthcoming *Persiles*, with which he ventures to compete with Heliodorus himself, and in his dedication of the second part of *Don Quixote* he promises the Count of Lemos that *Persiles*, which 'God willing' will be finished within four months, will be either the worst or the best book of entertainment ever written in Spanish — 'but I must say that I repent of having said "the worst", for according to the opinions of my friends, it will attain the highest possible excellence'. It is *Persiles*, not *Don Quixote*, that Cervantes hopes will bring him eternal fame.

The content of *Persiles* has been summarized as follows:

Persiles and Sigismunda — who for most of the book pass under the names Periandro and Auristela — are two royal children from the North, who love each other but cannot be united until they have visited Rome and received the permission and blessing of the Pope. On their travels they have many strange experiences, which all have a more or less manifestly symbolic meaning. The new Golden Age, the Paradise on earth which Don Quixote dreamt of, they find in a mountain valley on a wild and barbaric island. The entry to it is through a cave or tunnel. A fugitive Spaniard is their guide. In flight from the murderous inhabitants of the island, many years ago, he had himself found his way into the valley. A shepherd girl became his wife; now he lives with her and his children without fearing the noise of war, he drinks the water of the river and eats from the fruits of his own labour. . . .

The pilgrims do not find a permanent abode in this earthly paradise. Their journey continues: beyond Lisbon, most beautiful of cities, along the Tajo into Spain, where catholicism is preached more purely than anywhere else in the world . . . to Rome, where the Pope by virtue of his office looses

and binds souls and where Auristela receives instruction in the principles of
Christian faith which she could not get in her semi-barbarian northern
homeland. When her soul has in this manner been purified and ennobled,
she takes back her right name Sigismunda and is married to Persiles. Their
chaste love has passed the test; cleansed by their travails during their
thousand-mile pilgrimage, with the true faith inscribed in their hearts,
they return to the North as man and wife. And as the fairy-tale this novel
in fact is, it ends with the assurance that Persiles and his wife lived till they
saw their days prolonged in their great-grandchildren.

This 'Historia Setentrional', 'Northern Tale', as the subtitle reads
with a direct allusion to Heliodorus' 'Historia Etiopica', closely
follows its model's structure, but in reverse: north for south, Christianity (of the counter-reformation variety) for the sun cult, 'trabajos'
('travails' or 'passions' in the Christian sense) for 'amores'.
Everywhere there are motifs and narrative devices borrowed from
the master, but with an increased degree of complication: Cervantes
aims not only at imitation, but at emulation. Extraordinary events
succeed one another at a furious pace, and the explanations are
retrospective, as in Heliodorus and Achilles Tatius, the reader being
informed of what A has heard from B who had it from C. The
reader's curiosity is heightened and his patience tried to the utmost.
The pattern is hardly simplified by the independent sub-plots which
are woven into the narrative and sometimes threaten to deflect the
reader's interest from the main plot. It has been said that the parts
triumph over the whole as in a piece of Baroque art.
    Cervantes placed part of the action in 'Noruega más remota', far-
thest Norway, in order to have, like Heliodorus, the full *poetic*
freedom, but without imitating him slavishly in the choice of setting. A narrative in prose which took place in Spain or elsewhere in
the Mediterranean world would inevitably approach dangerously
near to historiography. To let the fictional characters come from
terra incognita and have the action played out at some distance in
time and space is, according to El Pinciano, the condition for the
verisimilitude of a prose epic; and 'verosimilitas' — not 'veritas',
'truth', in the prosaic sense — was the key concept of the author of
Philosophia Antiqua Poetica (1596), a work familiar to Cervantes.
In this connection El Pinciano recommends Heliodorus' model, but
Cervantes may have got the idea of a northern latitude from Tasso:
in his *Discorsi del poema eroico* (1594) — yet another of the neo-
Aristotelian 'Poetics' of this period — the Italian poet advises that if
an author is concerned about the 'authenticity' of a fictitious tale, he
should take his subject-matter from, say, 'Gotia, Norvegia, Svevia,

Islanda'. It has also been suggested that Cervantes somehow knew of *The Marvels beyond Thule* (above, p. 118), and that Antonius Diogenes' tale in its Byzantine summary, translated into Latin, influenced both his narrative technique and his choice of milieu; but the circumstances are obscure.

In the first part of *Don Quixote*, Cervantes is already proposing in outline what he tries to realize in full ten years later in his *Persiles*. Into the conversation between the Priest and the Canon on the pernicious influence of the romance of chivalry (chapters 47–8) a more positive tone intrudes itself. The purpose of entertainment is not evil in itself as long as it is combined with instruction and edification. Further absolute requirements are beauty, harmony and verisimilitude:

The falsehood is better the truer it looks, and the more it contains of the doubtful and the possible the more pleasing it is. Fabulous plots must be wedded to the reader's intelligence, and written in such a way that the impossible is made easy, enormities are smoothed out, and the mind is held in suspense, amazed, gripped, exhilarated, and entertained. (trans. E. C. Riley)

The Canon, who is Cervantes' mouthpiece both for the criticism of the existing romances of chivalry and for this manifesto, himself finds the chivalric genre tempting in principle:

For they [the books of chivalry] presented a broad and spacious field through which the pen could run without let or hindrance, describing shipwrecks, tempests, encounters and battles; painting a brave captain with all the features necessary for the part; showing his wisdom in forestalling his enemies' cunning, his eloquence in persuading or dissuading his soldiers, his ripeness in counsel, his prompt resolution, his courage in awaiting or in making an attack; now depicting a tragic and lamentable incident, now a joyful and unexpected event; here a most beautiful lady, chaste, intelligent, and modest; there a Christian knight, valiant, and gentle; in one place a monstrous, barbarous braggart; in another a courteous prince, brave and wise; representing the goodness and loyalty of vassals, and the greatness and generosity of lords. Sometimes the writer might show his knowledge of astrology, or his excellence at cosmography or as a musician, or his wisdom in affairs of state, and he might even have an opportunity of showing his skill in necromancy. (trans. J. M. Cohen)

Mutatis mutandis, this sounds like a programme for the sophistic Greek novel. But, above all, it is directly applicable to *Persiles*, and the Canon soon reveals that he has in fact himself tried to write such

an ideal romance. He has written more than a hundred pages but
has given the whole thing up, realizing that a general audience will
never appreciate its finer points.

If *Don Quixote* is an anti-novel, written deliberately to torpedo a
popular literary genre but not to create a new one, *Persiles*, on the
contrary, is intended as an exemplary novel, written with the same
aim as Cervantes' *Novelas ejemplares*, 'Exemplary Stories'. It is an
attempt to create a fourth type of novel, alongside the chivalric,
pastoral, and picaresque: a prose epic, edifying and perfect in form,
a successor of Homer, Virgil, and Heliodorus. 'For the epic may be
written in prose as well as in verse ,' says the Canon, who knows his
Pinciano.

Cervantes' own hopes of eternal fame through *Persiles* were not
fulfilled, as we know. It is true that the book was an immediate
success, did see some ten editions in a short time, and was translated
into several languages, but with the passing of time it has been completely eclipsed by *Don Quixote*. The brothers Schlegel in the
Germany of the age of romanticism still express their high esteem for
Persiles, but later critics who touch on this novel usually only reveal
their own failure to understand a work which lacks those qualities
which are so admired in *Don Quixote*. Against the 'realism' of *Don
Quixote* stands the 'wild fantasticality' of *Persiles*. Sometimes a
misguided apologia is attempted: those parts of *Persiles* set in the
South, being (almost) 'realistic', are cited as revealing the hand of
the master. Benevolent judges say that the novel is difficult and
inaccessible, others simply call it monotonous and dull. 'It is a tale
without meaning, without philosophy, and devoid of interest' — as
if there were not a whole world-picture in its structure alone: from
Chaos to Cosmos, from Fall to Redemption. The style may receive
some acknowledgement: 'from a purely stylistic point of view'
Persiles is the best book Cervantes ever wrote, says the same
Donquixotean who found the novel without any interest.

However, there seems to have been a change of opinion recently
among specialists. Titles like 'Heliodorus Christianus', *Cervantes'
Christian Romance*, and *Cervantes' Musterroman 'Persiles'* indicate
the points of departure for the new understanding. Critics do not
deny that the novel is difficult, but the reader is assured that on in-
tensive and repeated reading the impression of bewildering complexity turns into its opposite. *Leitmotifs*, recurring pictures and
symbols, a 'ritual' repetition of the main theme in the sub-plots, all
this serves to bind the 'independent' parts together and reveal a
striking unity and simplicity: 'a tale of life overcoming death, of

music calming tempests, a tale almost childlike in its thematic simplicity and repetitions' (A. Forcione).

But it is still not easy for those who do not read Spanish to form an opinion of the novel, since translations are few and difficult to get hold of. While *Don Quixote* is forever appearing in new editions in every language, one may scour libraries and bookshops in vain for *Persiles*: the last English translation seems to be that of 1854. Its literary merits apart, *Persiles* also contains interesting and amusing passages which deserve a wider readership. This is particularly true of the parts devoted to the homeland of Persiles and Sigismunda: here we discover how a learned and widely travelled Spaniard a hundred years after Columbus imagined Northern Scandinavia. We learn about the midnight sun and drift-ice, about skiing 'on the water', about werewolves and Arctic sea monsters. The big islands 'Tile' (Thule) and 'Frislanda' both have hints of Iceland about them, and on Greenland there is the monastery of St Thomas, which stands out as the northern centre for language teaching. In its imaginative mixture of fact and fiction this is a description which successfully competes with Heliodorus' picture of Meroë, that southern centre of the sun cult.

Racine in the Monastery School

In the year 1655, at the age of sixteen, the orphan Jean Racine entered the famous Jansenist school of Port-Royal. For three years he devoted himself to the study of Latin and Greek authors, making remarkably rapid progress. He read Plato and Plutarch in the original, though in copies purged of passages which were considered unsuitable for young and innocent minds. But poetry was his favourite reading: Homer, Pindar, and — even then — Sophocles and Euripides above all. He lost himself in them, walking through the forests around the monastery, and he almost learned them by heart. At least this is what his son, Louis Racine, relates in his *Mémoires sur la vie de Jean Racine* (1747). He continues:

[My father] had a remarkable memory. By chance he found the Greek novel about the love of Theagenes and Chariclea. Just as he was devouring this book, he was caught by the sacristan, Claude Lancelot [known as one of the creators of the Port-Royal grammar], who snatched the book from him and threw it in the fire. He succeeded in obtaining another copy, which however shared the same fate. So he had to buy a third copy, and in order not to have to fear the proscription of that one too, he learned the novel by heart and took it to the sacristan with the following words: 'Please burn this one too, like the others!'

This is an anecdote; if it is not literally true, it at least fulfills the requirement of verisimilitude. The reference is certainly not to the Greek original — which, incidentally, Rabelais a hundred years earlier had had Pantagruel use as a cure for insomnia! — but to Amyot's Heliodorus, which must at this time still have been easily accessible in any of its frequent reprints. That this novel, which in many respects approaches drama (and melodrama), made a real impression on the future dramatist is evident from his work.

Nor is Racine alone among seventeenth-century dramatists in his weakness for Heliodorus. Some tried to dramatize the whole novel, with its complicated plot and its host of characters — usually without much success. Others were inspired by individual episodes, motifs, or figures. About half a dozen 'Ethiopian' dramas are known in Germany alone, several of them 'school comedies' in Latin verse from the beginning of the century. In France and England Amyot's and Underdowne's success naturally induced a number of theatrical experiments, and in Spain no less a playwright than Calderón had 'Fortune's children', Theagenes and Charicleia, make their trip from the 'island' Delphi to Ethiopia in three acts (*Los hijos de la Fortuna*, 1664). Much is changed, but a scene such as Thisbe's death in the cave as a stand-in for Charicleia, the one Shakespeare alludes to, is gratefully seized on (see figure 61).

Not unexpectedly, the melodramatic qualities of Heliodorus' novel have attracted opera composers as well, Giuseppe Verdi being the most recent. In his *Aïda* (1871) the characters have other names and the novel's happy ending has been turned into the lovers' sacrificial death, but as Otto Weinreich has shown, enough remains of both atmosphere and concrete detail to make the debt unmistakable. Whether the connection was clear to Verdi himself is another question; at least the egyptologist who provided the librettists with the raw material knew where he could lay his hands on an effective story. Thus prose fiction, drama, and opera have drawn heavily on the *Ethiopica*, as has of course pictorial art (figures 62-5, and also figures 21-2); it only remains for film to discover this adventure story, with its crowd scenes and visual effects.

Back to Racine. He too is reported to have made an early attempt to dramatize the story of Theagenes and Charicleia, but no manuscript has survived. Critics have, however, detected various traces of the boy's admiration for Heliodorus in the great plays of his mature years. Antigone in *La Thébaïde* laments in strains reminiscent of Charicleia, and in *Iphigénie* there may be some influence from King Hydaspes, who in the last book of the *Ethiopica*, declares

Figs. 62–5 Key scenes from Heliodorus' novel. This cycle of paintings, consisting of nine (originally ten) pieces, each 116 ×/205 cm., now hangs in the Landgrafenmuseum in Kassel. It is anonymous; some ascribe it on stylistic grounds to David Klöker Ehrenstrahl (1628–1698), others to Karel van Mander the Younger (c. 1610–1670) or his circle. The paintings were therefore probably produced in Sweden or Denmark; they arrived in Germany in the eighteenth century as a gift from a Swedish king. Stylistically this cycle differs markedly from the typical court paintings of artists like A. Dubois (in Fontainebleau), A. Bloemaert (now in Sanssouci), and G. v. Honthorst (see figures 21–2); in the Kassel paintings we have expressive close-ups of the characters in dramatic situations.

Figure 62: Hydaspes and Persinna, Ethiopia's dark-skinned royal couple, with a painting of Andromeda; their daughter, Charicleia, got her white skin when the queen happened to fix her eyes on this painting at the moment of conception. Detail.

himself, like a second Agamemnon, ready to sacrifice his newly recovered daughter to the sun god for the benefit of the state. In *Bajazet* the hero himself has traces of Theagenes, whereas the passionate Sultana Roxane may have borrowed some colouring from the barbaric satrap's wife, Arsace, in Heliodorus. The constellation Arsace/Theagenes/Charicleia has also been considered one of the possible sources of inspiration for Phèdre/Hippolyte/Aricie in

Figure 63: Theagenes receives the torch from Charicleia's hand; compare Honthorst's treatment of the same scene, figure 21.

Figure 64: Charicleia threatens to stab herself if the robbers carry her away, leaving Theagenes wounded on the beach.

Racine's *Phèdre*. Racine's Princess Aricie, with whom Hippolyte is in love, has no counterpart in Euripides' *Hippolytus* — chastity is the young hero's shield — so Heliodorus with his completed triangle may well have influenced Racine. There is no way of proving it, however; the idea in itself is not very original, and there seem to be no specific similarities. Perhaps here is the place to point out the general risk of distortion modern neglect of the Greek novel has caused; literary historians, themselves unfamiliar with the Greek novel, tend to seek influences exclusively in the great classical authors, in this case Euripides and Seneca, whereas the subjects of their investigations sometimes had a much wider horizon. To return to *Phèdre*, we should also note that most engaging sub-plot in the *Ethiopica*, the life story of the young Athenian Cnemon, which is yet another variation on the Hippolytus/Phaedra motif. We do not know whether Racine first became acquainted with Euripides' Phaedra or with Cnemon's step-mother Demaenete, reckless in her violent passion; but Heliodorus' version, effectively told in the manner of a serial story within the novel, can hardly have escaped making an impression on his young reader.

There is also the possibility that Racine's treatment of his female characters was influenced in a general way by his reading Heliodorus. The force and violence of which Racine's heroines are capable in their passion contrast with the pale and timid appear-

Figure 65: Theagenes wrestles with an Ethiopian giant.

ance of the men; the women are the prime movers of the action. As we have already noted (above, p. 96), much the same is true of several of the Greek novels. If a novel is to be named after just one of the principal characters, the heroine is the obvious choice: *Callirhoe*, *Charicleia*, and so on — and *Phèdre*, not *Hippolyte*! Among the secondary characters as well, there are memorable female figures: Plangon in Chariton; Melite in Achilles Tatius; Arsace in Heliodorus. The same point may be made more negatively: the really remarkable thing is that the novels lack true heroes, that the principal male characters — with the exception of Clitophon, to whom the first-person narrative lends some character — are pale marionettes, who passively let themselves be tossed about the world by Fortune and are always on the defensive in the face of superior rivals and active women.

The Latecomers: Xenophon and Chariton

Longus and Achilles Tatius had appeared soon after Heliodorus. It is true that the first printed editions of these two novels in the original did not come out until after 1600, but translations into Latin and modern languages came some decades earlier. Achilles Tatius generally had to be satisfied with a place in Heliodorus' shadow — in the theoretical treatises he is mentioned only in tandem with the master — while Longus' pastoral managed to carve out a career for itself. As for Xenophon Ephesius and Chariton, however, it was to take nearly two hundred years after Heliodorus' revival before they became available. When in 1670 Pierre Daniel Huet attempted to trace *L'Origine des romans*, he still knew only the three sophistic novels (and Iamblichus in Photius' summary). To support his thesis that the Greek novel had an oriental origin he could consequently refer to the fact that the authors tended to be oriental by birth: Syrian, Babylonian, Egyptian. From an aesthetic point of view, he preferred Heliodorus; Iamblichus and Longus are sharply criticized for their artless way of telling the story in chronological sequence, instead of bringing the reader *in medias res* like Homer and Heliodorus. Chariton and Xenophon were unlikely to have aroused his enthusiasm.

In 1723 Xenophon's *Ephesiaca* appeared in print, in an Italian translation; some years later the *editio princeps* of the Greek text followed. The Indian summer of the Greek novel was long since past, and even if Xenophon had been discovered earlier, his novel was not of a kind to have inspired Renaissance or baroque poets and artists any more than it would have satisfied the literary theorist. But even so, in its first hundred years it went through a dozen different translations, some of which appeared in several editions. The few comments that can be traced in contemporary sources (prefaces, articles in encyclopaedias) are remarkably positive: there is a general admiration for the clarity and precision of the descriptions, for the narrative style, as noble as it is simple. Not until the latter part of the nineteenth century does the definitive condemnation come. Rohde calls the author a bungler, exceptionally unskilled in plot construction, and dull in style as well. Similar judgements fall upon the other novelists, even on the sophistic triad. To some extent it is probably the rise of the modern psychological novel that contributes to the fall of its old ancestors: be it explicitly or unconsciously, critics compared the novels with contemporary examples of the genre, and were naturally disappointed. As far as Xenophon is concerned, the pendulum has swung back somewhat during this century, as the similarities between his simple narrative style and that of folk-tale have received attention.

Chariton, like Xenophon, survived the Byzantine period in a single manuscript, and for one reason or another his novel was not printed until 1750. Then, as if by way of compensation, it was furnished with a Latin translation and a commentary (by J. P. D'Orville) which to this day remains the most detailed ever bestowed on a Greek novel. Translations into modern languages follow, but it is characteristic that at this time the ancient text is no longer looked up to as a model; instead, some translators try to improve upon it by their own invention. One German translator (1753) frankly states that he has let Chaereas only *pretend* to attempt suicide and that in his version the great king no longer cries unmanfully, as in the original, but 'sighs heroically'. Chariton's heroes were not heroic enough. The operation is justified like this: a novel is read just as a pastime, because one has nothing to do but does not want to be completely idle; hence it is immaterial whether the translation is exact or not. Another German translator (1807) is unsatisfied with the final section of the novel, with its long recapitulation. He livens it up by giving Polycharmus, Chaereas' constant companion, a more attractive bride than Chariton had found for him: in the original, Polycharmus is married to Chaereas' own sister, 'who for this purpose springs up like a mushroom from the earth', while in the translation he receives as a reward for his valour and loyalty the hand of Rhodogoune, the most beautiful woman in the whole Persian empire, excelled in beauty by Callirhoe alone!

Longus, Goethe's Favourite

The same year that Chariton was treated with such scant respect Goethe notes in his diary that he has read Longus' *Daphnis and Chloe* (in Amyot's French version). Here the tone is completely different; Goethe makes it quite clear that Longus' novel is a work of art to be respected and admired. He praises Longus for the richness of his motifs taken from the pastoral world, for his skilful composition and use of 'retardation'. The praise is still more lavish some years later, when Goethe reads the novel in Passow's German translation of the complete text — earlier editions had lacked the scene in which Chloe watches Daphnis bathing in the cave of the Nymphs. Even in his old age, in his conversations with Eckermann, Goethe still speaks enthusiastically of the sublime grace of the Lesbian idyll, with the sky as blue and clear as in a wall painting at Herculaneum. 'The whole poem testifies to the highest art and culture. . . . A taste, a perfection, a purity of feeling which is on a level with the best that has ever been achieved. . . . You would have to write a whole book to do full justice to all the merits of this poem. You should read it anew each year to learn from it over and over again and be influenced by its great beauty.'

These statements of Goethe's caused a sharp conflict of loyalties for German philologists. Professionally they were inclined to despise the Greek novel, and Longus with it: he was described as infantile and stale, intolerably rhetorical, and his erotic descriptions were marked by a nauseous obscenity, 'the base lustfulness of a pedantic phrasemonger'. On the other hand, they could hardly disavow Goethe. The usual way out of the dilemma was to point out that Goethe made the acquaintance of Longus in Amyot's 'stylistically very different' version. There is of course some truth in this: Amyot certainly made the rhetoric of both Longus and Heliodorus more easily digestible for modern readers. But, as we have seen, Goethe renewed the acquaintance in Passow's version and was no less enthusiastic; and his enthusiasm was inspired by the motifs and the atmosphere rather than by the style.

Of course there is no point in discussing whether Goethe or the philologists were 'right' in their opinion of Longus' artistry, or whether the Renaissance was right in extolling the work of Heliodorus, which later times have found pretentious and dull. Historically the Greek novel can no doubt lay claim to closer attention than most literary historians have paid it over the last hundred years; there is no honest way to define it out of the genre. But aesthetically it is impossible to put the clock back: the art of the novel has attained heights from which the first attempts in the genre look rather small — there is no 'classical' dimension to the Greek novel. And those who expect something of the same intellectual experience from a Greek novel as from Greek drama will inevitably be disappointed; the novels are hardly less 'timeless', but they were never truly profound. Yet, judged according to their kind and their time, it is not only the literary heavyweight Heliodorus and the graceful evergreen Longus who should be able to attract readers. Xenophon may rest in peace, but both the pure-hearted Chariton and the ironical Achilles Tatius display artistic qualities and proffer insights into ancient life and thinking to such a degree that they well deserve, like their heroines, to be resurrected now and then from their apparent death.

Daphnis and Chloe in the Mirror of Art

In contrast to the other Greek novels, Longus' *Daphnis and Chloe* has remained a title of current interest on the book market up to this day. Its motif, the pastoral idyll, has exercised its inherent power of attraction, and Longus' artistic style has inspired equally artistic translations. But its success on the book market is no doubt due primarily to the special attraction which *Daphnis and Chloe* appears to have had for book illustrators and book designers. Several of the editions of Longus are in themselves works of art, delicately illustrated from beginning to end and printed in an exquisite typography. Of this rich tradition our pictorial supplement can only give a few glimpses, samples of the ways in which different times and artists have interpreted Longus' novel and let its motifs assume visual form.

The following outline of the story will place the illustrations in context (see also pp. 35 – 40):

Young Daphnis is found being suckled by a goat, Chloe by a sheep (figures **66–7**). They grow up as foster-children in a goatherd's and a shepherd's family respectively, and start working with the flocks at the age of fifteen and thirteen. Their childish innocence receives its first blow when Daphnis, saved from a serious accident, undresses and washes himself in the fountain of the Nymphs: Chloe suddenly discovers how beautiful he is. A kiss, bestowed on Daphnis by Chloe as the prize in a beauty contest between him and a cowherd, communicates the infection of love to the boy.

The erotic games begin. Daphnis teaches Chloe to play on his pipe (figures **68–9**), and steals a kiss from her. A cricket, fleeing from a swallow, seeks shelter in Chloe's bosom; Daphnis puts his hand inside her dress and removes the cricket (figures **70–2**). Then a dramatic interlude: Daphnis is carried away by pirates, but is miraculously rescued. Chloe washes Daphnis in the cave of the Nymphs and for the first time herself takes a bath naked before his eyes (figures **73–4**). Book illustrators of the nineteenth and twentieth centuries often miss this point by anticipating the nakedness, making the children run about like Adam and Eve in Paradise from the start.

214

Autumn comes, and with it the harvest festival. The old cowherd Philetas tells Daphnis and Chloe about a visit Eros himself has made to his garden. He describes the nature of Eros lyrically (above, pp. 37 – 8), and the children realize what illness has been tormenting them. They try some of the remedies prescribed: the kiss and the embrace — without being cured. Their story is complicated by the outbreak of war; Chloe is carried away but is saved through the agency of the Nymphs and Pan. Reunited, the pious children sacrifice to their benefactors and swear eternal fidelity to each other.

Winter comes, separating the inseparable youngsters. Daphnis thinks of a stratagem: armed with glue and snares he sets out bird-hunting near Chloe's home and after a long wait is admitted into the house. At last spring returns. Love torments them, but they still cannot find an effective remedy, in spite of trying, to the best of their ability, to imitate the mating act of the goats (figures **75 – 6**). Then salvation presents itself: a woman from the neighbourhood, Lycaenion, young, beautiful and experienced in the ways of the town, falls in love with Daphnis, entices him, and deprives him of his innocence. But the summer passes, and he does not apply his new knowledge to Chloe. In the autumn Daphnis has been able to exact a half-promise from the foster-parents to be allowed to marry Chloe, in spite of the queue of noble suitors. After a long series of complications the wedding finally takes place, but not before Daphnis and Chloe have been recognized as the children of two rich townsmen.

'When night had fallen, everyone escorted them to the bridal chamber; some played the shepherd's pipe, others the flute, others again carried great torches (figure **77**) . . . Daphnis and Chloe lay down naked together, embraced each other and kissed, and they kept more awake during the night than owls (figure **78**). Daphnis did what Lycaenion had taught him, and then for the first time Chloe realized that what had taken place in the wood had been only shepherds' games.' This final scene has in some eighteenth-century editions attracted rather peculiar iconography, which in art history passes under the name *les petits pieds* (figure **79**); its originator is thought to be Count Philippe de Caylus (1692 – 1767).

Figs. 66–7 *Foundlings: Daphnis and Chloe are discovered by their foster-fathers. Figure 66: Crispin de Passe, 1626; and figure 67: Pierre Paul Prudhon, engraved by Vélard, 1850s.*

Figs. 68–9   *Chloe learns to play the shepherd's pipe. Figure 68: Raphaël Collin, etched by E. A. Champollion, 1890; and figure 69: Yngve Berg, 1928.*

Figs. 70–2 *Daphnis takes the cricket out of Chloe's bosom. Figure 70: P. P. Prudhon, engraved by B. Roger, 1802; figure 71: Luigi Conconi, 1892; and figure 72: Aristide Maillol, 1937.*

Figs. 73–4   *Chloe bathes naked in the cave of the Nymphs. Figure 73: Paul Avril, 1898; and figure 74: P. P. Prudhon, engraved by Annedouche, 1850s.*

Figs. 75–6   '*Look how the goats do it. . . .*' *Figure 75: Philip of Orléans and Benoît Audran, 1718; and figure 76: A. Maillol, 1937.*

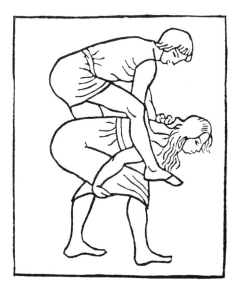

Fig. 77   Entering the bridal chamber. François Gérard, engraved by Godfroy, 1802.

Fig. 78 '. . . *and they kept more awake during the night than owls.' R. Collin and E. A. Champollion, 1890.*

Fig. 79 *'Les petits pieds', variation on a theme by Count Philippe de Caylus. Anonymous illustrator, 1749.*

The Text's Progress

In the dark Egyptian night a felucca glides down the Nile. Inside, by the flickering light of a lamp, a man sits deeply engrossed in a packet of parchment leaves which he has just acquired in Luxor, Homer's 'hundred-gated Thebes'. He tries to distinguish and transcribe the faint Greek handwriting, which some monk has evidently done his best to expunge to make room for a Coptic sermon. He has to confine himself to deciphering the better preserved writing on the parchment's flesh side; the text of the hair side will have to wait for the laboratory at home in Germany. He continues his laborious work in his tent at Abusir, and when he arrives in Cairo he borrows an edition of the Greek novelists from a friend. As he suspected, four of the leaves belong to Chariton's novel, so he is able to make a first and hasty comparison of his own transcript with the printed text. However, two other leaves belonging to the same codex appear to be fragments of a previously unknown novel about the beautiful Chione.

The parchment leaves, together with a packet of newly acquired papyri, are sent by boat to Hamburg, but there the capricious Tyche of the novels intervenes: while the ship is lying in the harbour, a fire breaks out on board, and the manuscript treasures are lost for ever. But the preliminary transcript which the German scholar — the distinguished papyrologist Ulrich Wilcken — made in Egypt in November 1898 still survives and bears witness, however incompletely, to the contents of what passes under the pathetic name *codex Thebanus deperditus*, the lost manuscript of Thebes.

The unlucky fate of this one text provides us with an allegory of *The Text's Progress* from antiquity to us by way of the middle ages; of the vicissitudes of textual tradition. The original lost for ever: that holds good for almost all ancient literature. All that survives are later manuscripts, executed during the middle ages under conditions as primitive, by our standards, as those of Wilcken in his felucca. And the copyist never dreamt that his transcript was destined to be the fragile link on which posterity's knowledge of the text would depend. Sometimes he had the opportunity to compare his transcript with another manuscript of the same work and to correct his text accordingly — for better or worse. This is what in textual criticism is called 'contamination', a mixture of the different branches of tradition which consequently makes it even more difficult to know what was in the prototype and what wasn't. If, on the other hand, the monk or scribe did not have this external means of control, we may be in greater trouble still: like Wilcken and the Chione fragment, he may be suspected of having made a number of errors in transcription; in some places he may have had to write something unintelligible or to leave a gap, because the prototype was damaged or difficult to read. In any case, each transcription distances us one step further from the original.

We shall now look more systematically at what there is for the translator of a Greek or Latin work into a modern language to work from; because he does not receive from his publishers a text authorized by the author himself. Instead he has to find the most reliable critical edition of the work in question. A modern critical edition of an ancient text is, ideally, a printed text which has been arrived at according to established scholarly principles with due account taken of all surviving manuscripts of the work. Manuscripts are dispersed through innumerable libraries, mostly in Europe, from giants like the British Library or the Vatican Library to the smallest monastery library on some Greek island. It is the editor's first task to track them down, to read them — nowadays mostly by means of microfilm — and to compare them. On this basis he tries to establish the best possible text, that is, one that comes as close as possible to the original wording. At the bottom of each page of the critical edition the editor prints the so-called 'critical apparatus', in which he accounts for the places where there are variants in the manuscripts or where he has himself departed from the reading(s) of the manuscripts. Thanks to this apparatus our translator is not at the mercy of the editor's choice, but can deviate from the printed text and establish his own.

These basic principles for a critical edition are generally followed in the texts published during the last hundred years or so in respected series like the German *Bibliotheca Teubneriana* and the British *Bibliotheca Oxoniensis*, though there are great differences in quality between the separate volumes of each series. Often one can find a good text with a critical apparatus in the French *Collection Budé* as well; this series has the additional advantage of always printing a French translation on the page opposite the Greek or Latin original. In the English counterpart, the *Loeb Classical Library*, the text accompanying the English translation is only infrequently an independent critical edition, and the apparatus is either reduced to a minimum or is non-existent; but this is the series in which one has the best chances of finding a text and a reliable English translation of any Greek or Latin author — with the Greek novelists as a deplorable exception. Most ancient works, however, including the novels, are nowadays to be found in at least one critical edition; medieval literature in Greek and Latin is less well catered for, though much progress has been made in recent decades. The older printed editions of ancient texts, produced from the early days of printing and onwards, are generally less reliable because they were based on fewer manuscripts and made less systematic use of them. As often as not, the one manuscript which happened to be to hand was reproduced in print, with the editor's own corrections.

What, then, does 'systematic use' of the manuscripts mean? If the editor has found only one medieval manuscript of his text, as is the case with Chariton's and Xenophon's novels, his procedure is similar to that practised in earlier centuries: he prints the manuscript's version with the corrections, 'emendations', that he considers necessary on the basis of his knowledge of the language and history, culture etc. of the period. He tries to arrive at an 'intelligible' text — an elastic concept, it is true — without 'violating' the tradition. In Chariton's case he may get some help from the papyrus scraps of the second and third centuries AD which have preserved small parts of the text, and from Wilcken's transcription of the *Codex Thebanus*, dated to the seventh or eighth century. The whole text will benefit from the experience he gains in this process of comparison: the editor will get some indication of the quality of his medieval manuscript, which is a thousand years younger than the papyri, and so can decide whether he should make frequent corrections, or rely on its testimony. It is true that the expectations with which the papyrus finds were greeted in the decades round 1900 have not quite been fulfilled: in spite of their antiquity and their comparative closeness to the originals the papyri are far from infallible witnesses to the truth; the text which has reached us by way of the medieval scribes is often of a better quality, because it relies on a more institutionalized tradition. But nevertheless the papyri provide us with an invaluable insight into earlier stages of the text's progress, and many errors which were previously attributed to ignorant monks or scribes of the middle ages turn out to have been there already in antiquity — and on closer inspection perhaps not to be errors at all. The early occurrence of a particular reading does of course not guarantee its authenticity, but simply the fact that it has since then passed a number of transcribers and readers, some of them no doubt both learned and vigilant, without being 'corrected', should at least give us pause: could it be that *we* are at fault, not knowing all varieties of language or not understanding the text correctly?

However, most of the literary works of antiquity which have survived to our times at all have done so in several manuscripts. This is true, for instance, for Longus, Achilles Tatius, Heliodorus, and Apuleius. In a typical case the prospective editor may have access to one manuscript from the tenth century, an additional two from the twelfth, and half a dozen written in the fourteenth and fifteenth centuries. Perhaps one of the fifteenth-century manuscripts — sometimes even one which is no longer extant — was the model for the first printed edition, the *editio princeps*. But of course our modern editor does not fall for the 'new'; he heads for the older witnesses. Can he then be sure that the *oldest* extant manuscript is also the best? No; only if he is able to prove that all the other manuscripts derive in their entirety, directly or indirectly, from that tenth-century codex, and have not been subject to contamination, can he dispose of them. And that is very rarely indeed the case.

First he has to deduce how the extant manuscripts are related to each other. In particular the lacunas and the 'obvious' errors — another subjective concept — help the editor to arrange the manuscripts in a 'stemma', or family tree, that is, to draw a schematic picture which shows their supposed dependences. Those manuscripts which present the same set of lacunas, errors, or other peculiarities are brought together as a 'family' or 'branch' in the stemma. Let us suppose that the manuscripts A, B, and C all miss a certain passage somewhere in the text; then they belong to the same family. We discover that in B this lacuna is caused by the loss of one of the manuscript's leaves: in A and C, on the other hand, the missing passage would have started somewhere in the middle of a page. This means that the relationship between the three manuscripts may in principle have been one of the following three:

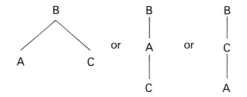

Nota bene, in principle, because there may of course have been intermediate links, now lost, between B and its descendants. We concentrate, then, on the relationship between A and C: are they brothers, or father and son? It turns out that C has a number of errors which we do not find in B, and that all these errors are also in A. In addition, A has a number of errors of its own, shared neither by B nor by C. In this ideally clear case — reality is seldom like this — we may safely choose the stemma at the right as representing the true relationship between A, B, and C.

Our editor is now no doubt disposed to 'eliminate' both A and C, that is, to pay no more attention to their readings, since both these manuscripts obviously descend from the extant B. But before doing so he must be quite sure that the scribes of A and C have not had any other manuscript to compare with, in addition to the main model; that none of the 'errors' is in reality a genuine reading derived from a better source. 'Contamination' is something which the textual critic must always take into account, even if it upsets his nice diagram.

Perhaps the other manuscripts will answer the question. The editor collects more families in the same manner, and at last his whole 'recensio' of

the manuscripts yields the following stemma, laboriously built up bit by bit
from the bottom:

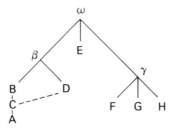

The Greek letters signify lost manuscripts, whose existence the editor is
able to postulate through his comparison of the extant ones. γ, for instance, is supposed to have existed because FGH, in addition to the errors
which are peculiar to each manuscript, present certain common
peculiarities not shared by B(CA), D, or E; the source of these peculiarities
is obviously a lost manuscript γ. As we can see, E has no close surviving
relative. B, on the other hand, turns out to have a brother, D, who shares
many of B's peculiarities but not, of course, its mechanical loss of one leaf.
A minute examination has also convinced the editor that the scribe of C
was able to correct his copy of B by comparing it to D; this is what the
broken line from D to C indicates. This correcting activity of his was,
however, carried out only in the first ten pages: the scribe never even noticed the large lacuna later in the text, which a comparison with D could
have helped him to remedy. He belonged to the species of scribes who have
a wonderfully clear handwriting, but do not care much about contents;
not surprisingly his copy — and its descendant, A! — were the basis of the
editio princeps.

   ω is the postulated 'archetype', that is, the manuscript from which all
three branches of the tradition descend. Perhaps it belonged to the ninth
century, when Byzantine humanists rediscovered the profane literature of
antiquity and transcribed the texts from the old majuscule manuscripts
which had survived into their own, more convenient minuscule style (majuscule: large letter; minuscule: small letter). Its text may be reconstructed
with some confidence, *if* the stemma is correct, in principle, and *if* no
more contamination has occurred. In that case, ω's version is certain
wherever β (that is, BD), E, and γ (that is, FGH) coincide. Furthermore,
wherever two of the three branches coincide, the majority should be right;
but the editor must beware lest his tripartite stemma prove to be in reality
a camouflaged bipartite stemma with, for instance, a common ancestor to
postulate for E and γ, before they meet β in ω. If that should be the case,
and there are accordingly only two branches with two different readings,
or if all three branches have different readings, it is the editor's task to try
to figure out which is the original reading — or whether they are all false,
deriving perhaps from something in the archetype which none of the

scribes succeeded in interpreting correctly. How errors of transcription arise, are diagnosed, and are emended is an art in itself, into which I shall not enter here. Anyhow, it may turn out that in our imagined case the readings of E, the tenth-century manuscript, are in most places to be considered as original; but the point of the whole exercise is that no single choice of reading must be made exclusively for the reason that E is the oldest and generally also the 'best' manuscript; even E may have nodded occasionally.

With his reconstructed medieval archetype our editor has at last arrived at the same point as his colleague who had just one manuscript to start from, and the real editorial work begins. The editor must not believe that it is the *ancient original* that he has reconstructed — and content himself with printing it; in all probability the medieval archetype too passes on a number of errors, as a result of the text's earlier, unknown vicissitudes. On the other hand, the editor must not imagine that he will ever, for all his knowledge and acumen, be able fully to recover the wording of the lost original. The editor's mastery reveals itself in his ability to choose the true middle way between fidelity to the manuscripts (that is, to their reconstructed archetype) and the boldness to intervene with changes, invented by himself or proposed by others, at places where the text would otherwise be incomprehensible or grammatically incorrect. The technical term for such proposals is, rightly, 'conjectures', guesses. Again, it is up to the translator, or whoever uses the critical edition, either to rely on the editor's judgement or to constitute his own text by means of the critical apparatus — still relying, necessarily, on the editor's accuracy in reading and reporting what the manuscripts offer by way of variants and on how generously he has listed other learned conjectures in addition to the one he has chosen to put in the text.

The Text's Progress: already in antiquity a succession of transcripts — with many opportunities for contamination, as far as the most widespread works are concerned — marked the way from the author's original (the 'autograph') down to the majuscule copy, or copies, that happened to survive the first 'dark centuries' of the middle ages and thus came to serve as model(s) for new medieval manuscripts, from which in turn our printed editions are descended. The way is indeed long and tortuous, but our situation is still not as bad as one might imagine. As long as we are dealing with literary works by recognized ancient authors, we have in most cases a fair chance of arriving at what the author really wrote and meant. The obscure points that remain after the scholarly treatment described above are mostly details without much interest for anyone apart from specialists. At least this is valid for such narrative texts as the Greek novels quoted in translation in chapter II, in spite of the fact that their authors did not belong to the established canon. The number of variants is moderate, even where there are many manuscripts, and the sense is generally clear; modern critical editions of a reasonably high standard are available for all of them.

Anonymous, popular tales like the *Alexander Romance* or the apocryphal Acts of the Apostles have a considerably more complex textual history (see pp. 140 – 1). Every other copyist was his own adapter and reviser: he changed, added, and subtracted, so that today's editor is confronted with a confusing multitude of versions and variants. He may be able to work out a stemma which in principle shows the relationships, but the original wording is seldom attainable. He may be forced to capitulate, in the sense that he decides to print the text of one of the medieval manuscripts, departing from it only where it offers an entirely impossible reading. Such a text — for instance, the one we followed in the translation of the *Alexander Romance* — must of course not be mistaken for the reconstruction of an ancient original, nor even that of a medieval archetype; but it is a snapshot of a living medieval work of literature, with an ancient core.

Finally, some words on the last stage these texts pass through on their way to the reader, the translation itself. To attempt to transfer a Greek or Latin literary work into a modern language, with the latter's different structure and the modern reader's different frame of reference, is — of course — in principle an impossible task. But there are differences of degree, at least as far as the reproduction of the style and tone of the original is concerned. Chariton and Xenophon write in such a way that a fair amount of their distinctive nature can be conveyed in English, for instance. The same is true for the *Alexander Romance*, *Apollonius of Tyre*, and *Paul and Thecla*. If perhaps the translation sometimes sounds clumsy or dull, if words or phrases are repeated more than modern stylistic rules would permit, then this is a way of reproducing some of the stylistic features of the originals — features, it should be noted, that are not typical of ancient literary style, but characterize these texts. In contrast, Longus' artistic prose, with its rhymes, assonances and syllable-counts, naturally defies any attempt at direct transference; here the obvious solution is to try to find a corresponding poetic tone in the recipient language, as Amyot apparently succeeded in doing in French. Achilles Tatius shifts between the stylistic levels: his plainly narrative passages, such as the description of the first kiss, cause no greater difficulties than the texts of the non-sophistic novels; his *ecphrases* and other excesses in poetic rhetoric are all the more intractable, owing to their subtle, compressed mode of expression. A translation into a modern language must become verbose and loose in comparison, and miss or overdo the points. Enough has been said above (p. 67) on Heliodorus, finally, and the impossibility of following his heavy periodic structure even for a short while.

Further Reading

An asterisk (*) marks editions on which the translated extracts in this book are based; however, the translators (listed in the preface) have at places chosen readings at variance with their respective editors.

References of the type [II:2] refer to sections of the present bibliography.

I Collected Translations; General Introductions; Bibliographies

1 The principal texts, both Greek and Latin, are available in complete **translations** into French and Italian, respectively, in P. Grimal (ed.), *Romans grecs et latins* (Paris, 1958); and Q. Cataudella (ed.), *Il romanzo antico greco e latino* (Firenze, 1973). It should be noted, however, that Xenophon Ephesius and *Apollonius of Tyre* are missing in Grimal's selection and that neither the Byzantine novels nor the pseudo-historical and Christian novels treated in chapters V–VI above are represented in either volume. A collection of new English translations of the Greek novels (the five extant 'ideal' novels, the principal fragments, Lucian's *True Story*, *Lucius or The Ass*, the *Alexander Romance*, and *Apollonius of Tyre*) will be published by the University of California Press under the editorship of B. P. Reardon. Till then, there is only the selection by M. Hadas (ed.), *Three Greek Romances* (New York, 1953), containing Longus, Xenophon, and Dio's *The Hunters of Euboea*. There is also a recent collection of translations into Spanish by J. Mendoza in the Biblioteca Clásica Gredos (Vol. 16, Madrid, 1979), which contains Chariton, Xenophon and fragments.

2 Both Grimal's and Cataudella's collections include competent **introductions** to the whole genre. In German, there are two separately published introductions of medium size, both called *Der antike Roman*. The one by R. Helm (2nd ed., Göttingen, 1956) deals comprehensively with all branches of ancient novelistic literature, providing detailed summaries of the plots, but is in some respects rather antiquated. The other one, by

235

K. Kerényi (Darmstadt, 1971), provides more inspiring reading, but it is highly selective, and the interpretation offered is Kerényi's own [III:5]. In Spanish, there is a comprehensive, up-to-date introduction by C. García Gual, *Los Orígenes de la Novela* (Madrid, 1972). A. Heiserman, *The Novel Before the Novel* (Chicago and London, 1977) cannot be recommended as an introduction — there are factual errors and instances of gross misjudgement — but at its best it offers fresh insights and an intelligent exploration of the material and technical conventions of the genre. G. Anderson, *Eros Sophistes: Ancient Novelists at Play* (Chico, California, 1982) pursues the humorous vein in the novels. Introductions restricted to one of the branches only (such as the ideal Greek novel) are mentioned in the appropriate place below.

3 A good starting-point for the **bibliography** of the ancient novel is G. N. Sandy, 'Recent Scholarship on the Prose Fiction of Classical Antiquity', originally published in *Classical World* 67 (1974) pp. 321–59 and reprinted in *The Classical World Bibliography of Roman Drama and Poetry and Ancient Fiction* (New York and London, 1978). It covers roughly 1950–70 and also lists earlier bibliographies. Part of the field is covered in greater detail by O. Mazal, 'Der griechische und byzantinische Roman in der Forschung von 1945 bis 1960', *Jahrbuch des Österreichischen Byzantinischen Gesellschaft* 11/12 (1962/63) pp. 9–55; 13 (1964) pp. 29–86; and 14 (1965) pp. 83–124. For literature later than 1970 there is the annual bibliography in *L'Année philologique* (Paris), in which the entries on the novels are to be found in the section 'Auteurs et textes' under the name of each novelist and under the heading 'Narrativa' (fragments, anonymous works), and in the section 'Histoire littéraire' under the heading 'Littérature narrative. . . '. From 1981 onwards, the scope of the *Newsletter* of the Petronian Society (ed. G. Schmeling, University of Florida, Gainesville, Florida) is being gradually increased to include bibliographical items on all ancient prose fiction.

4 The first international conference on the ancient novel was held in 1976 at the University College of North Wales, Bangor; the published proceedings of this conference, B. P. Reardon (ed.), *Erotica Antiqua* (Bangor, 1977), give a valuable survey of present trends in the research on ancient fiction. J. J. Winkler and G. Williams (eds.), *Later Greek Literature* (*Yale Classical Studies* 27, Cambridge 1982) contains important contributions on Chariton [II:3], Heliodorus [II:11], and the 'Second Sophistic' [III:6].

II The Ideal Greek Novel

1 There are several short **introductions** to the Greek novels. One is published separately: O. Weinreich, *Der griechische Liebesroman* (Zurich, 1962), an expanded version of Weinreich's 'Nachwort' to Heliodorus' novel in German translation [II:11]; it is an admirable survey of the whole genre, including the fragments, though the main emphasis is

on Heliodorus and his *Nachleben*. A penetrating study of the novels in their literary context is provided by B. P. Reardon, *Courants littéraires grecs des IIe et IIIe siècles après J.-C.* (Paris, 1971) pp. 309–403; the same author's view of the novels is stated more briefly in 'The Greek Novel', *Phoenix* 23 (1969) pp. 291–309. Another independent appreciation of the genre is that of C. W. Müller in his contribution to E. Vogt (ed.), *Neues Handbuch der Literaturwissenschaft*, Vol. 2: *Griechische Literatur* (Wiesbaden, 1981) pp. 377–412.

2 The **literary form** of the genre is often touched upon in the rich scholarly literature on its origins [III–IV], but there are also a few works concentrating on this aspect. S. L. Wolff, *The Greek Romances in Elizabethan Prose Fiction* (New York, 1912) analyses in some detail the narrative structure, characterization etc. in the three 'sophistic' novels. In an extensive introduction (pp. 1–227) to his Italian translation of Caritone di Afrodisia, *Le avventure di Cherea e Calliroe* (Torino, 1913), A. Calderini offers an inventory of the motifs used in the Greek novels. O. Schissel von Fleschenberg, *Entwicklungsgeschichte des griechischen Romanes in Altertum* (Halle, 1913), should also be mentioned in this connection as the first attempt to define, in a stricter sense, the form of the novels. T. Hägg, *Narrative Technique in Ancient Greek Romances* (Stockholm, 1971), applies the tools of modern literary criticism to the novels of Chariton, Xenophon, and Achilles Tatius; there is an annotated bibliography of previous studies of narrative technique. C. Ruiz Montero, *Análisis estructural de la novela griega* (Salamanca, 1979) attempts a structural analysis in the manner of Propp.

3 **Chariton**. Critical editions: W. E. Blake* (Oxford, 1938); G. Molinié (Collection Budé, Paris, 1979). English translation by W. E. Blake (Ann Arbor, Michigan, 1939); French by Grimal [I:1] and by Molinié (in the Budé edition); Italian and Spanish, see [I:1]. There is a recent translation into German by K. Plepelits (Stuttgart, 1976) with an excellent introduction and notes. The pride of place among literary analyses of Chariton is still taken by B. E. Perry, 'Chariton and his Romance from a Literary-Historical Point of View', *American Journal of Philology* 51 (1930) pp. 93–134, partly re-used in Perry's book of 1967 [III:3]. Characterization is studied by J. Helms, *Character Portrayal in the Romance of Chariton* (The Hague and Paris, 1966); language and date by A. D. Papanikolaou, *Chariton-Studien* (Göttingen, 1973). A literary study of the novel has been made by K. H. Gerschmann, *Chariton-Interpretationen* (Diss, Münster, 1974); C. W. Müller discusses Chariton in relation to historiography and epic: 'Chariton von Aphrodisias und die Theorie des Romans in der Antike', *Antike und Abendland* 22 (1976) pp. 115–36; and B. P. Reardon examines 'Theme, Structure and Narrative in Chariton', *Yale Classical Studies* 27 (1982) pp. 1–27. There is also a volume on *Chariton* by G. L. Schmeling in Twayne's World Authors Series (New York, 1974), with annotated bibliography. See also [II:2], Calderini, Hägg; [III:5], Petri; [IV:3], Bartsch.

4 **Fragments**. Collections: B. Lavagnini (ed.), *Eroticorum Graecorum fragmenta papyracea* (Leipzig, 1922); F. Zimmermann (ed.), *Griechische Roman-Papyri und verwandte Texte* (Heidelberg, 1936). English translation by S. Gaselee in the Loeb edition of Longus [II:8]; Spanish translation (including Lollianus) by J. Mendoza [I:1]. Important discussion of the fragments by R. M. Rattenbury, 'Romance: Traces of Lost Greek Novels', in J. U. Powell (ed.), *New Chapters in the History of Greek Literature* (Oxford, 1933) pp. 211–57; for the *Ninus Romance*, see also Perry [III:3] pp. 153 ff. A convenient short guide to the fragments, with dates, is Weinreich's introduction [II:1]. The most important recent finds were published by A. Henrichs, *Die Phoinikika des Lollianos* (Bonn, 1972), and H. Maehler, 'Der Metiochos-Parthenope-Roman', *Zeitschrift für Papyrologie und Epigraphik* 23 (1976) pp. 1–20; further contributions to Lollianus by C. P. Jones in *Phoenix* 34 (1980) pp. 243–54 and by J. J. Winkler in *Journal of Hellenic Studies* 100 (1980) pp. 155–81; to the *Parthenope Romance* by A. Dihle in *Würzburger Jahrbücher* N.F. 4 (1978) pp. 47–55. A new large fragment of the *Sesonchosis Romance* has been published by S. West in *The Oxyrhynchus Papyri*, Vol. 47 (London, 1980) No. 3319; compare J. N. O'Sullivan and W. A. Beck in *Zeitschrift für Papyrologie und Epigraphik* 45 (1982) pp. 71–83. On the *Iolaus* fragment, see [VII:3]; for the *Tinouphis* fragment (P. Turner 8), see M. W. Haslam in *Papyri Greek and Egyptian . . . in honour of E. G. Turner* (London, 1981).

5 Ancient **illustrations** to the novels are discussed in D. Levi, 'The Novel of Ninus and Semiramis', *Proceedings of the American Philosophical Society* 87 (1944) pp. 420–8, and in Maehler's article [II:4]. The subject is also dealt with in several of K. Weitzmann's works, for example in his *Ancient Book Illumination* (Cambridge, Massachusetts, 1959) pp. 99–104.

6 **Xenophon Ephesius**. Critical editions: G. Dalmeyda (Collection Budé, Paris, 1926), A. D. Papanikolaou* (Bibliotheca Teubneriana, Leipzig, 1973). English translation by M. Hadas [I:1], French by Dalmeyda (in the Budé edition), German by B. Kytzler (illustrated de luxe edition, Berlin, 1968); Italian and Spanish, see [I:1]. A short sensible appreciation of the literary qualities is offered in the introduction to Dalmeyda's edition; a detailed treatment of all the aspects of the novel, with full bibliography, by H. Gärtner in Pauly-Wissowa's *Realencyclopädie der classischen Altertumswissenschaft* 2. Reihe, IX (1967) pp. 2055–89. G. L. Schmeling, *Xenophon of Ephesus* (Twayne's World Authors Series, Boston, 1980), though directing itself to a wider audience, is also fully documented and contains an up-to-date, annotated bibliography. See also [II:2], Hägg. For the epitome theory, see K. Bürger in *Hermes* 27 (1892) pp. 36–67 and T. Hägg in *Classica et Mediaevalia* 27 (1966) 118–61.

7 **Iamblichus**. Photius' summary of the novel has been edited together with the fragments by E. Habrich* (Bibliotheca Teubneriana, Leipzig, 1960). The text, with a French translation, is also contained in R. Henry

(ed.), Photius, *Bibliothèque*, Vol. 2 (Collection Budé, Paris, 1960), Cod. 94. Italian translation, see [I:1]. Interpretation and attempt at reconstruction: U. Schneider-Menzel in F. Altheim, *Literatur und Gesellschaft im ausgehenden Altertum*, Vol. 1 (Halle/Saale, 1948) pp. 48–92. The first part of the summary is analysed in detail by A. Borgogno in *Hermes* 103 (1975) pp. 101–26.

8 **Longus**. Critical editions: G. Dalmeyda* (Collection Budé, 2nd edition, Paris, 1960): O. Schönberger (3rd edition, Berlin, 1980); M. D. Reeve (Bibliotheca Teubneriana, forthcoming). There are several English translations; among the more recent ones are those of M. Hadas [I:1] and P. Turner (Penguin, 1956). The edition by J. M. Edmonds in the Loeb Classical Library (London and New York, 1916) contains a revised version of G. Thornley's translation of 1657. French translation by Dalmeyda (in the Budé edition) and by Grimal [I:1]; German in Schönberger's edition, Italian in Cataudella's collection [I:1]. Schönberger's edition is especially to be recommended for its substantial introduction. Among the earlier studies of Longus that of G. Rohde is important: 'Longus und die Bukolik', *Rheinisches Museum* 86 (1937) pp. 23–49; among the more recent ones that of H. H. O. Chalk has been influential: 'Eros and the Lesbian Pastorals of Longus', *Journal of Hellenic Studies* 80 (1960) pp. 32–51. There is also an introduction to *Longus* by W. E. McCulloh in Twayne's World Authors Series (New York, 1970). On the connections between Longus and the pictorial art of the period, see Weinreich in his introduction [II:1], p. 19, and the article by M. Mittelstadt, 'Longus: Daphnis and Chloe and Roman Narrative Painting', *Latomus* 26 (1967) pp. 752–61.

9 **Dio Chrysostom**, *The Hunters of Euboea*. Text and English translation by J. W. Cohoon in the Loeb Classical Library: Dio Chrysostom, Vol. 1 (London and New York, 1932) pp. 285–373. English translation also by M. Hadas [I:1]. The quotation from A. Wifstrand is from his essay 'On the History of Prose Narrative' (in Swedish) in *Tider och stilar* (2nd edition, Lund, 1964) pp. 111–36: p. 115.

10 **Achilles Tatius**. Critical edition: E. Vilborg* (Stockholm, 1955), with a separate commentary (1962). Text and English translation by S. Gaselee in the Loeb Classical Library (revised edition, London and Cambridge, Massachusetts, 1969). German translation by K. Plepelits (Stuttgart, 1980) with exhaustive introduction and notes. French and Italian translations, see [I:1]. There is no monograph on Achilles Tatius, but Wolff's study [II:2] is especially detailed on this novel. The narrative technique of the novel has also been studied by D. Sedelmeier-Stöckl in a Vienna dissertation (1958), of which only a part was published in *Wiener Studien* 72 (1959) pp.113–43. See also [II:2], Hägg. The hypothesis of D. B. Durham, 'Parody in Achilles Tatius', *Classical Philology* 33 (1938) pp. 1–19, has been largely rejected; but an interesting reading of the novel as neither serious romance nor parody but as 'comedy' was recently presented by A. Heiserman [I:2] pp. 118–30. The comparison in attitude

between Achilles Tatius and Euripides derives from R. M. Rattenbury
[II:4] pp. 256 f.

11 **Heliodorus.** Critical editions: A. Colonna (Rome, 1938);
R. M. Rattenbury and T. W. Lumb* (Collection Budé, 2nd edition,
Paris, 1960). Only Colonna's edition contains testimonia and indices, while
the Budé edition has a long, valuable introduction and an annotated
French translation by J. Maillon; the Budé text is generally considered to
be superior. There are two separate English translations: by M. Hadas
(Ann Arbor, Michigan, 1957) and W. R. M. Lamb (London, 1961); and
two German: by R. Reymer, with 'Nachwort' by O. Weinreich (Zurich,
1950), and by H. Gasse in 'Sammlung Dieterich' (2nd edition, Leipzig,
1966) and in 'Reclam', with 'Nachwort' by H. Dörrie (Stuttgart, 1972).
French and Italian translations, see [I:1]. There is now also a monograph,
with bibliography, by G. N. Sandy in Twayne's World Authors Series
(Boston, 1982). Of earlier literary studies three deserve special mention:
V. Hefti, *Zur Erzählungstechnik in Heliodors Aethiopica* (Vienna, 1950);
T. R. Goethals, *The Aethiopica of Heliodorus: A Critical Study* (Diss,
Columbia University, 1959), and E. Feuillatre, *Études sur les Éthiopiques
d'Héliodore* (Paris, 1966). Two new major articles on Heliodorus should
also be mentioned: J. J. Winkler on his 'narrative strategy', *Yale Classical
Studies* 27 (1982) pp. 93–158, and J. R. Morgan on 'history, romance,
and realism' in the *Ethiopica*, *Classical Antiquity* 1.2 (1982). Heliodorus'
visual approach has recently been studied by W. Bühler in *Wiener
Studien* N.F. 10 (1976) pp. 177–85. The earlier argument about the
novel's *date* is conveniently summarized in Weinreich's 'Nachwort' and introduction [II:1]; more recently Feuillatre (above) pleads second century
AD; R. Keydell (in *Polychronion. Festschrift F. Dölger*, Heidelberg, 1966,
pp. 345–50), the latter half of the fourth century, and T. Szepessy (in
Acta Antiqua Acad. Scient. Hung. 24, 1976, pp. 247–76), again third
century, the earlier (more or less) common opinion. On the Meroitic
culture, see W. Y. Adams, *Nubia: Corridor to Africa* (London, 1977).
Heliodorus' and Achilles Tatius' different use of *ecphrasis* is examined by
J. Palm, 'Bemerkungen zur Ekphrase in der griechischen Literatur',
Kungl. Hum. Vetenskaps-Samfundet i Uppsala, Årsbok 1965–66
(Stockholm, 1967) pp. 108–211: pp. 183–96.

12 **Byzantine novels.** The novels of the twelfth century are described and
discussed by H. Hunger in *Die hochsprachliche profane Literatur der
Byzantiner*, Vol. 2 (Munich, 1978) pp. 119–42, with an up-to-date
bibliography, and also in his small monograph *Antiker und byzantinischer
Roman* (Heidelberg, 1980). The fragmentarily preserved novel by
Constantine Manasses has been edited and reconstructed by O. Mazal
(Vienna, 1967). The Byzantine reception of the ancient novels, especially
Heliodorus, is traced in H. Gärtner, 'Charikleia in Byzanz', *Antike und
Abendland* 15 (1968) pp. 47–69. The later, 'popular' kind of novel is dealt
with by H.-G. Beck, *Geschichte der byzantinischen Volksliteratur*
(Munich, 1971) pp. 115–53. Interesting viewpoints are also put forward

by Beck in 'Marginalien zum byzantinischen Roman', *Kyklos. Festschrift R. Keydell* (Berlin and New York, 1978) pp. 116–28. There is a critical edition with French translation of one of these novels: M. Pichard (ed.), *Le Roman de Callimaque et de Chrysorrhoé* (Paris, 1956).

13 **Eustathius Macrembolites.** Text in R. Hercher* (ed.), *Erotici scriptores Graeci,* Vol. 2. (Leipzig, 1859) pp. 159–286. There is also a separate critical edition by I. Hilberg (Vienna, 1876). The novel is analysed by M. Alexiou, 'A Critical Reappraisal of Eustathios Makrembolites' *Hysmine and Hysminias',* *Byzantine and Modern Greek Studies* 3 (1977) pp. 23–43. Rohde's negative judgement is to be found in his *Der griechische Roman* [IV:1] pp. 526 f.

III The Social Background and the First Readers of the Novel

1 The main contributions to the debate on the **origins** of the Greek novel will be listed below, according to the category within which each attempt at explanation falls: social or cultural [III:3]; religious [III:5]; educational [III:6], literary [IV]. For the history of this debate the reader is referred to G. Giangrande, 'On the Origins of the Greek Romance: The Birth of a Literary Form', *Eranos* 60 (1962) pp. 132–59, and to Reardon's *Courants littéraires* [II:1] pp. 312 ff.

2 For a general view of **Hellenistic society** in its various aspects J. Ferguson, *The Heritage of Hellenism* (London, 1973) may be recommended; it is attractively illustrated and contains the basic bibliography. A reliable, succinct survey of the period is provided by V. Ehrenberg, *Man, State and Deity* (London, 1974) pp. 64–106 (reprint of Ehrenberg's contribution to the *Encyclopaedia Britannica,* 1964). There is also, in several reprints, the standard work by W. Tarn and G. T. Griffith, *Hellenistic Civilisation* (3rd edition, London, 1952); and now the new volume in the 'Fontana History of the Ancient World': F. W. Walbank, *The Hellenistic World* (Glasgow, 1981). The cultural and religious aspects are especially stressed in M. Hadas, *Hellenistic Culture. Fusion and Diffusion* (New York, 1959); A. D. Nock's definition of a 'mystery' quoted above is taken from this book, p. 192. For a more serious study of the period M. Rostovtzeff, *The Social and Economic History of the Hellenistic World,* Vols. 1–3 (Oxford, 1941) is indispensable; for instance, the documentation for the picture of slavery and piracy given in the present study is to be found in — and is easily accessible through the index of — Rostovtzeff's work.

3 The problem of the **birth of the Greek novel** in the Hellenistic period is vigorously tackled in B. E. Perry's influential work, *The Ancient Romances: A Literary-Historical Account of their Origins* (Berkeley and Los Angeles, 1967): the biological approach — 'ancestors', 'development', etc. — is attacked; the new social conditions and cultural outlook are adduced to explain the new genre, and the deliberate intention of the indivi-

dual author is stressed. B. P. Reardon's book and article [II:1], the latter modestly called 'a gloss' on Perry's work, modify and develop the new approach and in a more systematic way bring it to bear on each of the extant novels. Of earlier studies with an approach reminiscent of Perry's, mention should be made of B. Lavagnini, *Le origini del romanzo greco* (Pisa, 1921), reprinted in *Studi sul romanzo greco* (Messina and Firenze, 1950).

4 No full study has been devoted to the **audience** for the ancient novel — its identity in terms of nationality, class, sex, and age — but there are some useful conjectures in the works of Perry [II:3] pp. 133 f.; [III:3] p. 98; and Schmeling [II:3] pp. 30ff.; [II:6] pp. 131 ff. Discussion and further references are to be found in Gual [I:2] pp. 39−61 and in D. N. Levin, 'To Whom did the Ancient Novelists Address Themselves?', *Rivista di Studi Classici* 25 (1977) pp. 18−29. Some interesting points are made by C. W. Müller [II:1] pp. 392−6. Specific reference is made in my text to a suggestion of G. Highet [VIII:1] p. 165. A. Scobie, *Aspects of the Ancient Romance and its Heritage* (Meisenheim/Glan, 1969) pp. 9−29 discusses the possible role of itinerant professional story-tellers; see also Scobie in *Rheinisches Museum* 122 (1979) pp. 229−59. For illustrated papyrus books, see K. Weitzmann [II:5] p. 100. Egypt as the birthplace of the Greek novel was proposed by J. W. B. Barns in *Akten des VIII. intern. Kongr. f. Papyrologie* (Vienna, 1956) pp. 29−36 and discussed in Reardon's book [II:1] pp. 327−32 and article [II:1] p. 306 n. 39. The quotation of O. Murray is from his *Early Greece* (Glasgow, 1980), p. 81.

5 The view that the extant novels are **Mysterientexte** was argued with force and ingenuity by R. Merkelbach, *Roman und Mysterium in der Antike* (Munich and Berlin, 1962); Chariton, however, is an exception to this rule, according to R. Petri, *Über den Roman des Chariton* (Meisenheim/Glan, 1963). Merkelbach develops and systematizes the thoughts of K. Kerényi, *Die griechisch-orientalische Romanliteratur in religionsgeschichtlicher Beleuchtung* (1927; 2nd edition, Darmstadt, 1962). The religious factor in the genesis and growth of the genre has also been stressed by F. Altheim, *Roman und Dekadenz* (Tübingen, 1951). The religious explanation, in the extreme form advocated by Merkelbach, has met with little favour (see, for example, Kerényi, p. 291 n. 2; R. Turcan in *Revue de l'Histoire des Religions* 163, 1963, pp. 149−99; and Gärtner [II:6] pp. 2076−80), but the discussion is not closed; each new papyrus find provides new fuel: Lollianus [II:4]; Iolaus [VII:3], etc.

6 The Greek cultural revival or '**Second Sophistic**' is dealt with by E. Rohde [IV:1]; solidly based on the literary evidence, his description of the movement and of the school of rhetoric is still valid, and my own account is heavily indebted to it. There is also the article of more recent date by E. L. Bowie, 'Greeks and their Past in the Second Sophistic', *Past and Present* 46 (1970) pp. 1−41, as well as a collection of new *Approaches to the Second Sophistic*, edited by G. W. Bowersock (University Park,

Pennsylvania, 1974), including a contribution by B. P. Reardon on 'The Second Sophistic and the Novel', pp. 23–9. The sociology of the movement is carefully mapped out in G. W. Bowersock, *Greek Sophists in the Roman Empire* (London, 1969); a response to this book is the article by E. L. Bowie in *Yale Classical Studies* 27 (1982) pp. 29–59. Rohde's reason for treating the Second Sophistic in such detail in a study of the Greek novel was his conviction that the school of rhetoric of that period was the very birthplace of the genre: the novel, while utilizing motifs from Hellenistic love poetry and fantastic tales of travel, grew out of school exercises in creative writing. Papyrus finds have proved this to be chronologically impossible, but the same educational explanation of the new literary genre has been tried by Cataudella [I:1] Prefazione; and Giangrande [III:1], only with a shift of emphasis to the *Hellenistic* school of rhetoric.

IV The Literary Pedigree of the Novel

1 The Greek novel's literary inheritance from the established genres was the focus for E. Rohde, *Der griechische Roman und seine Vorläufer* (1876; 5th edition, Darmstadt, 1974); from the 3rd edition (1914) the book also contains a valuable corrective essay by W. Schmid; from the 4th edition (1960) in addition an appreciation of Rohde's achievement by K. Kerényi. While Rohde stressed the influence of love elegy, travel tales, and rhetoric, E. Schwartz stressed 'story-telling' epic and historiography in his *Fünf Vorträge über den griechischen Roman* (1896; 2nd edition, Berlin, 1943, with an instructive introductory essay by A. Rehm).
2 For **epic and novel** as 'basically the same genre', see Perry [III:3] pp. 44 ff.; and also Weinreich [II:1] pp. 21–31 and Müller [II:3]. A comparison between certain aspects of narrative structure in ancient epic and novel, with references to the relevant studies of the epic technique, is to be found in Hägg [II:2] pp. 306–35.
3 On **historiography and novel**, from different points of view, see Schwartz [IV:1] (my quotations are from pp. 73 and 116 of the first edition); J. Ludvíkovský, *Recký Román Dobrodruzný* (Prague, 1925, with French summary), who advocates a development *Cyropaedia – Alexander Romance – Ninus Romance –* Chariton; and the two works by M. Braun, *Griechischer Roman und hellenistische Geschichtsschreibung* (Frankfurt/ Main, 1934) and *History and Romance in Graeco-Oriental Literature* (Oxford, 1938). Xenophon's *Cyropaedia* is edited with an English translation by W. Miller in the Loeb Classical Library (London and New York, 1914). Photius' summary of Ctesias' *Persica* and *Indica* is available, with a French translation, in R. Henry (ed.), Photius, *Bibliothèque*, Vol. 1 (Collection Budé, Paris, 1959), Cod. 72. The question of whether Chariton shaped his novel according to Hellenistic rules for historiography is answered in the affirmative by W. Bartsch, *Der Chariton-Roman und*

die Historiographie (Diss, Leipzig, 1934); for the corresponding argument with regard to characterization, see Helms [II:3].

4 A survey of the extant **biographies** of philosophers with novelistic traits is given by R. Helm [I:2] pp. 61–5. The *Life of Aesop* should also be mentioned in this connection: text B. E. Perry, *Aesopica*, Vol. 1 (Urbana, 1952) pp. 35–77; translation L. W. Daly, *Aesop without Morals* (New York and London, 1961). Philostratus' *Life of Apollonius* is available with English translation by F. C. Conybeare in the Loeb Classical Library (London, 1912); there is also an abridged English translation by C. P. Jones (Penguin, 1970). Complete French translation by Grimal [I:1], Italian by D. Del Corno (Milano, 1978, Biblioteca Adelphi 82).

5 The **tales of travel** of Euhemerus and Iambulus are dealt with by Rohde [IV:1] pp. 220–42 and, more recently, by J. Ferguson in his *Utopias of the Classical World* (London, 1975) chapters XII and XIV. Diodorus Siculus' summaries of their works (5.41–6 and 2.55–60) are to be found, with English translation, in the Loeb Classical Library edition by C. H. Oldfather (Vols. 2–3, London and New York, 1935–9). Lucian's *True History* is available in several English translations: by P. Turner, *Satirical Sketches* (Penguin, 1961); by L. Casson, *Selected Satires* (New York, 1962); and by B. P. Reardon, *Selected Works* (New York, 1965); text and English translation by A. M. Harmon in the Loeb Classical Library, Vol. 1 (London and New York, 1913). French translation by Grimal [I:1], Italian in Cataudella's collection [I:1].

6 Antonius Diogenes, **The Marvels beyond Thule**. Critical edition with French translation: R. Henry (ed.), Photius [II:7] Cod. 166. Italian translation in Cataudella's collection [I:1]. The 'novel' is dealt with, together with Lucian's *True History*, by K. Reyhl, *Antonios Diogenes* (Diss, Tübingen, 1969). C. W. Müller gives it a prominent place in his history of the genre [II:1], as did Rohde [IV:1]. Its remarkable composition is studied by F. Lacôte in *Mélanges d'indianisme S. Lévi* (Paris, 1911) pp. 249–304 and by W. Fauth in *Würzburger Jahrbücher* N.F. 4 (1978) pp. 57–68.

7 **Erotic poetry**. Apollonius Rhodius' *Argonautica*, often described as a 'romance', is most easily accessible in the English prose rendering by E. V. Rieu, *The Voyage of Argo* (Penguin, 2nd edition, 1971); Heiserman discusses it together with the novels [I:2]. Parthenius' *Erotica pathemata*: text and English translation by S. Gaselee in the Loeb edition of Longus [II:8]. The principal treatment of Hellenistic poetry in relation to the novel is Rohde's [IV:1]; the importance of the local legends, 'leggende popolari', was stressed by Lavagnini [III:3].

8 The relation between '**novella**' and novel in antiquity has been much discussed, with very different conclusions: compare, for example, Rohde [IV:1] pp. 4–9, who denied any historical connection between the two, and Schissel [II:2], who saw a development from '*Novellenkranz*' (Aristides' *Milesiaca*) via '*Rahmenerzählung*' (Antonius Diogenes) to '*Roman*'. The early history of the novella is traced by S. Trenkner, *The*

Greek Novella in the Classical Period (Cambridge, 1958); a collection of the novellas in Italian translation, with an extensive history of the genre (pp. 1 – 172), has been made by Q. Cataudella, *La novella greca* (Naples, 1957). The importance of the novella for the emergence of the novel is again stressed by F. Wehrli, 'Einheit und Vorgeschichte der griechisch-römischen Romanliteratur', *Museum Helveticum* 22 (1965) pp. 133 – 54. See also Perry [III:3] pp. 79 – 84.

V From Historical Novel to Medieval 'Popular Book'

1 The **Alexander Romance**. Critical edition of 'Rec. A' by W. Kroll (Berlin, 1926); English translation by E. H. Haight, *The Life of Alexander of Macedon by Pseudo-Callisthenes* (New York, 1955). The basic edition which tries to reconstruct 'Rec. B' is by L. Bergson (Stockholm, 1965), whereas H. van Thiel* (ed.), *Leben und Taten Alexanders von Makedonien* (Darmstadt, 1974), is based on one manuscript of that 'recension'; it contains facing German translation and a lucid introduction on the novel's sources, textual tradition, and 'Fortleben'. Spanish translation of van Thiel's text by C. García Gual in the Biblioteca Clásica Gredos, Vol. 1 (Madrid, 1977). The modern standard work on the sources and the textual tradition of the novel is R. Merkelbach, *Die Quellen des griechischen Alexanderromans* (1954), now available in a revised and enlarged 2nd edition (Munich, 1977).

2 The **Chion Novel** is edited, with introduction, English translation, and commentary, by I. Düring: Chion of Heraclea, *A Novel in Letters* (Göteborg, 1951).

3 The **Medieval Alexander**. Survey, with the basic bibliography, in *Lexikon des Mittelalters*, Vol. 1 (Munich and Zurich, 1980) pp. 354 – 66. There is also the fine monograph by G. Cary, *The Medieval Alexander* (Cambridge, 1956). The complex European tradition is perhaps most easily accessible through D. J. A. Ross, *Alexander Historiatus* (London, 1963), which lists manuscripts and early prints. The Old Swedish *Konung Alexander* was edited by J. A. Ahlstrand (Stockholm, 1862); character-ized by C. I. Stähle in *Ny ill. svensk litteraturhistoria*, Vol. 1 (Stockholm, 1955) pp. 85 – 91; and analysed in detail by H. H. Ronge, *Konung Alexander* (Diss, Uppsala, 1957).

4 **Illustrations to the Alexander Romance**. The origins are explored by K. Weitzmann, *Greek Mythology in Byzantine Art* (Princeton, 1951) pp. 186 – 8, and *Ancient Book Illumination* [II:5] pp. 105 – 107. The il-luminated manuscripts are listed in Ross [V:3], and there are two richly il-lustrated publications: A. Xyngopoulos, *Les miniatures du Roman d'Alexandre le Grand dans le codex de l'Institut Hellénique de Venise* (Athens and Venice, 1966), and D. J. A. Ross, *Illustrated Medieval Alexander-Books in Germany and the Netherlands* (Cambridge, 1971). Further bibliography in the lexicon article [V:3].

5 **Troy Romances.** Dictys Cretensis, both Latin text and Greek fragments, in the critical edition by W. Eisenhut (Bibliotheca Teubneriana, Leipzig, 1973). For Dares Phrygius, there is only the old edition by F. Meister (Bibliotheca Teubneriana, Leipzig, 1873). Both novels are available in English translation, with a good introduction, by R. M. Frazer: *The Trojan War. The Chronicles of Dictys of Crete and Dares the Phrygian* (Bloomington and London, 1966). Illustrations in H. Buchthal, *Historia Troiana. Studies in the History of Mediaeval Secular Illustration* (London and Leiden, 1971), which also surveys the literary tradition. The Swedish version is again characterized by Ståhle [V:3] pp. 118 f.

6 **Apollonius of Tyre.** Critical edition by D. Tsitsikli (Beiträge klass. Phil., Vol. 134, Königstein/Ts., 1981). Latin text and German translation in F. P. Waiblinger* (ed.), *Die Geschichte vom König Apollonios* (Munich, 1978). English translations by P. Turner (London, 1956) and Z. Pavlovskis (Lawrence, Kansas, 1978). Latin text and Old English translation in P. Goolden (ed.), *The Old English Apollonius of Tyre* (Oxford, 1958), with extensive introduction. The old standard work on this novel is by E. Klebs, *Die Erzählung von Apollonius aus Tyrus* (Berlin, 1899), who concludes that the story is Latin in origin, without a specific Greek model. See also Perry [III:2] pp. 294 – 324. The medieval tradition is surveyed, with up-to-date bibliography, in *Lexikon des Mittelalters*, Vol. 1 (Munich and Zurich, 1980) pp. 771 – 4.

VI The New Heroes: Apostles, Martyrs and Saints

1 **Paul and Thecla.** The Greek text (with Greek and Latin adaptations and additions) was edited by R. A. Lipsius in R. A. Lipsius and M. Bonnet* (eds.), *Acta Apostolorum Apocrypha*, Vol. 1 (Leipzig, 1891) pp. 253–72. English translation in E. Hennecke, *New Testament Apocrypha*, Vol. 2 (London, 1965). There is now a detailed analysis, with an up-to-date bibliography, of all these Acts by E. Plümacher, 'Apokryphe Apostelakten', in Pauly-Wissowa's *Realencyclopädie der classischen Altertumswissenschaft*, Supplement XV (1978) pp. 11–70. The connections between the Acts and the pagan novels were explored by R. Söder, *Die apokryphen Apostelgeschichten und die romanhafte Literatur der Antike* (1932; 2nd edition, Darmstadt, 1969). The genre of the 'aretalogy' is the subject of R. Reitzenstein, *Hellenistische Wundererzählungen* (1906; 2nd edition, Stuttgart, 1963). Thecla in early Christian art is dealt with by C. Nauerth and R. Warns, *Thekla. Ihre Bilder in der frühchristlichen Kunst* (Wiesbaden, 1981); her continued literary life may be studied in G. Dagron (ed.), *Vie et miracles de Sainte Thècle* (Brussels, 1978), with an exhaustive introduction. For the Swedish eighteenth-century novel *Thecla*, mentioned in the text, see T. Stålmarck, *Jacob Mörk* (Stockholm, 1974) pp. 154–209, with a summary in German.

2 **Joseph and Asenath**. Critical edition with extensive introduction by M. Philonenko (Leiden, 1968). The story's similarities to the Greek novels are stressed by S. West in *Classical Quarterly* 24 (1974) pp. 70–81. Up-to-date bibliography in J. H. Charlesworth, *The Pseudepigrapha and Modern Research. With a Supplement* (Chico, California, 1981) pp. 137–40; pp. 291 f.

3 **Pseudo-Clementines**. Critical editions of the Greek and Latin texts by B. Rehm and F. Paschke: *Die Pseudoklementinen*, Vol. 1: *Homilien* (2nd edition, Berlin, 1969); Vol. 2: *Rekognitionen in Rufins Übersetzung* (Berlin, 1965). Rehm summarizes his view of the novel in *Reallexikon für Antike und Christentum* 3 (1957) pp. 197–206, where the basic bibliography is given. The novelistic plot is reconstructed by Perry [III:3] pp. 285–93.

4 **Hagiographic novels**. On hagiography as a Byzantine literary genre, see H.-G. Beck, *Kirche und theologische Literatur im byzantinischen Reich* (Munich, 1959) pp. 267–75, with further bibliography. The origins and literary domicile of the genre are the subject of H. Delehaye's important study of 1921, *Les passions des martyrs et les genres litteraires* (2nd edition, Brussels, 1966).

5 **Barlaam and Ioasaph**. Greek text with English translation by G. R. Woodward and H. Mattingly in the Loeb Classical Library: [St John Damascene], *Barlaam and Ioasaph* (London and Cambridge, Massachusetts, 1967); this new edition is provided with an introduction (with bibliography) by D. M. Lang, who explores the origins and concludes that Euthymius is the translator; the candidature of John Damascene, on the other hand, is defended by Beck, *Volksliteratur* [II:12] pp. 35–41. The Old Norse *Barlaams ok Josaphats saga* was recently critically edited by M. Rindal (Oslo, 1980).

VII The Roman Comic Novel

1 There is an excellent **introduction** by P. G. Walsh, *The Roman Novel* (London, 1970), which judiciously steers a middle course between the extremes of recent research on Petronius and Apuleius; my own brief treatment is indebted to Walsh's more detailed discussion of the problems involved. The two novels' *Nachleben* in the picaresque is dealt with by Walsh (pp. 224–43) and Scobie [III:4] pp. 91–100.

2 **Petronius**. There is a recent critical edition, with German translation, by K. Müller and W. Ehlers (Tusculum Bücherei, 2nd edition, Munich, 1978); of earlier editions that of A. Ernout, with French translation, may be mentioned (Collection Budé, Paris, 1950). Text and English translation by M. Heseltine in the Loeb Classical Library (2nd revised edition, London and Cambridge, Massachusetts, 1969). English translation also by J. P. Sullivan (Penguin, revised edition, 1969); French and Italian in Grimal's and Cataudella's collections [I:1]. M. S. Smith's recent commen-

tary on the *Cena Trimalchionis* (Oxford, 1975) contains a useful introduction and bibliography. Among the abundant scholarly literature on Petronius, special mention should be made of J. P. Sullivan, *The Satyricon of Petronius. A Literary Study* (London, 1968), with extensive bibliography. See also Perry [III:3] pp. 186–210. Annotated bibliographical surveys by H. C. Schnur and G. Schmeling in *The Classical World Bibliography* [I:3]; bibliographical 'handlist' in G. L. Schmeling and J. H. Stuckey, *A Bibliography of Petronius* (Leiden, 1977); and current bibliography as well as critical reviews in the *Newsletter* of the Petronian Society [I:3].

3 The **Iolaus** fragment (P. Oxy. 3010) was first published by P. Parsons, 'A Greek *Satyricon?*', *Bulletin of the Institute of Classical Studies, University of London* 18 (1971) pp. 53–68, then in *The Oxyrhynchus Papyri*, Vol. 42 (London, 1974); compare R. Merkelbach in *Zeitschrift für Papyrologie und Epigraphik* 11 (1973) pp. 81–100.

4 The Greek **Story of the Ass.** Critical editions by van Thiel* (below) and M. D. Macleod (*Luciani Opera*, Vol. 2, Oxford, 1974); Greek text and English translation by M. D. Macleod in the Loeb Classical Library (Lucian, Vol. 8, London and Cambridge, Massachusetts, 1967). The latest comprehensive study of the Greek story and its relationship to Apuleius' novel is by H. van Thiel, *Der Eselsroman*, Vol. 1: *Untersuchungen* (Munich, 1971); in Vol. 2: *Synoptische Ausgabe* (1972), the two works are printed on opposite pages. See also Perry [III:3] pp. 211–35.

5 **Apuleius.** Critical edition with German translation by R. Helm* (7th edition, Berlin, 1978). The edition by S. Gaselee in the Loeb Classical Library (London and New York, 1915) contains W. Adlington's English translation of 1566. Mention should also be made of the highly readable, but free English version by R. Graves (Penguin, 1950), and of the recent translation by J. Lindsay (Bloomington, Indiana, 1962). French and Italian translations in Grimal's and Cataudella's collections [I:1]. The following commentaries on various parts of the *Metamorphoses* have recently appeared, all with extensive bibliographies: Book I by A. Scobie (Meisenheim/Glan, 1975); Book IV, 1–27 by B. L. Hijmans and others (Groningen, 1977); and Book XI, *The Isis-Book*, by J. Gwyn Griffiths (Leiden, 1975); Scobie's commentary will when completed cover Books I–III, the Groningen commentary Books IV–X. Besides Walsh's introduction [VII:1], there is now also J. Tatum, *Apuleius and The Golden Ass* (Ithaca and London, 1979), which presents the novel against the background of Apuleius' other literary activities. An important collection of essays by various authors was recently published by B. L. Hijmans and R. Th. van der Paardt, *Aspects of Apuleius' Golden Ass* (Groningen, 1978). Bibliography for the years 1938–70 by C. C. Schlam in *Classical World* 64 (1971) pp. 285–309, reprinted in *The Classical World Bibliography* [I:3].

VIII The Renaissance of the Greek Novel

1 **Heliodorus'** literary *Nachleben* has been investigated by M. Oeftering, *Heliodor und seine Bedeutung für die Literatur* (Berlin, 1901); there is a shorter, more readable essay by Weinreich [II:1] pp. 56–71, as well as an account by Maillon in his introduction to the Budé edition of the novel [II:11] pp. xciii–ci, and now also a chapter in Sandy's introduction [II:11]. Heliodorus, Achilles Tatius, and Longus are dealt with, though rather fragmentarily, in G. Highet's monumental study of *The Classical Tradition* (London, Oxford and New York, 1967), from which I have borrowed the scheme translation/imitation/emulation. Highet relies heavily on Wolff's study of the three sophistic novels and their influence on Elizabethan prose fiction [II:2], which is still the most detailed investigation of the reception of the Greek novels in any period of European literature. There are also two recent articles by G. N. Sandy: 'Ancient Prose Fiction and Minor Early English Novels', *Antike und Abendland* 25 (1979) pp. 41–55 (to which I owe the quotation at the beginning of chapter VIII), and 'The Theory and Practice of the Novel in France', in the sixteenth and seventeenth centuries, (forthcoming in the same journal). Underdowne's version of *An Aethiopian Historie* was edited, with an introduction by Charles Whibley, in *Tudor Translations*, Vol. 5 (London, 1895). Another 'less faithful' translation is analysed by R. Pruvost, 'Le *Daphnis and Chloe* d'Angel Day 1587', *Revue Anglo-Américaine* 10 (1932–33) pp. 481–9. On *Shakespeare and the Greek Romance* there is a monograph by C. Gesner (Lexington, Kentucky, 1970).

2 **Sidney**. My account of the Heliodorean influence on the two *Arcadias* is chiefly based on Wolff [II:2], R. W. Zandvoort, *Sidney's Arcadia. A Comparison between the Two Versions* (Amsterdam, 1929), and the introductions to J. Robertson (ed.), Philip Sidney, *The Countess of Pembroke's Arcadia* (*The Old Arcadia*) (Oxford, 1973), quotation from p. 128; and to G. Shepherd (ed.), Philip Sidney, *An Apology for Poetry* (London, 1965), quotations from pp. 100 and 103. On Sidney and Richardson, see Highet [VIII:1] p. 341. On the Greek novel's influence on Robert Greene, in particular his *Menaphon* (1589), there is now, in addition to Wolff [II:2], the study by W. R. Davis, *Idea and Act in Elizabethan Fiction* (Princeton, 1969) pp. 138–88.

3 **Cervantes**. *Persiles* is available in a recent German translation with introduction and commentary by A. M. Rothbauer, Cervantes, Vol. 1 (Stuttgart, 1963); for a complete list of translations, see T. Diego Stegmann, *Cervantes' Musterroman 'Persiles'. Epentheorie und Romanpraxis um 1600* (Hamburg, 1971). Apart from these two works, my account is based on W. Boehlich, 'Heliodorus Christianus' in *Freundesgabe für E. R. Curtius* (Bern, 1956) pp. 103–24, E. C. Riley, *Cervantes's Theory of the Novel* (Oxford, 1962), and A. K. Forcione, *Cervantes' Christian Romance* (Princeton, New Jersey, 1972), quotation from p. 149.

I quote also from J. M. Cohen's translation of *Don Quixote* (Penguin, 1970). The summary of the novel's plot is translated from G. Fredén, *Miguel de Cervantes* (Stockholm, 1956) pp. 90 – 2.

4 **Racine.** The description of Racine's experiences at Port-Royal is to be found in L. Racine, *Mémoires sur la vie de Jean Racine* (Lausanne and Geneva, 1747); the translated passage on pp. 23 f. The potential influence from Heliodorus on Racine's plays is discussed by Maillon [II:11] pp. xcviii-ci. On *Aida*, see Weinreich [II:1] pp. 70 f.

5 The subject of **Heliodorus in art** is surveyed by W. Stechow in *Journal of the Warburg and Courtauld Institutes* 16 (1953) pp. 144–52.

6 The European **reception of Xenophon** is traced by G. Schmeling [II:6] pp. 146–53. In the introduction to Plepelits' translation of **Chariton** [II:3] p. 23 the first German translations by Ch. G. Heyne (Leipzig, 1753) and C. Schmieder (Leipzig, 1807) are described and quoted.

7 **Goethe and Longus.** The relevant texts are collected by E. Grumach, *Goethe und die Antike*, Vol. 1 (Berlin, 1949) pp. 316–20; in my treatment reference is to Diary, 22 July 1807; Letter to Passow 20 November 1811; and Conversation with Eckermann 20 March 1831. More detailed discussion in Kerényi [I:2] pp. 11–29 and Schönberger [II:8] pp. 20–2; for examples of the German philologists' conflict, see Rohde [IV:1] p. 516 and Helm [I:2] p. 51.

8 **Longus in art.** In the Swedish edition of the present book, *Den antika romanen* (Uppsala, 1980) pp. 307–19, there is an essay by S. Karling on this topic.

IX The Text's Progress

1 There is an excellent introduction to the **textual tradition** by L. D. Reynolds and N. G. Wilson, *Scribes and Scholars: A Guide to the Transmission of Greek and Latin Literature* (2nd edition, Oxford, 1974). The procedure to be followed by the modern editor is described in detail by M. L. West, *Textual Criticism and Editorial Technique Applicable to Greek and Latin Texts* (Stuttgart, 1973).

2 The story of **Codex Thebanus** is told by U. Wilcken in *Archiv für Papyrus-Forschung* 1 (1901) pp. 227–72.

List of Illustrations

1. 'Venus de Milo', detail. Aphrodite statue of Parian marble, from Melos, probably last quarter of 2nd cent. BC. Musée du Louvre, Paris. Photo: Hirmer Fotoarchiv, Munich.

2. Tyche-Fortuna. Carved sardonyx stone, *c.* 50–25 BC, h. 1.84 cm. Kunsthistorisches Museum, Vienna (catalogue Zwierlein–Diehl, 1973, no. 208). Photo: Isolde Luckert.

3. Callirhoe and Chaereas on board ship. Ill. by C. L. Desrais, engraved by N. Thomas, for Chariton (8.6) in French trans. by M. Fallet (Amsterdam, 1775). Photo: British Library.

4. Ninus with portrait of Semiramis. Detail of floor mosaic from Antioch on the Orontes, *c.* AD 200. Museum of Historic Art, Princeton. Photo: the museum.

5. Parthenope and Metiochus (standing). Detail of floor mosaic from Antioch on the Orontes, *c.* AD 200. Photo: Menil Collection, Houston, Texas.

6. Parthenope and Metiochus (sitting). Fragments of floor mosaic from Antioch on the Orontes, *c.* AD 200. Institute for the Arts, Rice University, Houston, Texas. Photo:

7. The later Artemisium, Ephesus, second half of 4th cent. BC. Reconstruction drawing by F. Krischen, *Die griechische Stadt* (1938).

8. Artemis. Terracotta statuette of Tanagra type, h. *c.* 20 cm. After drawing in R. Kekulé von Stradonitz, *Griechische Tonfiguren aus Tanagra* (1878), table 17. Photo: University Library, Oslo.

9. Helius. Rhodian tetradrachm, 3rd cent. BC, diam. 2.5 cm. Photo: Hirmer Fotoarchiv, Munich.

10. Isis. Carved cornelian, *c.* 50 BC, h. 1.66 cm. Kunsthistorisches Museum, Vienna (catalogue Zwierlein-Diehl, 1973, no. 204). Photo: Isolde Luckert.

27. Illustrated papyrus fragment (Bibl. Nat. Cod. suppl. gr. 1294), 2nd cent. AD. Photo: Bibliothèque Nationale, Paris.

28. Illustrated book-roll, containing *Odyssey* 22.169–232. Reconstruction drawing by K. Weitzmann, *Illustrations in Roll and Codex* (1947).

29. 'Sappho'. Wall painting from Pompeii, 1st cent. AD, diam. 29 cm. Museo Nazionale, Naples. Photo: Scala, Florence.

30. Young woman with jewels. Mummy portrait (on wood) from Hawara, Egypt, *c.* AD 100–50. Royal Scottish Museum, Edinburgh. Photo: the museum.

31. Apollonius of Tyana. Roman contorniate medallion, second half of 4th cent. AD, diam. 3.7 cm. Bibliothèque Nationale, Cabinet des Médailles, Paris, inv. 17162 (obverse). Photo: Bibl. Nat.

32. Dancing couple. Detail of Lucanian red-figure volute-crater from Ceglie del Campo, *c.* 410 BC. Museo Archeologico Nazionale, Taranto. Photo: the museum.

33. Alexander the Great; Queen Olympias. Obverse and reverse of Roman contorniate medallion, second half of 4th cent. AD, diam. 3.0 cm. Bibliothèque Nationale, Cabinet des Médailles, Paris, inv. 17145. Photo: Bibl. Nat.

34. Alexander the Great; Alexander on horseback. Obverse and reverse of Roman contorniate medallion, second half of 4th cent. AD, diam. 3.7 cm. British Museum, London (Alföldi, *Die Kont.-Med.*, 1976, no. 45). Photo: the museum.

35. Queen Olympias and the snake. Woodcut in *Alixandre le Grant* (Michel le Noir: Paris 1506), fol. B.ii. After G. Cary, *The Medieval Alexander* (1956).

36. Letter-writing. Miniature in 14th cent. manuscript of the *Alexander Romance* in Greek (Rec. γ, ms. D), fol. 89v. Istituto Ellenico, Venice. Photo: the institute.

37. Alexander visiting the Gymnosophists. Miniature from same ms., fol. 113v.

38. Portent announcing Alexander's death. Miniature from same ms., fol. 185r.

39. Alexander on his death-bed. Miniature from same ms., fol. 192r.

40. Alexander carried to the sky by griffins. Ill. for German 'Historien-bibel' in late-15th-cent. manuscript. Zentralbibliothek, Solothurn, prov. no. 217, fol. 292r. Photo: the library.

41. Alexander in his gondola. Stone relief in Fardhem church, Gotland, Sweden. Second half of 12th cent. Photo: Key L. Nilsson.

Index

Note: The 'Further Reading' section (pp. 235 – 50) is not included in the index.